Kubrick's Monolith

Kubrick's Monolith

The Art and Mystery of
2001: A Space Odyssey

JOE R. FRINZI

To Earl,
Enjoy the book. The
Odyssey continues!
Best wishes,
Joe R. Frinzi

McFarland & Company, Inc., Publishers
Jefferson, North Carolina

LIBRARY OF CONGRESS CATALOGUING-IN-PUBLICATION DATA

Names: Frinzi, Joe R., 1955– author.
Title: Kubrick's monolith : the art and mystery of 2001:
a space odyssey / Joe R. Frinzi.
Description: Jefferson, North Carolina : McFarland & Company, Inc.,
Publishers, 2017. | Includes bibliographical references and index.
Identifiers: LCCN 2017028979 | ISBN 9781476664422
(softcover : acid free paper) ∞
Subjects: LCSH: 2001, a space odyssey (Motion picture) |
Kubrick, Stanley—Criticism and interpretation.
Classification: LCC PN1997.T86 F75 2017 | DDC 791.43/72—dc23
LC record available at https://lccn.loc.gov/2017028979

BRITISH LIBRARY CATALOGUING DATA ARE AVAILABLE

ISBN (print) 978-1-4766-6442-2
ISBN (ebook) 978-1-4766-2867-7

Front cover: Keir Dullea as David Bowman in Stanley Kubrick's
2001: A Space Odyssey, 1968 (MGM/Photofest)

Printed in the United States of America

McFarland & Company, Inc., Publishers
Box 611, Jefferson, North Carolina 28640
www.mcfarlandpub.com

To the memory of Stanley Kubrick and Arthur C. Clarke, the creative minds behind the making of *2001*. It is more than a curious irony that the conception and completion of this literary project should have been heralded by the passing of these two great men who had such an enormous impact on my own artistic ambitions. I will be forever grateful to them.

To the memory of Stanley Kubrick and Arthur C. Clarke, the creative minds behind the making of *2001*. It is more than a curious irony that the conception and completion of this literary project should have been heralded by the passing of these two great men who had such an enormous impact on my own artistic ambitions. I will be forever grateful to them.

TABLE OF CONTENTS

Acknowledgments

While active work on this book began in the spring of 2000 and continued, on and off, through 2016, the reality is that this is a work that was 40-plus years in the making. Over that time period, I accumulated an enormous amount of information on *2001* and also Stanley Kubrick, Arthur C. Clarke, science fiction, movies, writing, filmmaking and the space program, all of it fueled by the passions of my youthful exuberance. Along the way, I shared my love for *2001* with many and varied family members and friends, each of whom, in their own way, helped contribute to this book. They include Wayne Cardinalli, Susan Chase, Kevin Convery, Tom Coombe, Elaine Drago, Neil Frederick, Mike Gontkosky, Gershon Hinkson, Janie Hodges, Isadore LaDuca, Joe and Pam LaDuca, Monica McAghon, Simone Odino and Darrell Van Citters. I thank them all. An extra special thanks goes to Jim Hicks and Carole Heffley, the original publishers of *The Irregular*, for their continued guidance, support and enthusiasm for this project. Jim, especially, was instrumental in helping me do the photo shoot in New York that appears in the book.

My brother Anthony put up with my obsessions about *2001* more than he probably wanted to, while my sister Stephanie has been one of my biggest champions in this book's creation, as well as all my other creative endeavors. She and I can talk about anything and everything, and I truly value our close relationship. My parents, Anthony and Barbara, have supported my interests, even if they didn't always quite understand them. Their love and indulgence over the years have helped in ways they'll never know. I can't imagine completing this project without the generosity and love of my family.

Of course, I am also indebted to those I've met and worked with in the publishing world who helped guide this project to completion. I would be remiss if I didn't thank George Case, author of *Calling Dr.*

Strangelove, who provided me with the means of contacting my publisher in the first place. I am also grateful to *2001* actors Keir Dullea and Dan Richter for their generosity and support.

There are others, too, who also had an influence on this book. Over the course of time, people come and go in your life, some you know well, others only casually. Wherever I went and whoever I talked to, *2001* would eventually come up in conversation. All the interactions from all these people are filtered into this book in one form or another, and have helped color my own perceptions and feelings about the film. If you weren't mentioned by name, earlier, then you are thought of with much gratitude here.

PREFACE

This is a very personal work, but I hope it will have a wide appeal to anyone who appreciates good movies. *2001* was my entry into the world of director Stanley Kubrick. I first saw the film as a very impressionable 16-year-old in 1971 when it played at the cinema in my home town. From the first frame to the last, I was completely under the spell of this unique motion picture and, though I didn't realize it at the time, it would become the epiphany of my life. Over the next decade I saw it many times as it made the rounds at the various sub-run theaters, and I began amassing a formidable collection of Kubrick memorabilia (books, posters, soundtracks, stills, etc.) that were available in the pre-home video era of the 1970s.

My appreciation for *2001* and Kubrick grew as I became familiar with the work of other notable directors (Bergman, Fellini, Kurosawa, Lean, Welles, etc.) that I was fortunate enough to see in the burgeoning art house movement. Over the ensuing years, my movie book library grew as well, as I devoured both critical and popular studies of these master filmmakers. This is when the first inklings entered my consciousness that I might someday want to contribute a book on *2001*. Being a small-town writer with no connections to the academic or publishing world, my desire remained, for many years, simply a pipe dream.

It wasn't until the passing of Stanley Kubrick in 1999 that I realized that if I wanted to do a book on *2001*, I'd better get at it. With hundreds of books about film in my library, 40 or so on Kubrick, I knew that I was as knowledgeable on the subject as I needed to be. I quickly decided, with some hubris, that I wanted to write the ultimate, definitive study of *2001*, including every aspect of the movie from its conception to the world's reaction as we approached the new millennium. I wanted it to be a scholarly work, but also one that would resonate with pop culture

1

fans of the film. It would be the book I always wished someone else had written, satisfying all the passions the movie had evoked in me. That was the task I set for myself. I thought it would take a year.

The project took me five years to write and another ten to find a publisher. I tried to cover everything from the script and symbolism to production design, special effects and music, and present them in a way that was more complete than other authors had done. My sources were the books I'd read, the memorabilia I owned, and the 30-plus years of passion I had. I deliberately shied away from seeking new interviews with people involved in the film (I didn't have access to them anyway). I relied on what was already a part of the written record, much as a historian might work. Even so, contradictions occasionally surfaced. There were plenty of anecdotes to draw upon, but I also wanted this to be an exploration of the film from my own perspective. This approach seemed to be the better way to go, and one that would set my book apart from those that came before it. I took advantage of many of the previously published books and articles on Kubrick for inspiration, which is reflected in the accompanying bibliography. I did my best to avoid being overly dry in my writing, something that has plagued many an academic tome. I'd been told by others who had read my previous articles and my work as a local film critic that I had a warm and inviting literary "voice." Those who read my *2001* manuscript felt I'd brought that same quality to the book.

I am particularly appreciative of actor Keir Dullea's approval. I first met the star of *2001* in the late 1980s when he did a one-man show in a little hole-in-the-wall venue in Allentown, Pennsylvania. It wasn't even a proper theater, just a large room with folding chairs (and no raised stage to perform on). Still, Keir came out and proceeded to charm the audience (made up mostly of middle-aged women) who, no doubt, had first become enthralled with the lanky, handsome actor during his 1960s heyday. Back then, Keir made a string of notable films including *The Hoodlum Priest, David and Lisa, The Thin Red Line, Bunny Lake Is Missing, Madame X and The Fox.* His crowning glory during this period was playing astronaut David Bowman in *2001: A Space Odyssey.* That film left such a huge imprint on the cinematic universe that nothing Keir did afterward (*De Sade, Black Christmas, The Haunting of Julia, The Next One*) could escape from its long, monolithic shadow. But Keir pressed on, doing theater, television and the occasional movie. In 1984, he reprised his David Bowman role in the *2001* sequel *2010: The Year We Make Contact*, based on Arthur C. Clarke's follow-up novel and directed by Peter Hyams.

My goal with this work was to add something new and interesting to the collective study of Kubrick's oeuvre in general, as well as what he achieved with *2001*, specifically. As it is filtered through my own personal experience, I hope it resonates with most fans, though I doubt it will please everyone equally. But for those seeking to know just how bold and original *2001* remains today as a work of cinematic art, I feel I did the film justice and honored its legacy.

INTRODUCTION

2001: A Space Odyssey is a classic. I knew that from the day I first saw it in May 1971 when I was 16. For those who take movies seriously, it is perhaps the most innovative film since Orson Welles made his 1941 masterpiece *Citizen Kane*. Many ensuing works, like *The French Lieutenant's Woman* (1981), *Pulp Fiction* (1994) and *Memento* (2001), owe a debt to director Stanley Kubrick, who paved the way for the success and acceptance of structural experimentation found in many movies today. *2001*'s revolutionary mix of form and content make it a subject worthy of analysis and celebration. After all, how often can you truthfully say that you went to the movies and had a profound experience? Since its 1968 release, *2001* has become an enduring part of cinema history. Like *Kane* and other classic films, it will never go out of style.

2001 was my generation's cinematic epiphany. Just as Walt Disney's 1940 animated concert feature *Fantasia* had a profound impact on those who would find their way into the classical music and animation fields, Kubrick's movie inspired many Boomers to seek careers in space science and, especially, the film industry. It certainly got to me, and while I didn't pursue filmmaking myself, beyond a few Super-8 shorts and some work on independent productions, I did become passionate about cinema. At the very least, *2001* proved to me (and the rest of the world) that there were other ways to make and watch movies than had generally been the case up until that time. The current movie generation takes much of what was unique about *2001* for granted: elaborate sets, realistic models and effects, striking cinematography and unconventional story structure, all of which are part of modern cinema's language. Kubrick didn't invent these things, but he did help to perfect them and make them viable. Ironically, the dual-edged sword of *2001*'s legacy is that, thanks to the proliferation of home video, many more people have an opportunity to see it, but most have never experienced this extraordinary movie in a theater environment. If ever there was a film meant to be seen on the big screen, it is this one.

Beyond the movie itself, there is the man who made it. Simply put, Kubrick was one of the giants of cinema, and his untimely death in 1999 was heartbreaking for those of us who admired him and expected that he'd be around to hold court during his greatest film's signature year. Unfortunately, it was not to be. But as the years passed, his reputation has grown in stature and become more mythic. He was an original visionary, like Hitchcock, Welles, Bergman and Fellini, one of the masters who helped shape and define cinema for our modern world. He has inspired and influenced scores of filmmakers, many of whom have paid homage to him in their own movies. A hundred years from now, people will be interested in Kubrick and his films will still be relevant.

Can pop culture be wedded to high culture? I believe so. Just as the monolith in *2001* was, as the novel's writer Arthur C. Clarke once remarked, "a sort of cosmic Swiss army knife—it does whatever it wants to do" (*Stanley Kubrick: A Biography* by Vincent LoBrutto, 284), so too, this book encompasses a multitude of levels about the movie as it relates to a variety of subjects. From filmmaking and special effects, to science and mythology, to sociology and nostalgia, there is something here for everyone. To some, this format may appear to make the book "neither fish nor fowl." I choose to see it as being more of a chameleon: When it needs to be highbrow, it is; when it needs to be pop, it becomes that, too. The intent of this book is to bridge the gap between intellectual analysis and pure movie fandom. Fortunately, *2001* is one of the few films that fits comfortably in both these worlds. Perhaps that is also why it will endure.

1

VISION OF THE COSMOS
The Minds and Philosophy Behind *2001*

I have no doubt that in reality the future will be vastly more surprising than anything I can imagine. Now my own suspicion is
that the Universe is not only queerer than we suppose, but queerer
than we *can* suppose.
—biologist J.B.S. Haldane, 1927

Just what did Stanley Kubrick and Arthur C. Clarke have in mind
when they decided to collaborate on a film in the spring of 1964? Though
they were over a decade apart in age (Kubrick was born in 1928, Clarke
in 1917), the two men's sensibilities were similarly molded by the events
of World War II, along with the Cold War politics that followed. Both
were highly successful, respected professionals in their fields, Kubrick
a film director, Clarke a writer of science and science fiction. Both were
keenly intelligent, with creative minds that spoke with distinctive voices.
Kubrick's desire from the beginning was to make the proverbial "really
good" science fiction movie—to take a B-movie genre and raise it to A-
movie status. Clarke saw the opportunity to inject intelligence and dignity into the sci-fi film genre, something it was sorely lacking, and which
written science fiction had in spades. In joining forces, these two talents
would end up creating *the* grandest, smartest, most artistically innovative
motion picture to explore man's place in the universe.[1]

Before we can delve into *2001*'s underpinning philosophy, it is important to understand the time period in which it was made, along with the
mindset of the populace and the achievements of film as an art form.
And we need to know the background of the two men most responsible
for its creation, Kubrick and Clarke.

Stanley Kubrick

Stanley Kubrick was born on July 26, 1928, at Manhattan's Lying-In Hospital.[2] He was raised in the Bronx by his parents Gertrude and Jacques. In school, young Stanley proved to be an indifferent student, though not for a lack of ability. An intelligence test revealed him to be so far above the norm that conventional education bored him. A childhood photo shows a dark-haired boy with a wide face and his legendary piercing eyes already evident.

The teenage Kubrick had three main passions: photography, chess and drumming. He would dabble at the drums for most of his life but, encouraged by his father, it was the other two that came to dominate his world.

Stanley's first camera was a Graflex, a single lens reflex with a large negative, a type of camera used by professional news photographers of the day.[3] Even this early in his life, it seemed, he approached picture-taking as a pro. His passion for chess, on the other hand, appealed to young Stanley's intellect and desire for order. He became good enough that, as a young adult, he played for money (and often won) against the chess masters in New York City's Washington Square.

Photography ultimately became the path for Kubrick. While still in high school he began submitting photos to *Look* magazine. His 1945 photo of a news vendor despondent over the death of President Roosevelt perfectly expressed the feelings of millions of Americans over the president's passing and revealed Kubrick's ability, even as a teenager, to expressively use an image to fully convey the essence of a story.[4] For the next four years he worked at *Look* as a photo-journalist, using the still picture format to refine his skills in composition and storytelling.

Eventually Kubrick felt the limitations of shooting still photography and yearned to try his hand at filmmaking. At first he felt that documentaries were the way to go. During his youth in the 1930s and '40s, the documentary short and newsreel film were staples in movie theaters. But by 1950, with the mainstream arrival of television, theatrical documentaries were a dying form. Still, between 1951 and 1953, Kubrick managed to shoot and complete three documentary film shorts. His first, *The Day of the Fight*, was a 16-minute chronicle of middleweight boxer Walter Cartier as he prepared for a bout. Kubrick chose wisely for his first foray, picking a subject with which he was already familiar. (In 1949, Kubrick photographed Cartier for *Look*.) The film had a limited run and barely broke even, but Kubrick plowed ahead, completing *Flying Padre* (8.5 minutes) and *The Seafarers* (30 minutes) by 1953. But the writing was on the wall. If Kubrick wanted a career in cinema, he would have to move up to features.

In 1953, at the age of 24, Kubrick became a feature film director with the completion of his first motion picture, the self-financed *Fear and Desire*, an existential exercise about the madness of war. Kubrick would later dismiss this first effort as amateurish and pretentious. Despite its crudeness, Kubrick already showed signs of his talent through inventive camerawork, editing and frame composition. For his next project, he abandoned overt allegory for film noir moodiness with *Killer's Kiss*, the tale of a down-on-his-luck boxer who finds redemption, of a sort, when he rescues an attractive woman from the clutches of a seedy small-time crime boss. Though the boxing milieu returned Kubrick to familiar territory, the script and his work with the actors was much less assured than his talent with the camera. *Killer's Kiss* was released in 1955 to mediocre reviews and, like its predecessor, it didn't make a dime. Things were looking tough for the budding director.

At this time, Kubrick hooked up with James Harris, a minor league film distributor who wanted to produce features. In Kubrick, Harris saw the opportunity to work with a raw, young talent who would obviously become a great director someday. In Harris, Kubrick saw someone who could negotiate with the studios to obtain financing for his films. Their first effort, *The Killing*, was based on the novel *Clean Break* by Lionel White. (The title change may have reflected a bit of monetary wishful thinking on Kubrick's part.) The book recounted the story of a racetrack robbery and its aftermath. What made it especially interesting, and a cut above the average pulp potboiler, was its fragmented flashback structure, which followed the robbery from the point of view of all the participants. It was primarily this structural uniqueness which intrigued both men. With a more substantial budget than his earlier films, Kubrick was able to hire solid character actors like Sterling Hayden, Elisha Cook Jr., Marie Windsor and Jay C. Flippen. The result was a brilliantly edited, lit and photographed crime film, with slightly clunky dialogue delivered by competent actors. Kubrick proved he was a great technical filmmaker, but only a so-so writer. Still, it was enough to get Hollywood to take notice.

Kubrick's "graduation piece" was 1957's *Paths of Glory*, based on the 1935 novel by Humphrey Cobb. It starred A-list actor Kirk Douglas along with notable screen veterans Adolphe Menjou and George Macready. The film was produced by Harris under the umbrella of Douglas' company, Bryna. Douglas took over a third of its $950,000 budget for his fee as star and producer. It was money well spent since it legitimized Kubrick as a bona fide professional.

During this period, Kubrick met his third wife, Christiane Harlan (who went by the stage name Suzanne Christiane), who would remain his lifelong soulmate. (She played the part of the German girl at the end of *Paths of Glory*.) The film was a powerful indictment of the military class hierarchy of World War I; Kubrick rose to the challenge with a series of brilliant set pieces, from tracking shots through the trenches, to the troop ground assault (with hundreds of extras), to the kangaroo court martial envisioned as a diabolical chess game. Though the movie was not a box office success, it has since been hailed as one of the greatest anti-war movies ever made, and is one of Douglas' favorites; he called it "possibly the most important picture Stanley Kubrick has ever made."[5]

Douglas was so taken with Kubrick's talent that he called upon him to take over the directorial reins on *Spartacus* when the original director, Anthony Mann, left over disagreements with the producer-star (Douglas). Though Kubrick would later disown *Spartacus*, saying Douglas, the writer and the producer refused to accept any of his suggestions,[6] it remains one of the best and smartest "spear and sandal" epics, and allowed Kubrick to work with such hallowed actors as Laurence Olivier, Charles Laughton and Peter Ustinov, the latter winning a Best Supporting Actor Oscar.

While Douglas admired Kubrick's talent, a major rift developed between them over the question of the screenplay credit (*Spartacus* was written by the blacklisted Dalton Trumbo). Douglas took umbrage when Kubrick suggested that he (Kubrick) take the credit. For Kubrick, an up-and-coming director trying to make a name for himself, having such a credit on a major motion picture (regardless of what he privately thought of the script) was as much a practical consideration as it was opportunistic. Since they needed a real name, and using Trumbo's was still considered risky (though Douglas was certainly for it), Kubrick no doubt reasoned, "Why not me?"[7] Douglas ultimately chose to go with Trumbo's name, effectively breaking the blacklist.

Vowing never to be in a "*Spartacus* situation" again, Kubrick and Harris produced their next piece, an adaptation of Vladimir Nabokov's controversial 1955 novel *Lolita*, the story of a middle-aged man's infatuation with a 12-year-old nymphet. Such material was guaranteed to generate free publicity. For Kubrick and Harris, the challenge of making an acceptable mainstream movie from such provocative material was met by downplaying the story's sexual aspects through the skillful use of innuendo and humor. The stellar cast featured James Mason, Shelley Winters, Peter Sellers and 14-year-old Sue Lyon as the title character. Amazingly, Kubrick and Harris managed to pull it off. While the movie was only a modest success, it firmly established Kubrick as a talented and innovative maverick who thrived on making edgy, original films that challenged the viewer to re-evaluate what movies could say and do.

At this point, Harris had gotten the bug for directing and decided he needed to move on. Now in his early thirties, Kubrick became his own producer and would retain full artistic control of his projects. He decided his next project would be about the dangers of nuclear annihilation. What began as a serious dramatic treatment of the subject, based on Peter George's 1958 novel *Red Alert*, quickly evolved into the "nightmare comedy" called *Dr. Strangelove: or How I Learned to Stop Worrying and Love the Bomb*. Released in early 1964, it cemented Kubrick's reputation as one of the most gifted filmmakers of his generation. Full of sardonic wit and hilarious sight gags, *Strangelove* boasted truly phenomenal comic performances by a legendary cast that included Sterling Hayden, George C. Scott, Slim Pickens, Keenan Wynn and, in three separate roles, Peter Sellers (who should have won an Oscar for sheer inventiveness). A resounding success in America *and* abroad, *Strangelove* was nominated for four Oscars—Best Picture, Director, Actor (Sellers) and Screenplay—but won none. It did win a plethora of other awards (New York Film Critics Award for Kubrick; Society of Film and Television Arts and a Hugo for Best Picture). Kubrick had tapped into something new and exciting in the pop culture mentality then emerging. In the year that the Beatles conquered America and the world with their music, Kubrick had done much the same in the realm of cinema.

A man and his camera. Director Stanley Kubrick mulls over his next move.

In the spring of 1964, Kubrick stood at the pinnacle of professional success and worldwide acceptance. He could more or less write his own ticket and was in the enviable position to tackle virtually any project he desired. And it was in this climate that he decided the time was right to make a motion picture about man's place in the cosmos. He'd been reading up on the subject for many months but, even with all the knowledge he'd absorbed, knew he'd need some help from an "insider." He told his friend Roger Caras (later the publicist for *2001*) that he was planning to make a film about extra-terrestrials and was currently reading every major science fiction writer in order to find the right collaborator. Caras responded, "Why waste your time? Why not just start with the best? Arthur C. Clarke."[8]

Arthur C. Clarke

Arthur Charles Clarke was born on December 16, 1917, in the small coastal town of Minehead, near the Bristol Channel in Somerset in southern England.[9] The eldest of four children, he took an interest in science at an early age, even building his own telescope when he was 13.[10] Tragedy struck a year later when his father died, leaving his mother to support the family.[11] Clarke began writing imaginative fiction while still in school, and was a fan of the magazine *Astounding Stories*. These early leanings toward space and the fantastic would point the way for his future as a published author. With the coming of the war, his dreams were put on hold as he served in the Royal Air Force from 1941 to 1946, specializing in the relatively new technology of radar. In 1945 he wrote a technical paper titled "Orbital Radio Relay," published the following year in the October issue of "Wireless World," which posited the idea of orbiting communications satellites.[12] During this time, he also began selling his first science fiction stories to the very same magazines he loved as a boy.

After the war, Clarke enrolled at King's College in Cambridge where he earned his Bachelor's Degree in math and physics.[13] He found work as an assistant editor for *Physical Abstracts* from 1949 to 1951, and then went on to be a full-time writer. Prior to this post, he wrote the short story "The Sentinel" over Christmas for a BBC competition (in which he did not place); in 1964, "The Sentinel" would become the basis for his collaboration with Kubrick.[14] While continuing to create short magazine stories in the early 1950s, he also turned out the sci-fi novels *Islands in the Sky, The Sands of Mars* and *Against the Fall of Night*, which established his penchant for scientific speculation and poetic circumstance.

Clarke's first great sci-fi novel *Childhood's End* (1953) dealt with the next step in the evolution of man, when aliens intervene to create a race of super-intelligent Earth children; a variation of this theme is at the heart of his story for *2001*. A prodigious writer, he churned out novels, short stories, non-fiction science books and technical papers that put him in the forefront of respected literary intelligentsia. He maintained a rigorous scientist's mind and filled his science fiction stories with hard science fact, grounding even the most fanciful tales in a solid bedrock of reality. But his fiction, far from being dry or boring, contained a wistful poetry that never failed to touch his readers.

In the 1950s, he developed an interest in scuba diving as the next best alternative to experiencing weightlessness while he waited for an actual space program to be developed.[15] He fell in love with the island of Ceylon (now Sri Lanka), off the coast of India, when he visited there in 1956 to do research for a book project. The beautiful locale offered the opportunity for year-round underwater exploration in a climate that was much more inviting then his gray, chilly days in England. So taken was he with his new hobby that he added it to the plots of some of his published works (both fiction and non-fiction).

An intensely private man, Clarke married in 1954 and would divorce a decade later. There was some speculation as to his sexual orientation (virtually none of his fiction concerns any interpersonal relationships between women and men); in a 1986 *Playboy* interview, he indirectly admitted to bisexual inclinations. He seemed much more at ease talking about technology, the space program and humanity's destiny.[16] By 1960, as an acclaimed author with nearly 30 books to his name, Clarke had been the recipient of many awards, including the Hugo (sci-fi's equivalent of the Oscar) for his story "The Star," and was the guest of honor at the 1956 World Science Fiction Convention.

The 1960s saw the arrival of the space age, which couldn't come soon enough for the farseeing author. As a former Royal Air Force fellow, not to mention the man who "invented" the communications satellite, Clarke found some highly sympathetic allies in the halls of NASA. He had friends in many varied fields, from scientists and technicians to writers and scholars. It was an exciting time for the space-minded author, who knew that man's destiny lay in the stars.

In early 1964, Clarke received a cable from Roger Caras, a man he'd first met in 1959 during a weekend with the famed French underwater explorer, Jacques Cousteau. It read, "STANLEY KUBRICK—DR. STRANGELOVE, PATHS OF GLORY, ET CETERA, INTERESTED IN DOING FILM ON ET'S. INTERESTED IN YOU. ARE YOU INTERESTED? THOUGHT YOU WERE A RECLUSE."[17]

Clarke had heard of Kubrick, had seen *Lolita* and admired it, and had heard good things about *Dr. Strangelove*. He replied with his trademark droll wit: "FRIGHTFULLY INTERESTED IN WORKING WITH ENFANT TERRIBLE-STOP-CONTACT MY AGENT-STOP-WHAT MAKES KUBRICK THINK I'M A RECLUSE?"[18]

Kubrick and Clarke met for the first time on April 22, 1964, at New York's Plaza Hotel in Trader Vic's bar.[19] Clarke made the trip from Ceylon to complete work on a Time-Life book called *Man in Space*, so the cable from Kubrick was fortuitous in its timing. The two men immediately hit it off, as they each realized they'd found an intellectual soulmate. Their work habits, however, were quite at odds: Clarke was an "early to bed, early to rise" sort while Kubrick was a confirmed night owl.[20] Still, the two managed to find enough common ground upon which to establish a productive working relationship.

Before coming to the States to meet Kubrick, Clarke went through his published fiction and selected a 1948 short story which he thought would be suitable material for a movie.[21] "The Sentinel" recounts the discovery of an alien artifact (a 12-foot-tall crystalline pyramid) on a lunar mountaintop by a group of scientists. The device is surrounded by a still-functioning force field, operating for untold millions of years. It takes the scientists 20 years to break through and, in the process, they destroy the artifact. At the end of the story, the man who discovered the device reflects that those who placed it on the moon may return once they've learned it's been tampered with, due to the cessation of its signal. He fears their arrival could prove ominous for humanity.

Kubrick responded favorably to Clarke's story and they agreed to use it as the climax of the movie, which would be about the early days of planetary exploration.[22] The idea, evidently, was that man's quest for knowledge, illustrated by the exploration of the planets, would be rewarded in the end with the discovery of another (and higher) intelligence; a sort of vindication of scientific faith. Eventually, it was deemed preferable to make "The Sentinel" the beginning of the movie and to follow that with man's search for the beings that left the lunar artifact. Clarke spent the next six months, with Kubrick's input, expanding this premise into a novel-length treatment and another year and a half refining it into its final book form. The screenplay was derived from the various drafts of the novel and was continually amended even as the movie was being shot.[23]

The late 1950s saw the dawn of the space age and by 1964 the United States and Russia each had competitive and well-developed manned space programs. Their goals were the conquest of space and the establishment of a human presence off the Earth. In many ways, to both super-powers, space was simply an extension of the land acquisition policies they'd been practicing for most of their histories. For Kubrick and Clarke, the new frontier of space was akin to the sea voyages of our ancestors. The mystery and awe that the ancient Greeks and others had for the world's vast oceans was very much how modern man felt about the cosmos.

2001 **author Arthur C. Clarke poses for a publicity photograph on the pod bay set.**

Kubrick and Clarke determined that the best approach to take with their story was to couch it in mythological terms. Thus was born the concept of a "Space Odyssey": The modern explorer (astronaut) sets out on a journey (space mission) dictated by the gods (aliens) and is profoundly changed by the experience. Kubrick was so keen on developing a mythic theme that he gave Clarke a copy of Joseph Campbell's classic analysis on myth, *The Hero with a Thousand Faces*, to study. Clarke found it to be very stimulating material.[24] At a press conference for *2001*'s Washington, D.C., premiere, Clarke said:

> Our aim was to give a mature treatment of the theme of space exploration.... What we were trying to do was to convey the wonder and beauty and, above all, the promise of space exploration.... At the same time, we were attempting an even more ambitious theme, and this was nothing less than an attempt to convey the possible, indeed the probable, place of man in the hierarchy of the universe.

On another occasion, Clarke stated, "We set out with the deliberate intention of creating a myth. The Odyssean parallel was in our minds from the beginning, long before the film's title was chosen."[25] The normally tight-lipped Kubrick allowed this revelation in a *Playboy* interview after the movie was released:

> I will say that the God concept is at the heart of *2001*—but not any traditional, anthropomorphic image of God.... When you think of the giant technological strides that man has made in a few millennia—less than a microsecond in the chronology of the universe—can you imagine the evolutionary development that much older life forms have taken? ... Their potentialities would be limitless and their intelligence ungraspable by humans.[26]

The early days of the Kubrick-Clarke collaboration in the spring of 1964 found them meeting daily for discussions. They visited the just-opened World's Fair in Flushing, Queens, where they were surrounded by visual stimulus about the promise of the space age future. They visited many other sites in New York and saw a number of sci-fi films to check out the competition.[27] The consensus was that the opposition was very poor, though Clarke seemed to be a bit more lenient in his criticism than was Kubrick, who saw mainly bad sets, bad effects and bad acting. The schism in their tastes was illustrated most strongly after Clarke told Kubrick to see the 1936 film *Things to Come*, which depicts a future where the search for knowledge by noble scientists is seen as the true destiny of humanity. While laudable in its intent to show intellectual pursuit as a positive force, the film is hopelessly naive in portraying man and his institutions as benevolent and beyond corruption. The visual effects and art direction are quite stunning, however, and the huge underground city has the look of a World's Fair utopia. Kubrick's response to Clarke after screening the film was, "What are you trying to do to me? I'll never see another movie you recommend!"[28]

Despite this crack in their solidarity, the two men began in earnest to develop their project. Kubrick gave Clarke a spot at his Central Park West offices to begin writing, but after a day there, Clarke decided he'd be more comfortable at his usual home away from home in New York City, the Chelsea Hotel; he could hobnob with other legends of bohemia in residence there, including William Burroughs, Allen Ginsberg and Henry Miller.[29] Kubrick began assembling a crew of designers to help him realize his vision of the film. From clothing to spaceships, everything in *2001* would have to be designed from scratch.

The amount of effort Kubrick was investing in the design and the script for *2001* was nearly unprecedented at the time for any movie, much less for the second-class genre of science fiction. At this point in time (mid–1964), sci-fi films did not have a very high reputation in the industry. Though the genre could trace its origins back to the very beginnings of cinema with Georges Méliès' *A Trip to the Moon* (1902), it was in the postwar 1950s that sci-fi hit its stride. Unfortunately, this was mainly through cheesy films about monsters and aliens attacking our way of life; or about the dangers of atomic radiation (which resulted in monsters and mutants attacking our way of life), clearly a reaction to the fears of Communism. As noted earlier, Kubrick and Clarke checked out the competition and found it wanting. However, there were several films from sci-fi's past that were made with some care and seriousness. *Conquest of Space* (1955) was ultimately defeated by its overtly stilted earnestness. *The Thing from Another World* (1951), despite its snappy dialogue and brilliantly built-up sense of dread, was undone by a silly monster. Still, it is worth a brief glance back at some of the better ones prior to the making of *2001*.

The Author's Top Ten Sci-Films (Before 2001)

Destination Moon (1950). Produced by George Pal, with a screenplay based on a novel by science fiction author Robert Heinlein, this was Hollywood's first real attempt to do a serious film in what was considered a minor kiddie genre. It was shot in a dry documentary style by director Irving Pichel; the sets, costumes and even the lunar landscape were made as accurately as was possible, given what was technically available or known at that time. Noted astronomical artist Chesley Bonestell was a technical advisor for the outer space views and lunar landscape vistas seen in the film.[30] In place of the Flash Gordon heroics, the filmmakers strove for realism, but forgot to include any believable drama. The look of the film, shot in Technicolor, is quite impressive, even if it bears little resemblance to how events were actually done by NASA nearly 20 years later. The movie won an Oscar for its special effects, which for the most part *are* remarkable. However, despite a contrived racing-against-the-clock launch sequence and other melodramatic moments, the finished film is curiously flat and unengaging, mostly due to its overemphasis on the technical side of the story. It was evidently felt, perhaps correctly, that the audience needed to be educated on the nuts and bolts of space travel. To sugarcoat the school lesson, and to provide a bit of levity to the movie, the producers presented some of this information via a film-within-the-film cartoon short with Woody Woodpecker. Whatever its shortcomings, *Destination Moon*, being one of the first science fiction movies from the post–World War II era, was certainly ahead of its time, and proved that you *could* approach the genre in a grown-up manner. Kubrick was enamored enough of this film, despite its crudities, to have a copy available for multiple viewings during the early phases of production on *2001*.

The Day the Earth Stood Still (1951). This is a literate and intelligent allegory about birth, death and redemption, and one of the most ambitious stories to come out of the period. An emissary from an alien federation comes to Earth to warn us that we must mend our primitive, violent ways or face annihilation. The alien, looking quite human and played in an understated manner by British actor Michael Rennie, is very much molded as a Christ figure, even adopting the subtle alias "Mr. Carpenter." Directed with great sensitivity and warmth by Robert Wise (who started his career by editing *Citizen Kane*, and went on to direct the Oscar-winning films as *West Side Story* and *The Sound of Music*), the movie was a far cry from the sensationalist offerings of the genre at the time. While it is restrained and unusually intelligent for science fiction, the marketing was anything but, relying on images of the alien's giant robot, Gort, depicted with rays shooting out of his visor, carrying a provocatively clad woman in his arms. This was evidently part of the "bait-and-switch" tactic to lure Cold War audiences in to see a "monster flick" that was, in reality, a cogent anti-war statement.

Invaders from Mars (1953). Perhaps one of the most unusual films, sci-fi or otherwise, to come out of the 1950s, this atmospheric horror show about aliens taking over mankind is clearly an example of form blending seamlessly with content, a concept that Kubrick utilized to an even greater effect in *2001*. Directed by the brilliant production designer William Cameron Menzies, *Invaders* is a literal nightmare, thanks to its use of dramatic color, lighting and exaggerated stylized sets. Told from the point of view of a young boy who awakens in the middle of the night to see a flying saucer landing behind a hill near his house, the story quickly escalates as, one by one, his family and other authority figures are taken over by the aliens. This vulnerable state of helplessness was meant to emulate the paranoia many Americans felt about the threat of Communist infiltration during this time. The film ends with the boy waking up, realizing the whole thing was a dream, and then seeing the saucer, again, land behind the hill. This circular structure gives the film a truly nightmarish and mythic quality, and makes it a definite cut above the usual alien invasion story.

Invasion of the Body Snatchers (1956). Despite its lurid title, this is a dark, sinister exploration of the loss of individuality. Based on the gripping thriller by Jack Finney, the movie concerns a doctor returning from a medical convention and noticing that his friends and neighbors seem to be different. He soon learns that the townsfolk are systematically being replaced by alien seed pod replicants, who lack emotion or the desire for free will. It was seen by both the left and the right as an indictment of the other, but it is really a warning against conformity in whatever guise it takes. Production values were minimal, as were the effects, but the black-and-white cinematography creates just the right sense of mounting dread. At the distributor's insistence, a hopeful ending was bookended around the story, to take the edge off its bleakness. Still, the film is finely acted and tautly directed (by Don Siegel, who would later do *Dirty Harry*) in an understated yet noirish fashion, and it remains a potent portrayal of paranoia. In 1978 the story was remade by Philip Kaufman and again proved to be a winner.

Forbidden Planet (1956). This big budget sci-fi movie carries the pedigree of being based on Shakespeare's *The Tempest*. The plot involves a space cruiser out to investigate the disappearance of a scientific expedition to the planet Altair IV, 20 years earlier. There they find the last survivor of the mission, Dr. Morbius, and his grown daughter, Altaira, living comfortably with their robot servant Robby. Morbius is reluctant to leave his isolated planetary paradise, due to his discovery of the remains of an alien race called the Krell. The Krell machinery, still functioning, taps directly into the user's mind and unleashes an invisible "id" monster. Despite its intellectual ambitions, the film is geared mainly toward juveniles through stock characters (a comic relief cook) and stock situations (rivalry over "the girl"). The tour of the Krell labs, however, is very impressive and ranks as the visual high point of the film (much like *2001*'s Star-Gate sequence). And like *2001*, much time and money was spent on creating elaborate sets and believable special effects, all showcased in full color and CinemaScope. Unfortunately, again, the marketing for this movie was decidedly lowbrow. The "monster carrying off the damsel in distress" poster features a fearsome-looking Robby cradling a blonde beauty who faintly resembled Altaira. Not surprisingly, no such scene appears in the movie itself.

The Incredible Shrinking Man (1957). While its title has all the hallmarks of sensationalist claptrap, this movie, directed by Jack Arnold and written by Richard Matheson (from his own novel), is a superb meditation on the loss of "self." Six months after encountering a mysterious fog while vacationing on a boat with his wife, Scott Carey (Grant Williams) discovers that he is shrinking at the rate of about an inch a week. The effect that this has on his life, his marriage and his self-esteem are palpably shown. The diminution from man to midget to doll is handled with such care and finesse, it never becomes silly or unbelievable. At mouse size, he has a run-in with the house cat but escapes into the basement, somewhat bloodied. His wife believes he has been killed. In the film's scariest sequence, he fights a tarantula for a few crumbs of food. After this victory, and now less than an inch tall, he feels himself shrinking into oblivion. In a poignant voice-over (the entire film is punctuated with his narration), Carey expounds that "the unbelievably small and the unbelievably vast eventually meet, like the closing of a gigantic circle." As he literally becomes one with the universe, we see a series of astronomical images dissolve from one to another while he proclaims, "To God, there is no zero. I still exist." Pretty heady stuff for a film with such a tabloid title.

I Married a Monster from Outer Space (1958). Speaking of tabloid titles, it's hard to imagine one more risible than this. Another example of the "Reds under the bed" obsession then permeating the culture, the movie is actually quite sophisticated in creating a moody sense of helplessness in the face of losing one's humanity to an alien takeover. Produced and directed by Gene Fowler, Jr., from a Louis Vittes screenplay, the story concerns aliens from a dying world who come to our planet, in need of women for the purpose of procreation. They kidnap human males and acquire their memories and appearance to gain access to compliant partners. The film's major innovation was in its exploration of sexual interplay, something not usually touched upon in science fiction,

21

then or now. Though the idea of marriage as a metaphor for the loss of male freedom certainly wasn't new at the time, the novelty of alien abduction as the catalyst provides a nice quirky twist. And since the aliens want offspring, the notion of them bedding down with human females, even under the sovereignty of holy matrimony, was kind of shocking and racy for the time. To be fair, this was a film never intended to promote big, philosophical ideas, but simply to entertain in as lurid a manner as was possible for the times. The ad campaign reflected this as well, showcasing the alarmed-looking star Gloria Talbott, in full bridal regalia, being menaced by a silhouetted monster against a blood-red background. That the film still managed to elicit some serious thoughts on alien interaction lent credibility to the story's somewhat schlocky premise.

The Space Children (1958). This lesser-known Jack Arnold effort harkens back to the "aliens intervening on our behalf" scenario seen in *The Day the Earth Stood Still*. However, in place of *Day*'s Christ-like emissary, we have instead a "space brain" consciousness (God?) which mentally controls a group of children whose scientist-parents work at a military base. The scientists are planning to send a hydrogen bomb into space, and the children are enlisted by the brain to sabotage the launch. Such a pacifist stance in a movie was unusual for the Cold War era, though there was certainly plenty of public outcry against the increased militarization at that time. While the reaction of the film's adult characters to their plans being thwarted is one of shock and surprise, the performances of the children, especially Michel *Lawrence of Arabia* Ray as "Bud," are striking in their Zen-like centeredness, which raises this film to a very high level. Like the Star-Child in *2001*, these "space children" are now wise beyond their years due to their contact with an alien presence. When one realizes that in the original ending of *2001*, the Star-Child was going to detonate the nuclear bombs orbiting the Earth (which is still retained in the novel),[31] the coincidental connections between these two films, made a decade apart, is quite astonishing.

La Jetée (1962). Chris Marker's extraordinary experimental film, made up entirely of still photos (with the exception of one key shot), stands above the rest as a singular work of art, much as *2001* does. As still after still clicks by, the narrator tells us how a group of ragtag sci-

22

entists in a post-apocalyptic future have created a time portal through the use of hallucinogenic drugs. Their plan is to return to the past to gather information and prevent the war from happening. One time traveler becomes involved with a woman from the past and sees a location by an airport pier that seems strangely familiar to him. It turns out that, as a child, he was actually a witness to his own death, which occurs at the film's end. If the story of the film also seems familiar, that's because it was remade, rather well, as *12 Monkeys* (1996), directed by Terry Gilliam. The original, which runs a half-hour, is a unique cinematic experience. It takes the concept of time travel—always a dicey issue—and turns it inside out. More importantly, the use of still photos gives it a sense of reality that is palpable, as if you were actually looking in on real events. In a way, photography itself is a sort of time machine, since it freezes moments of time forever. Marker uses the metaphor of still photos to underline the idea of memory and time coming together to illustrate the main character's fate. The short running time kept it from having any sort of conventional release, though it did make the rounds on the art house circuit and on college campuses. However, to the general moviegoing audience, Marker's film was practically unknown. Even now, despite a Criterion DVD release and widespread availability, it remains a largely obscure title.

Alphaville (1965). Directed by French New Wave filmmaker Jean-Luc Godard, this odd, allegorical film is part sci-fi, part film noir thriller, as well as a modern retelling of the Orpheus and Eurydice myth. The main character, secret agent Lemmy Caution (Eddie Constantine), passes himself off as a reporter when he arrives in Alphaville, a city where words and emotions have no meaning. After an encounter with a "hospitality woman" and a thug, he meets Natacha von Braun (Anna Karina) at his hotel. His mission is to find her father Dr. von Braun, the creator of Alpha 60, a super-computer which runs the dehumanized city. The film is intentionally filled with the clichés and tropes of B-movie thrillers and comic strip sensibilities, as it weaves its story through the use of parable, of the loss of individuality in the modern world. The fear of technology is best exemplified in the gravelly, throaty voice of Alpha 60, which is as annoying to listen to as Douglas Rain's Hal 9000 is soothing. *Alphaville* has both its admirers and detractors among cineastes. In strictly science fiction terms, it fails to deliver the elements that most genre fans require. There are no special effects or space-age sets and props, just conventional architecture and technology of the mid–1960s. As an allegorical film, it was able to transcend those needs since Godard clearly had other goals in mind in telling his story. Once *2001* came out, however, it became far more important for filmmakers to incorporate realistically projected futuristic technology into their sci-fi speculations. Given the explosion of sophisticated and technically-oriented science fiction films that followed in the wake of *2001*, Godard's parable approach, where cars are spaceships and cities are galaxies, has aged less gracefully than most of its admirers are willing to admit.

These were the best sci-fi movies that were available for Kubrick and Clarke to examine prior to the beginning of principal filming in December 1965, some or all of which may have influenced their own vision. During production on *2001*, and up to its release in 1968, a number of other science fiction films were made that at least attempted to tell grown-up stories and to present some realism in the production design. These included such obscure and/or noteworthy titles as *Fantastic Voyage, The Bamboo Saucer, Countdown, Mission Mars* and of course *Planet of the Apes* (released one month before *2001*), as well as the popular television series *Star Trek*. With regular news broadcasts showing NASA space launches, what had once been only science fiction (men in spaceships) was quickly becoming a reality in day-to-day life. Popular entertainment had to adjust accordingly to this new paradigm.

2001 was not alone in exploring intelligent themes in the science fiction genre. However, it must be said that intelligent sci-fi films were the exception and that, for the most part, their promotion was designed to capitalize on their stories' most lurid and sensational aspects. By and large, sci-fi films of the 1950s and '60s were made quickly and cheaply, created mainly to cash in on the UFO mania of the time, and to provide fodder for the rising teen market at drive-in theaters. There was little or no serious intent. This was considered comic book stuff, made primarily for kids. Their budgets were practically non-existent, and the special effects and art departments were often asked to conjure up spaceship sets and monster suits out of thin air. Nowadays we take it for granted that set design and effects will be top-notch; nothing less is acceptable to audiences. We have *2001* to thank for establishing this expectation of technical excellence. Unfortunately, the intellectual influence of *2001* has lagged behind, considerably, which suggests that its story structure was even more complex, and less easily imitated. Or, perhaps, that aspect was just viewed as less commercial.

However, it is in the realm of the screenplay (or story structure) that *2001* boasts its most innovative contribution to cinema. Rather than engage in the standard three-act play format, Kubrick and Clarke decided upon a much bolder approach: They would establish a series of vignettes, or set pieces, that initially do not appear to have any connective narrative threads, though in reality they are inextricably linked to one another. Added to that was Kubrick's determination to strive for a completely visual approach to telling his story. Originally, the film was conceived to have narration, as well as numerous expository dialogue sequences, but Kubrick ultimately chose to eliminate the former and drastically cut back on the latter, to the point where virtually nothing of importance is communicated through the spoken word. This has led to the mistaken impression by some that *2001* is badly written. For those who expect and require conventional dramatic performances in their entertainment, *2001* was obviously a disappointment. The intent, I believe, was to show modern man at an evolutionary dead end, socially and spiritually; that language (the thing which separates us from animals) no longer served man in any useful capacity. It may also be the reason why, when we first see a human being in *2001* on the space plane, he is asleep. This may have been Kubrick's way of saying that man, as an entity, is still unconscious and needs to awaken (which he accomplishes at the end of the film when the astronaut is reborn as the Star-Child with enormous, wide open eyes).

Unlike written science fiction, which delivers its full wealth on the printed page, reading a transcript of *2001* yields very little of its dazzling originality. Its strengths lie primarily in its visual impact, and in propelling the story through imagery rather than words. The passage "a space plane approaches and docks with a large, orbiting space station to the strains of the 'Blue Danube' waltz" doesn't begin to do justice to the actual sequence as seen and heard in the finished film. Kubrick gave us nothing less than a "ballet mechanique," a machine ballet, where objects of 21st century design danced to 19th century Old Vienna. And this is just one example of many in which *2001* raised its storytelling to the mythic level.

Mythology

While the *2001* characters may not seem to be important as individuals, their place in the cosmic order was a major concern for Kubrick. The big theme behind *2001* was "man's place in the universe." Clarke's belief was that, since our solar system is relatively young, there should be many other older civilizations scattered throughout the heavens. And as we made our own first tentative steps into space in the mid–1960s, it seemed reasonable to speculate on what it would be like to meet our cosmic betters. But since interstellar travel for us is still a far-off dream, they would have to make the first move. It is a short leap to imagine such a meeting set in mythological terms. Much has been made of how George Lucas used mythic elements, culled from such literary sources as King Arthur and *The Lord of the Rings*, in his *Star Wars* movies. While this may be true in a pop psychology sort of way, the evidence supports *2001* as the first (and one could argue, the only) significant science fiction film to explore classic mythical themes in a truly substantial manner.

In Joseph Campbell's landmark book on mythology, *The Hero with a Thousand Faces*, he had this to say:

> Mythology has been interpreted by the modern intellect as a primitive, fumbling effort to explain the world of nature (Frazer); as a production of poetical fantasy from prehistoric times, misunderstood by succeeding ages (Muller); as a repository of allegorical instruction, to shape the individual to his group (Durkheim); as a group dream, symptomatic of archetypal urges within the depths of the human psyche (Jung); as a traditional vehicle of man's profoundest metaphysical insights (Coomaraswamy); and as God's revelation to his children (The Church). Mythology is all of these. The various judgments are determined by the viewpoints of the judges. For when scrutinized in terms not of what it is but how it functions, of how it has served mankind in the past, of how it may serve today, mythology shows itself to be as amenable as life itself to the obsessions and requirements of the individual, the race, the age.[32]

Campbell continued:

> The standard path of the mythological adventure of the hero is a magnification of the formula represented in the rites of passage: separation—initiation— return: which might be named the nuclear unit of the monomyth.
>
> "A hero ventures forth from the world of the common day into a region of supernatural wonder: fabulous forces are there encountered and a decisive victory is won: the hero comes back from this mysterious adventure with the power to bestow boons on his fellow man."[33]

While both *2001* and *Star Wars* neatly parallel all these examples of "the myth," only *2001* carries it to an unpredictable conclusion. Kubrick found a way to stay true to the myth without sacrificing its revelation. His film never falls into the trap of familiar convention.

Though *2001* takes Homer's *Odyssey* as its namesake, it is not a point-by-point update. Kubrick and Clarke took the mythical idea of a great journey (Homer's epic is considered the definitive version in western literature) and then created their own mythical fable, layering it with modern conceits about technology. Still, they were smart enough to sprinkle it with Homeric signposts: When astronaut Bowman enters the computer Hal's brain to disconnect its higher functions, this can be seen as an eerie echo of Odysseus blinding the Cyclops, Polyphemus. That Hal is represented in the film as a single, red-eyed lens strengthens the analogy. (Originally, the computer was going to be female and named Athena, the goddess who served as Odysseus's protector.[34]) Bowman's trip through the Star-Gate (and the wonders he sees) could be taken as a visual representation of the sirens' songs that so enraptured Odysseus. And after all his adventures, Odysseus returns home alone, just as the transformed Bowman does in *2001*. Bowman's name may even be a play on how Odysseus, returning home disguised as an old beggar, revealed himself by stringing the great bow that he alone could wield.[35]

Without a doubt the most potent mythic icon in *2001* is the Star-Child (a term devised by Clarke for the novel but never used in the movie), even more so than the monolith. In a film replete with birth imagery, the culminating sequence, where the dying astronaut is transformed (reborn if you will) into a cosmic fetal super-being, carries with it undeniable mythic connotations. While Clarke is credited with the concept of the Star-Child ("Bowman will regress to infancy, and we'll see him at the end as a baby in orbit"—journal entry, October 3, 1965[36]) as well as its rationalization ("Suddenly found a logical reason why Bowman should appear at the end as a baby. It's his image of himself at this stage of his development. And perhaps the Cosmic Consciousness has a sense of humor"—journal entry, October 5, 1965[37]), it was Kubrick who gave it iconic status through the filming and editing of the end sequence. See Chapter 5 for further speculation about the Star-Child.

Many have debated the symbolism of *2001*'s Star-Child and whether it was meant to be seen as optimistic or pessimistic. In *The Hero with a*

Thousand Faces, Campbell probably best describes the intentions of Kubrick and Clarke: "Only birth can conquer death—the birth not of the old thing again, but of something new. Within the soul, within the body social, there must be—if we are to experience long survival—a continuous 'recurrence of birth' to nullify the unremitting recurrences of death." There is a lot of death in *2001* but it is offset by "a continuous recurrence of birth," most spectacularly with the appearance of the Star-Child. While the *2001* storyline is mythologically "the hero's journey," it is also about spiritual renewal. The hero is transformed and he is born anew. Where one world ends, a new one begins. *2001* is life-affirming in its view of humanity's potential. Even though the film ends with man in the image of an infant, it is at least an infant god. The race endures. Birth conquers death.

Conceiving Aliens

Creating an intelligent story and designing realistic and believable special effects were vital to Kubrick's grand scheme. Equally important, and even more daunting, was the challenge of just how to depict a totally convincing alien being. Sci-fi films usually depicted aliens as a threat, the result of our unconscious mind trying to identify the "unknown," which taps into our deepest fears. At the time, there were two schools of thought regarding alien biology: They'd either be very close to human or else they'd be nothing at all like human. Hollywood had followed this formula as well; they either employed actors with little or no makeup or else they created hideous (and often silly) monsters of every description. This was well before our culture became inundated with alien abductions, *The X-Files* and rehashing the phenomenon of the 1947 Roswell incident (where an alien spacecraft supposedly crashed) so there were no preconceived notions then about what an alien "should" look like.

Kubrick leaned toward a humanoid alien, very tall and thin, like a Giacometti sculpture. As a practicality, he reasoned that he could film an actor using an anamorphic lens, and then project the footage without a compensating anamorphic element on the projector. The result would distort the actor into a thin, elongated figure.[38] During production,

Kubrick made some tests with this method, trying first a skin-tight, all-white costume, then an all-black costume with white polka dots, shot against a black background with the actor pirouetting. Though the results were interesting, Kubrick was unsatisfied and continued to experiment.[39]

Clarke had his own views on alien life forms, based more on scientific reasoning than on moviemaking convenience. Though the bilateral symmetry of the human form seems ideal—not too many limbs, sense organs together at the highest point on the body—Clarke's scientific mind told him that the odds were decidedly against anything like man appearing elsewhere in the universe. The genetic dice had been thrown too many times for this combination to come up again. For *2001*, he toyed with the idea that the aliens might be machines,[40] having passed beyond the need for flesh and blood; or that the beings encountered at the end were in fact human, whose ancestors had been taken from Earth when the aliens first visited.[41] Though these ideas were certainly intriguing, they lacked the magical and otherworldly quality demanded by Kubrick.

With time growing short before Kubrick was to move to England to begin production, Clarke made a call to a friend, a young, brash, relatively unknown astrophysicist named Carl Sagan, who would later go on to fame and fortune with his 1973 book *The Cosmic Connection* and the popular 1980 PBS series *Cosmos*. The three men met at Kubrick's New York penthouse for dinner to discuss the matter, weigh the options and see if there was a way to solve the dilemma of how to portray aliens in a serious manner. Sagan only confirmed what Clarke had felt all along: that the chance of the humanoid form being repeated elsewhere was not very likely.[42]

Sagan believed that the best approach to take was to "suggest" rather than actually show the aliens. His reasoning was that no matter what Kubrick and his team came up with, "any explicit representation of an advanced extraterrestrial being was bound to have at least an element of falseness about it."[43] Whether or not he realized it, Sagan helped plant the seed that would lead Kubrick to perhaps his most profound decision regarding *2001*: leave the aliens unseen.

For the duration of production on *2001*, Kubrick would wrestle with the idea of showing his aliens while Clarke furiously wrote draft after draft of what an encounter with them might be like. The truth they finally came to, after much wandering through these blind alleys and dead ends, was that depicting beings who were millions of years advanced from us was, by its very nature, impossible. As Clarke noted in his 1970 book, *The Lost Worlds of 2001*, "One might as well expect Moon-Watcher [the man-ape leader from the beginning of *2001*] to give a lucid description of [astronaut] David Bowman and his society."[44] The solution, as originally suggested by Sagan, was to bypass the aliens completely. In their stead, Kubrick chose to show only the enigmatic monolith, letting it represent the alien presence with its blank perfection. As an abstract symbol, the monolith provided Kubrick with the perfect icon to achieve a metaphor-rich patina for his story about an encounter with a higher intelligence. The minimalist monolith thus became both a mirror of, and a doorway into, our own concepts of the unknowable, tapping directly into the unconscious.

The existential philosophy of the plot and myriad mythological story elements, coupled with a scientifically sophisticated production design and the decision to portray the aliens as an enigmatic and unknowable force, helped to form the intellectual skeleton that would eventually become *2001*. Kubrick was determined to create a modern fable about man and his place in the universe. The allegorical aspect of science fiction made it a logical successor to mythology; made it, in fact, the new mythology for our time. And with Clarke as his collaborator, Kubrick knew the script would reflect the mythic grandeur he desired. But the bones still needed flesh. Kubrick now needed to turn his attention to designing a technical musculature and symbolist skin for his movie if it were to have the artistic depth he required. As it turned out, the visual symbolism of *2001* would carry just as much weight as the story. And it would be more important than any actor.

2

THE ART OF MONOLITHS
Symbolism in *2001*

> Brancusi once said about sculpture, "Why talk about sculpture when I can photograph it?"
> —sculptor Andy Goldsworthy in the 2000 documentary *Rivers and Tides*

Like most great mythic tales, *2001* abounds in symbolism. From the first frame to the last, every shot seems designed to provide the viewer with multiple levels of meaning. Colors and shapes portend a significance beyond mere actuality. Objects and even characters have a totemic presence about them that speaks more to our subconscious minds than to our waking consciousness. Ever the perfectionist, Kubrick saw to it that everything within every scene carried its own distinctive mythic "fingerprint." The composition, as well as the subjects being photographed, often defined the filmmaker's intention. Form conveyed content.

Any attempts to decipher the subtext in *2001*, and thus divine its mythological core, should begin with the symbols and themes that Kubrick meticulously layered into every fiber of his movie. An understanding and appreciation of these touchstones makes the movie that much easier to interpret. Also, such information helps to enrich the experience of watching the film, allowing the viewer to connect with it on a deeper, more spiritual level than perhaps even they realized existed. The central symbolic device in *2001* is the enigmatic monolith.

The Monolith

The monolith is the ultimate symbol in this most symbolic of movies. At the time, it was a cinematic litmus test for audience endurance in a film that gave no quarter to simple explanations. It served as both Rorschach inkblot and free-association assessment where one could find the truth (or at least *a* truth), by looking inward. Like the title characters in *Moby Dick* and *The Wizard of Oz*, the monolith was an impenetrable enigma, and was called everything from "God" to "that damn black two-by-four!"[1] As an icon, it remains potent and undiminished in its capacity to evoke awe and mystery. Literally a tabula rasa, it is a metaphoric blank tablet upon which viewers could inscribe their own interpretation. Born out of the minimalist art movement of the 1950s and '60s, the monolith, as it appears in the film, had a long and complex gestation.

In Clarke's short story "The Sentinel," the object found by the astronauts on the moon was a tetrahedron—a four-faceted pyramidal structure composed of three equilateral triangles with a triangular base (as opposed to the more familiar five-faceted Egyptian pyramid composed of four triangles with a square base). The tetrahedron represents the simplest design of a three-dimensional solid shape (four triangular faces, compared to a cube's six rectangular faces). According to Clarke, there was much that recommended the tetrahedron as an object both of fundamental simplicity and enduring mystery. As he stated in *The Lost Worlds of 2001*, "It was a shape which inspired all sorts of philosophical and scientific speculations (Kepler's cosmography, the carbon atom, Buckminster Fuller's geodesic structures...)."[2] Despite these pedigrees, however, what worked beautifully on the printed page, or in the abstract recesses of the analytical mind, was less than satisfactory as a visual metaphor.

Kubrick's art department whipped up model artifacts of various sizes and placed them in lunar and African landscapes but they just didn't look right.[3] Even while the TMA-1 moon pit set was being constructed at England's Shepperton Studios, Kubrick had a full-size tetrahedron planned and built. However, while it was spiritually akin to church steeples and ancient pyramids, the tetrahedron was just a little too close in appearance to its earthly counterparts, and perhaps too fundamental in its form, to fully fill the bill. As an emissary of a higher intelligence, Kubrick's artifact needed to be both simple and advanced, minimalist in design, yet something that looked "made," something not found in nature. The cube was the next logical step but it, too, lacked the grandeur of God. Finally they hit upon the rectilinear slab as a shape that would most inspire a sense of wonder.[4]

If in Clarke's mind the tetrahedron evoked the wonders of Kepler and the carbon atom, then the monolith, as the artifact came to be known, tapped into an equally rich and much more mysterious vein of analogy which included everything from ancient tablets like the Rosetta Stone and the Ten Commandments, to structures like Stonehenge and Islam's most holy shrine, the Ka'aba—an enormous 40-foot cube draped in black fabric which contains a sacred black stone that fell from the sky (!), most likely a meteorite. In a more mundane yet equally intriguing example, the monolith recalls a door (and by implication, a doorway) through which one may pass, or at least knock upon to gain entry. In an astonishing similarity, in 1962 Austrian artist Ernst Fuchs painted "The Unhinged Doors of Gaza" which depicts a pair of floating mono-lithic slabs as a set of wide open doors hovering just overhead in the sky.[5] Evidently the time was right for just such a visual metaphor.

The minimalist art movement of the 1950s and '60s gave rise to many examples of blank canvases and slab-like sculptures (Ad Rein-hardt's 1964 piece "Blank Painting No. 34" and the mid–1960s works of sculptors Ronald Bladen and Donald Judd come to mind). Certainly this was an influence on much of the visual design of the time, from architecture (New York's Seagram Building and the United Nations annex) to consumer goods (furniture and appliances with clean lines and smooth surfaces). Ornamentation was eschewed in favor of simple functionalism. It was the art world's attempt (some say a failed one) to distill the essence of art and expression into a universal form. Free of any dependence on influences derived from cultural provincialism, the minimalists aimed to bypass consciously made choices rooted in the artist's own limited experience, and to tap directly into the unconscious where form could (and would) attain an absolute meaning, regardless of the observer's own inclinations.

While such a quest may seem a noble pursuit, it is easy to under-stand why such a movement foundered. Functionalism in design is a far cry from the needs of art; a toaster is not the same as sculpture. Any attempt to cut off a viewer's personal experience with art in favor of some universal dictate runs counter to the reason most people are drawn to art in the first place. One's relationship to a work of art, be it paintings, sculpture, music, literature or whatever, is generally a very subjective, interpersonal and passionate experience. The pursuit of a selfless, egoless, cultureless art form denies the viewer most of the inherent criteria they require for a satisfying connection to the work. However, this detached aloofness was absolutely perfect for Kubrick's needs. The monolith represented the unknowable, the incomprehensible, even. In selecting a black rectangular slab to embody his alien enigma, Kubrick was able to give form to something which had no form. And its shape provided a key counterpoint to the natural order of the universe. Indeed, in choosing a hard-edged rectangle for his artifact, Kubrick set the stage for one of the major visual motifs that would define the symbolism in his film.

Shapes

The use of shapes in *2001* played an enormous role in dictating its themes and subtext. In Kubrick's formalized universe, objects fell into two distinct categories, circles and rectangles. Following classic symbolic references, the first represented the feminine, the natural and the intuitive, while the latter echoed traits that were masculine, artificial and analytic. The aesthetic of the soft, yielding curve vs. the hard geometric right angle would find artistic full flower in *2001*'s mythic cosmos. Occasionally Kubrick would apply his symbolism in mixed, even complex ways, as when he shows a tiny round space pod rising over the large round hull of its parent ship, artificially echoing the natural sun-Earth-moon alignment that opens the film. The large circular space station wheel being pursued by the small linear space plane certainly can be seen as a sexual dance—again, the artificial imitating the natural.

At its most basic level, the entire universe in *2001* can be viewed as a natural cosmic sphere of immense proportions, while the monolith is an embodiment of the intellect, contained, yet no less immense. The two come together in Jupiter's orbit when the irresistible force (the monolith) meets the immovable object (the fabric of space) and thus is created the Star-Gate. While this event provides a profound example of these elements interacting, the natural and the technological dovetail most sublimely in the character of Hal the computer. That Hal is made up of both the circle and the rectangle speaks eloquently to his dualism. He is the artificial brain with the human soul, and his asexual voice further hints at his blended nature. His fisheye lens is almost always seen affixed to a rectangular plate that bears his name. And while he is mostly identified by this ubiquitous lens (he is, after all, the Cyclops whom Bowman-Odysseus must defeat), Hal, in fact, cleaves closer to the masculine artificial rectangle—the memory units in his "brain" are like tiny, clear monoliths while the interior walls of the brain room feature hundreds of rectangular slots, and the entire room is a rectilinear construct. This artificiality illustrates, most succinctly, what separates Hal from the truly organic curves of the human Bowman.

One of the more sly uses of the circle by Kubrick in *2001* is the waterhole. In prehistoric Africa, two tribes of man-apes fight for control of this life-giving puddle in their arid desert. Four million years later Kubrick revisits this dynamic on board the space station: two tribes—Russian and American this time—again square off, but with a veneer of civilized politeness subduing their raw animal aggression. They sit in the station lounge at a modern version of the waterhole: a low, round tabletop upon which sit their drinks. Ironically, Dr. Floyd (the doppelganger for the victorious man-ape, "Moon-Watcher") does not accept a drink, and it is he who leaves the "waterhole" while the Russians remain to nurse their drinks. Despite this reversal, we know that Floyd is the victor since he obviously knows something the Russians do not. And soon we will find out that he, "Moon-Traveler," like the man-ape, Moon-Watcher, is privy to knowledge of the monolith.

Perhaps the most intriguing use of the circle occurs when we are introduced to Dave Bowman, the astronaut who will ultimately be transformed into the Star-Child that is seen at the film's end, floating in a bubble by the Earth. In an eerie foreshadowing of his fate, Bowman is first seen in the movie as a rotating reflection in Hal's circular lens. From the very beginning, then, we are subconsciously informed of Dave Bowman's ultimate destiny. Bowman also appears several times in Hal's lens, as if to reinforce this notion.

Birth and Death Imagery

2001's grand theme is that of life, death and rebirth. From the sub-human to the super-human, the movie is about the journey of the human race from animal pre-self- consciousness to god-like enlightenment. And hand in hand with this theme was Kubrick's unrelenting insistence on interlacing his fable with concepts and imagery that evoked both birth and death. Very often, the two concepts were tied together—the birth of one predicated on the death of another. Though I believe the movie is ultimately life-affirming, Kubrick understood that you couldn't have the rebirth without the death; that you can't make the omelet without breaking the eggs. The constant eating that is shown throughout the film is another echo of how one's sustenance depends on the demise of another. So, in all its incarnations, the notion of birth and death overwhelmingly permeates the subtext of the movie, as well as its *mise-en-scène*.

Conception and Birth

Even before the film's titles appear up on the screen, Kubrick presents us with a moon-Earth-sun alignment that speaks eloquently to the idea of birth and enlightenment: A glorious, sunlit Earth seems to be literally born out of the dead, dark moon. And if one views the Earth as representing the cradle of humanity, the rising sun behind it becomes a metaphor for the dawning of awareness in human beings. It is the light bulb going on over the head of a person who has just discovered the answer. Incidentally, that shot of the entire Earth, partially lit, hanging in space, came nearly nine months before the reality was seen by the Apollo 8 astronauts during their Christmas mission around the moon at the close of 1968.[6] The very title of the movie portends the birth of a new millennium, a future 33 years ahead of the film's release. Back then, the "distant future" of the year 2001 may have looked promising, and our entry into space exploration our salvation. As if to reinforce the birth concept, immediately after the opening title we are shown another, this one proclaiming "The Dawn of Man," set against a serene African sunrise. Though life is hard for our prehistoric forebears, and death abounds, we are shown our ape ancestors in family units which include babies (played by real chimpanzees, no less).

Our first view of the future world of 2001 is a "space ballet" between the orbiting space station and an approaching space plane. The dance, and it *is* a dance, ends as the plane prepares to enter the docking port

36

slot at the station's center. You don't have to be Freud to figure this one out; it's clearly a mechanized version of coitus, and like all tasteful directors, Kubrick cuts away prior to penetration. On the space station, Floyd talks on a videophone with his young daughter (actually Kubrick's own daughter Vivian),[7] who is having a birthday party the next day. Cut from the final film was a second call Floyd made to Macy's to purchase a bushbaby for his little girl.[8]

The second half of the waltz, and the completion of Dr. Floyd's trip to the moon from the space station, takes place in a globe-shaped vessel and could be interpreted as the fertilized egg making its way to the uterus. The finale shows the vessel on the moon base landing pad being lowered into a womb-colored enclosure. Likewise, the cockpits of both the moon shuttle and moon bus are bathed in red light and, like the underground moon landing port, resemble electronic wombs.

Aboard the spaceship *Discovery* we are introduced to a new life form, Hal the computer, who seems to be nearly as sentient (and a lot more personable) than his human crew mates. One of these human astronauts, Frank Poole, receives birthday greetings from his parents from a video transmission, thus establishing another family unit. When it becomes necessary to leave the ship to repair the antenna, Mission Commander Dave Bowman uses a small, one-man space pod to do the task. As the pod exits the front of the "mother ship" through a set of parting double doors, the tiny sphere emerging from the larger one resembles an actual birth. The weightless astronaut exiting the pod to spacewalk his way to the antenna (in his red, ribbed spacesuit) recalls a newborn baby. Later in the film, when Bowman has to force his way back into the ship, he blasts into the emergency airlock—a red-lit womb if ever there was one—again wearing the red, ribbed spacesuit that makes him look like a newborn infant. In fact, this symbolic "birth" of Bowman comes on the heels of his taking decisive action against the computer who'd locked him out of the ship. In this way Bowman is reborn as a true human being (as opposed to the automaton-like astronaut he had been before), and has thus earned the right to learn the truth about the mission and the monolith. It is also a harbinger of his later, actual rebirth in the hotel room at the film's end.

Once the ship arrives in Jupiter's orbit, the planet and its countless moons, huddled together, evoke an image of a mother and her children.

During this sequence, we see a tiny *Discovery* (previously it had always appeared huge) against the immensity of the planet, looking like a spermatozoon attached to the female egg. Several shots later, the spaceship "ejaculates" a space pod (sperm), which will then enter the Star-Gate (vagina), at the end of which will be born the Star-Child (baby). The pod emerging from the maw of the ship also has echoes from Greek mythology of the goddess Athena, who was born fully grown out of the head of her father, the god Zeus.[9]

Death and Dying

There is also a great deal of death shown and alluded to in *2001*. In the opening "Dawn of Man" sequence, we see a number of African desert landscapes, all devoid of life save the hardy scrub plants and the birds whose cries we hear. The first signs of mammalian life we see are some bones. Life and death are immediately linked; one does not exist without the other.

Once the man-apes are introduced, it is obvious that they are struggling to survive and are under the constant threat of a marauding leopard. The leopard attacks a man-ape who is foraging for food; his companions scurry away, leaving the shrieking ape to his bloody fate. At night, while the man-apes huddle for safety in their cave, they can hear the leopard's menacing growls of contentment as it feasts on the carcass of a freshly killed zebra (actually a dead horse painted to look like a zebra, actual dead zebras evidently being hard to come by on Kubrick's set).[10]

After his encounter with the monolith, head man-ape Moon-Watcher is inspired to use a bone as a weapon. While he smashes a tapir skeleton in an orgy of ecstasy, we see images of real tapirs being felled. Moon-Watcher's meat-eating tribe, now stronger and smarter, overpowers a rival tribe for control of the local waterhole, beating to death its leader. The victorious Moon-Watcher hurls his weapon into the air and as it falls back to earth it is transformed, in one of the single most brilliant cuts in movie history, into a satellite orbiting the Earth. Originally this and other satellites seen were to be identified as weapons platforms (essentially, orbiting bombs), the idea being that we go from the first weapon to the ultimate one.[11] Much of this is lost upon the viewer, especially with the pleasant "Blue Danube" waltz serenely playing on the soundtrack. The only connection that can now be gleaned is that we are going from the most primitive tool (the bone) to the most sophisticated (an orbiting satellite). This works fine in the film's larger philosophy, but the death context is gone.

Dr. Floyd arrives at the excavation site on the moon (called TMA-1 for Tycho Magnetic Anomaly One), which resembles an immense, exaggerated-scale, open grave. The shot of the six spacesuited astronauts standing before the rim of the pit could easily be interpreted as mourners attending a funeral. The stygian monolith standing upright in the pit looks very much like an upright tombstone that, in an almost comical Magritte-like fashion,[12] is being mistakenly buried in place of the casket. Floyd and his comrades descend the ramp into the pit as if willingly walking toward their own deaths. Given the nature of the monolith, and what ultimately happens to Bowman at the film's end, it does seem that man as an entity indeed dies out, to be replaced by the Star-Child.

Next the huge interplanetary spaceship *Discovery 1* makes its way through the vast emptiness of deep space. This vessel, with a large spherical hull at one end, a long, segmented spine in the middle and its chunky propulsion system at the rear, looks like the gigantic skeleton of some bizarre extinct creature, especially when shown in elongated profile. Three of the five crew members are in a state of hibernation and will be "awakened" when the ship reaches Jupiter. The hibernation chambers, or "The Hibernaculum," as they were called in the novel, are long, horizontal units with clear Plexiglas tops; inside are white form-fitting shells that contain the hibernating astronauts. These shells, each with a tiny window showing the sleeping astronaut's face, look exactly like some futuristic mummy inside its sarcophagus box. This mummy motif evokes not only death but also rebirth. In earlier versions of the film, the hibernauts were referred to as "sleeping beauties,"[13] a reference to their glass coffins as well as their enchanted (i.e., false) state of death.

The other two astronauts, Bowman and Poole, use their chambers, without the shell, as conventional beds. Both are shown sleeping in them at one time or another, which suggests an open casket funeral. Eventually, the Hibernaculum become just that—coffins—when the three hibernauts are killed by Hal in what *New Yorker* movie critic Penelope Gilliatt called "the most chillingly modern death scene imaginable: warning lights simply signal 'computer malfunction' and sets of electrophysio-logical needles above the sleepers run amok on graphs and then record the straight lines of extinction."[14] These deaths occur when Bowman is outside the ship in a pod to rescue Poole, whose own pod turned on him, snipping his air hose and sending him careening off into space. Poole's death was subtly foreshadowed earlier in the film when he played a game of chess with Hal and lost. In keeping with the notion of sacrifice that is often necessary in chess, after retrieving Poole's body Bowman must let him go so he can use the pod's mechanical arms and hands to open the emergency airlock. The shot of Poole's receding, spinning corpse, framed in the oval window of the space pod as Bowman looks on in stony silence, is one of the most heartrending in the movie.

Bowman's victorious re-entry into *Discovery* through the emergency airlock, after Hal refused to open the pod bay doors, precipitates his single-minded determination to deactivate the rogue computer. Earlier, when Bowman and Poole discussed Hal's behavior in private, their conversation provided the expository information on what they would need to do to subdue him; it's not simply a matter of "pulling the plug." So when Bowman enters Hal's brain room and begins to deactivate him, we can see that it is a complex procedure, almost akin to a medical operation. Bowman inserts a screwdriver-type device into a row of small, square entry ports and gives each a one-quarter turn. This action causes the clear rectangular modules directly above each port to rise from their flush position in the control panel slots. With module after module sliding out, Hal pleads in his monotone voice for Bowman to stop, then regresses to an infantile state (shades of Bowman's fate!) as he recites his first lessons which includes the song "Daisy." The computer's voice continues to slow down during this monologue, becoming almost a death rattle at the end. Ironically, it is the most poignant death scene in the entire movie. For all intents and purposes, Hal was a sentient, living being and his "death" carries a greater sense of loss than any of the organic deaths of real human beings.

Not until very near the end of the movie, after the Star-Gate sequence, does the concept of death reappear. In the room at the end we see Bowman go through several stages of sudden aging which raises the specter of its inevitable conclusion. One can easily surmise that mankind itself is coming to an end, based on Bowman's unnaturally rapid progression towards death. This theme is also vividly illustrated when we see the dying Bowman in bed and the monolith appears in the room, looking, again, very much like a tombstone. The featureless black slab rises from the foot of the bed (seen in an elegantly symmetrical, totally Kubrickian composition of the room) that leaves little speculation as to its symbolic meaning. The surprise (if one can call it that) comes when the dying Bowman is then transformed (reborn) as the Star-Child.

So what is one to make of Kubrick's interplay between the symbols of birth and death? On which side of the equation does the filmmaker stand? Though Kubrick was notorious, at least in his films, for being a cynical realist with a dark disposition toward the human race and a not very favorable believer in the goodness of man, it seems that *2001* would be the exception to the rule. In almost all of his films, the main characters tended to be unlikable and usually came to no good in the end. But in *2001*, a film which bombarded us relentlessly with imagery and situations that suggested both birth and death, in the final moments—the final frame, even—it is birth and life, as illustrated in the visage of the luminous Star-Child, which wins out and carries the day.

Color

For all practical purposes, artistically speaking, *2001* was Kubrick's first color movie. In 1953, he had shot the color documentary short *The Seafarers*, but that "for hire" job afforded him little opportunity to control what images came before his lens. Likewise, with *Spartacus*, Kirk Douglas' big-budget Roman epic, Kubrick was denied control of the artistic reins, at least regarding sets and costumes, all of which were in place when he came aboard as a last-minute replacement.[15] Up until that time, Kubrick's *mise-en-scène* was largely dictated by his black-and-white photo essays for *Look* magazine, followed by his noir-inspired film work of the 1950s. Given what little experience he had then, it is all the more remarkable that his *2001* work is so innovative and assured in its use of color. *2001* marked a turning point in Kubrick's oeuvre; from this point on, all his films would be shot in color. The director who made his name photographing stark, graphic images in noirish black-and-white found that he was equally adept when it came to the rest of the spectrum.

In symbolic terms, Kubrick favored the color red; it was his hue of choice, the pigment of his imagination. Though there are wonderful splashes of red throughout *Spartacus*, we can't be sure how much was added by Kubrick and how much was already there when he came on board. In later films, red would almost exclusively signal danger or foreboding. (The red bathroom and the cascading river of blood in *The Shining* are standout examples.) While this is certainly true in *2001*, most notably when Bowman blasts his way into the emergency airlock and when he enters Hal's brain room to disconnect him, red also served to display a sense of wonder: the sweeping white curve of the space station interior, dotted with bright red Olivier Mourgue chairs; the controlled energies of spaceship cockpits bathed in red light like photographic darkrooms (an environment Kubrick knew well!); Bowman, in his red spacesuit, traversing the white octagonal storage bay; the lunar shuttle being lowered into the cavernous red-lit moon base landing port; and Bowman, again in his red spacesuit, standing in the hotel room at the film's end.

As the first truly transitional film in Kubrick's leap from black-and-white to color, it is interesting to note that the first three-quarters of *2001* are shot almost like a black-and-white movie: the subdued palette of the opening African scenes, white spaceships against black star fields, white interiors with, generally, one focal color (the red chairs in the space station, the yellow walls of the moon shuttle, the blue chairs at the moon base) or are bathed in red monochromatic light (cockpits, Hal's brain, the emergency airlock, the moon base landing port). It is only when the Star-Gate opens up before Bowman that the audience is engulfed in an overwhelming deluge of colors. It's as if Kubrick has been holding back and holding back, using color very judiciously for maximum impact (I've seen few films where I was so aware of the use of color as in *2001*), and then, during the Star-Gate, he opens the floodgates and the colors literally come rushing at us.

Editing

Kubrick was a keen proponent of the power of editing, which he considered the most satisfying and intrinsically artistic element in the hierarchy of filmmaking. He once said, "The most instructive book on film aesthetics I came across was Pudovkin's *Film Technique*, which simply explained that editing was the aspect of the film art form which was completely unique, and which separated it from all other art forms."[16] On his own, he studied the techniques of varied directors and editors, especially the noted Russian filmmakers Sergei Eisenstein and the aforementioned V.I. Pudovkin, specifically their theories on editing, or montage. The concept of montage, as practiced by Eisenstein and detailed in his essay compilations *Film Form* and *Film Sense*, influenced Kubrick in many of the editing choices he made throughout his career, though he didn't think much of the filmmaker himself. "Eisenstein's greatest achievement is in the beautiful visual compositions of his shots, and his editing. But as far as content is concerned, his films are silly, his actors are wooden and operatic."[17] The most dramatic editing technique employed by the Russian filmmaker was "collision," in which the juxtaposing of two images creates a separate, almost kinetic reaction.[18]

While the "bone-to-bomb" cut is the most flamboyant (and symbolic) edit in Kubrick's entire oeuvre, there are three other noteworthy examples of collision in *2001*: (1) the cut from a peaceful nighttime landscape of the man-apes' cave, to the raucous flurry of activity of the screeching man-ape tribes at the final waterhole scene prior to the murder of the other tribe's leader; (2) the static two-shot, from behind, of Bowman and Poole listening to mission control okaying their plan to replace the antenna unit, to the tracking shot behind Bowman, breathing heavily in his red spacesuit as he walks through the white, eight-sided storage room to enter the pod bay; and (3) a space pod is seen racing toward the camera in dead silence; then there's a close-up of Bowman in the pod, with the radar tracking sound as backdrop. In every one of these editorial collisions, Kubrick also uses the collision of silence and sound to underscore the visual elements. Strictly speaking, while these techniques do not necessarily function as metaphor or symbolism, Kubrick found the use of them added a heightened ambience to his mythological tale. As a form of cinematic language, Kubrick's use of collision editing can perhaps be equated to the use of stylized verse by Homer to tell his epic poems. In both cases, the artistry helps to enhance the story.

While many of Kubrick's earlier films dabbled in the use of symbolism to convey the director's vision (the chessboard courtroom in *Paths of Glory*, the Gainsborough-esque portrait, riddled with bullet holes, of a young woman in *Lolita*, the airplane refueling-copulation in *Dr. Strangelove*), they were evidently just a warm-up for what he was to achieve in *2001*. His films after that continued to use symbolism in provocative ways, but the sheer amount to be found in *2001* would not be duplicated. Kubrick's usage and sophistication with symbols and metaphor, however, can be demarcated clearly between his pre–*2001* and his post–*2001* work. And the lessons learned at this juncture would serve him well in his career where his experimentation found a new maturity and subtlety.

For some, this Kubrickian trait of pushing the cinematic envelope was seen merely as parlor tricks or the showboating antics of an insecure talent. However, Kubrick never believed that a filmmaker should remain an invisible element in the process, and considered film to be a legitimate art form.[19] He often wrestled with the dilemma of form vs. content, always wanting to extend the visual range of the medium (special effects in *2001*; period lighting in *Barry Lyndon*; fluid camera movement in *The Shining*), yet realizing that you needed to ground such experimentation in a strong story to keep the audience interested. In *2001*, he found the perfect marriage of the two, crafting a tale of mythological proportions and then dressing it up in a symbolist veneer that helped make it one of his best works—a film regarded as one of the greatest of all time. At the very least, *2001*'s success made it viable for movies to indulge in a higher artistic ambition and still appeal to a mass audience. This is something that we now take for granted, the notion that an art film could reach across the class chasm and find a home with middlebrow sensibilities. Prior to the release of *2001*, and its phenomenal worldwide success in the late 1960s, this simply wasn't the case. There is little doubt that its success paved the way for further unconventional explorations like *Eraserhead* in the 1970s, *Koyaanisqatsi* in the '80s and even *Pulp Fiction* in the '90s. Movies today are both dumber and smarter than they've ever been and the success of such innovative fare as *A Beautiful Mind*, *Memento* and *Amelie*, to name just three films from the year 2001, is proof that the seeds of Kubrick's 1968 masterpiece have continued to provide a rich cinematic harvest that still nourishes us to this day.

3

SCIENCE AND TECHNOLOGY
The Future That *2001* Predicted

Well, given the level of detail in the movie, it was an absolute setup to be proven wrong. I've got to say that I'm really impressed by how much the movie got right. And I think a lot of the mistakes are really interesting mistakes—mistakes that one learns something from by seeing why they were made.
—computer expert Stephen Wolfram in *HAL's Legacy*

For many Americans, the 1950s was an era of profound optimism. Anything seemed possible; standards of living were rising, allowing for widespread home ownership for many working class people for the first time. This postwar prosperity continued into the 1960s with the Kennedy administration and the Camelot era). Young, vibrant and, dare we say, sexy, John F. Kennedy epitomized America's new direction and savvy sophistication. Civil rights were on the move to bring equality to the dispossessed; technologically, we had entered the space age, with manned orbital flights around the Earth and a commitment to go to the moon. It seemed as if each day some new challenge was faced and met; apparently nothing was beyond man's capability. All he needed was the will to do it. Computers had begun to take on many varied tasks, speeding up production and making life easier, better and more efficient. The communications satellite Telstar allowed people to see live television broadcasts from almost anywhere in the world, making us more of a global community. Propeller-driven passenger airplanes were giving way to jet travel, making trips to faraway locales less of an ordeal. The world, it seemed, was shrinking. And Pan American Airlines had announced that when the time came—perhaps during the 1980s or so—they would be the first to offer passenger service into space.[1] Orbiting hotels and resorts on the moon were only a step away. Welcome to the future!

Well, then, what the hell happened? When we finally stood on the other side of the millennium, many of the dreams of *2001*'s "Expo '01" technological future had not yet materialized. What seemed possible, and even inevitable, in 1964, when Kubrick's space adventure was still in its embryonic stage, ultimately crumpled under the weight and expense of the Vietnam War and of later administrations that were unwilling to commit to the long-term goal of establishing a presence in space. Add to that the miscellaneous unforeseen setbacks that inevitably crop up whenever technology is asked to break new ground, yet must still answer to the whims of political and social realities, and it is almost a certainty that some percentage of predictions will miss the mark. It is the cold fear that clutches the heart of anyone who strays into the field of prognostication. But despite the missteps, Kubrick's crystal ball still functioned remarkably well (thanks to Clarke and others whose job it was to do the gazing), and for far longer than most other cinematic attempts.

The visual design of *2001* functioned as both symbolic representation and scientific speculation. In addition to the abstract and metaphoric dimension of the film, there was also the simple nuts-and-bolts aspect of its production design. In telling his mythological fable, Kubrick knew it had to be grounded in an absolutely real environment. Sets, clothing, spacecraft, props, signage, sound effects, etc.—all of it had to be 100 percent believable. This documentary approach had served Kubrick well in his previous film *Dr. Strangelove*, where all the hardware and military settings were as real as possible. Against that backdrop he could then play out his nightmare comedy and even be allowed the indulgence of the fantastical War Room set that was a classic example of metaphoric design and has since become a staple in other movies.

Fantastic sets would be the order of the day for Kubrick's film, but they would all have to carry the stamp of authenticity from genuine design engineers. Up until the making of *2001*, not much thought or effort went into the design of futuristic sets or props, at least not in the direction of realism. Production design might be stylish, though usually with little regard to functionality or what made sense. If computers were

Director Stanley Kubrick, standing over actor Gary Lockwood on the interior pod set, lines up a shot.

called for, you simply put together some boxy shapes with lots of blinking lights. Spaceships were either saucers or tubes with fins. Costumes could range from the banal to the outlandish, as long as the women's outfits were revealing and/or skintight. Kubrick would have none of this. He had higher aspirations than mere titillation.

Director Stanley Kubrick (with beard) on the centrifuge set with actors Keir Dullea and Gary Lockwood (seated).

The Design Team Triumvirate

To achieve the realism he desired, Kubrick sought out the help of technology design firms to supplement the work of his production designer Tony Masters. He also secured the services of NASA designer Harry Lange, who was instrumental in giving *2001* its sleek, clean, believable look. Scientific advisor Frederick I. Ordway also helped keep the production on the straight and narrow regarding what was likely to be a reality 30 years down the line. These three men were largely responsible for the overall design of Kubrick's masterpiece. A closer look at their backgrounds and contribution to the film sheds an illuminating light on the creative design process.

One of the preeminent production designers working in film at the time, Tony Masters was perhaps best known for his work with John Box on David Lean's epic *Lawrence of Arabia*. The tall, affable Brit started making a name for himself in movies in the 1940s, with work on such films as *Don't Bother to Knock*, *Expresso Bongo*, *The Day the Earth Caught Fire*, *Ferry Cross the Mersey* and *The Heroes of Telemark*. His efforts on *2001* in planning out the design of nearly all the sets, from the spacecraft interiors to the surreal hotel room at the end, are considered by many to be the pinnacle of his long career. It would also be Masters' only Oscar nomination; his *Lawrence of Arabia* colleague John Box won for the musical *Oliver*.

In addition to the grandeur of the space station interior and the TMA-1 lunar excavation site, *2001*'s centerpiece sets were the *Discovery* spaceship interiors, most notably the drum-shaped centrifuge and the pod bay. The 38-foot diameter, ten-foot-wide centrifuge was designed to provide the astronauts with an artificial gravity along the rim, thanks to its ability to rotate at a constant speed. The actual set was built by the Vickers-Armstrong Engineering Group at a cost of $750,000 and could, in fact, rotate at three miles per hour, which allowed Kubrick to obtain some remarkable shots.[2] In the introductory sequence, Frank Poole (Gary Lockwood) is seen jogging around the entire 360-degree interior in what appears to be a fixed camera shot. In reality, the actor remained at the bottom of the rotating set, running in place as it were, while the camera was attached to the moving centrifuge. Since the entire set rotated, the camera didn't "know" it was moving.[3] On screen it appears as if the actor is traveling around the motionless interior of the centrifuge space. Kubrick also used this technique with the stewardess in the Aries moon shuttle to great effect. As innovative as this camera trick appeared, it had previously been done in the 1951 movie *Royal Wedding*, where Fred Astaire is seen dancing around an entire room (floor, walls, ceiling). As in *2001*, the camera was attached to a rotating set.

While Kubrick's efforts with the centrifuge paid off handsomely, when it came to the pod bay set he was slightly less successful in depicting the weightless environment that would exist there. Having already established the Velcro "grip shoes" on the Orion space plane, the director decided that his Jupiter-bound astronauts would use them as well. The actors walk in a sort of loping, buoyant fashion as if they were underwater and their feet were "Velcro-ed" to the carpet. Most audience members did not pick up on this and assumed that there was some other kind of artificial gravity in the pod bay or that Kubrick had decided to just overlook this element of physics. It didn't help that he had his actors lean on consoles, step up into pods and climb ladders in a conventional gravity manner. One early concept idea for a zero gravity Athena computer control room, submitted by Eliot Noyes and Associates in 1965 and rejected by Kubrick, was to have each astronaut secured in a hip yoke mechanism on an extended boom arm that would allow them to work safely in a gravity-free environment.[4] Perhaps if digital effects technology had been available in the mid–1960s to "erase" support wires, the director would have had his astronauts floating around in the pod bay just like the actual astronauts of the actual year 2001 did on the space shuttle and the International Space Station.

While Masters was busy building the inside of Kubrick's futuristic world, based on Harry Lange's design input, Lange was concentrating on the outside, specifically spacecraft design, spacesuits and various props needed to bring the 21st century to life. His NASA background and his friendship with such illustrious scientists as Wernher von Braun made Lange an ideal component to the *2001* design team. In the world of moviemaking, the hiring of an actual scientific designer was practically unprecedented and Lange's input would be as far-reaching as anyone's regarding the technical hardware look of the film.

Carrying the "think tank" notion a step further, Kubrick drew on the considerable talents of Frederick I. Ordway III, a liaison consultant for NASA. Hired as a scientific advisor in January 1965, Ordway supplied the production with up-to-the-minute information regarding the scientific credibility of virtually everything in the movie.[5] He also served as a public relations conduit between Kubrick and the many technology design companies that provided concept drawings and real hardware for the film. These firms included private civilian corporations Bell Telephone Laboratories, Boeing, Chrysler, Honeywell, IBM, Eliot Noyes and Whirlpool, as well as government agencies that were providing technology systems for NASA.[6]

Lange and Ordway were colleagues who, together with others, had founded the consulting company General Astronautics Research Corporation. The men had also co-authored a speculative science text titled *Intelligence in the Universe*. By chance, Arthur C. Clarke met the two in January 1965 at the American Institute of Aeronautics and Astronautics convention held at New York's Hilton Hotel. After a bit of a chat, it became clear to Clarke (who was there to publicize his own science book *Man and Space*), that Kubrick needed to meet these guys. A quick call to the director allowed him to set up a get-together with the two men, who quickly agreed to become a part of the project. What was anticipated to be a six-month stint ballooned into a two-year-plus commitment for the pair.[7]

One of the hardest aspects of Ordway's job was that he never knew where Kubrick would point his camera, or how close he'd get to the technology on display, so everything had to look completely realistic.[8] Given the level of sophistication and integrity they brought to their work on *2001*, Ordway, Lange and Masters could take pride in the knowledge that they contributed a great deal to Kubrick's movie and that they kept the science in it as honest as possible.

Where's Hal?

Many of *2001*'s predictions about our technological future have not yet come true, though an argument could be made that it was more a matter of economics and short-sightedness, rather than a failure of science, which has kept us from reaching these goals. When it came to the Hal 9000 computer, however, it must be acknowledged that science and know-how failed to appreciate the complexities involved in creating this particular kind of machine intelligence. It was assumed that cognitive ability was merely a matter of raw brain power, and that as computers acquired more "memory" and computing power, a type of awareness by the computer of itself would inevitably follow. Well, it turns out that crunching numbers is one thing, but trying to teach a computer to understand the subtleties of human language—its inflection and context, the emotionally charged relationship of certain words or phrases to others, the experiential quality of various words which can trigger our emotions and memory recall—all of these intangibles still remain beyond the computer's ability to understand, much less reproduce.

The notion of a sentient machine was certainly not new prior to *2001*. Robots and talking computers, a staple of science fiction, can be found in the writings of classic authors Isaac Asimov (*I, Robot*) and Robert Heinlein (*The Moon Is a Harsh Mistress*), as well as in a plethora of films (*Metropolis, The Day the Earth Stood Still, Forbidden Planet*). Very often the use of these devices serves as an analogy for the human condition, either how we as a species are becoming more machine-like and losing our own humanity, or as an evolutionary extension of where we are headed and how a more powerful brain might function. In the case of Hal, the idea of a machine intelligence in a movie about the evolutionary leap of the human race from ape to man to superman served mainly as a satiric jab at man's attempt to play at being God, a pale reflection of the god-like force of the monolith that was, according to the film, the progenitor of the human race.

Hal's own evolution was similar to the creative evolution of most of the other elements in the film; just as the man-apes, spacecraft and sets followed a path toward their final design, Hal, too, changed. In the first draft of Clarke's novel, Hal was a talking robot named "Socrates."[9] Perhaps Kubrick had seen one too many bad films with robots or maybe there was just something inherently comical about the robot persona; whatever the reason, it was decided to make the robot a computer and to give it a female personality. This new incarnation was christened Athena,[10] named for the goddess of war, wisdom and fertility. Athena is also in Homer's *Odyssey*, and plays a sort of "divine counterpart" to Odysseus (as Sheila Murnaghan said in her introduction to Stanley Lombardo's 2000 translation of the epic poem). The idea of male astronauts interacting with the female computer certainly plays to Kubrick's sense of humor and irony and would even have added an interesting take on the role that gender plays in society. The Athena name was retained by the production people in identifying one of the sets and appears on the blueprints the set builders used.[11] On a less serious note is this entry in Clarke's diary after a typical story bull session: "Stanley has invented the wild idea of slightly fag robots who create a Victorian environment to put our heroes at ease."[12] Ultimately, it was decided to give the computer a male voice and persona and thus was born Hal, for *Heuristically* programmed *al*gorithmic computer. The fact that HAL is one letter shifted from IBM in the alphabet was, according to Clarke, a coincidence.[13]

While the movie was being shot, British actor Nigel Davenport was briefly engaged to provide in-person on-set line deliveries for the other actors to engage with. Kubrick also used one of his production assistants on occasion. However, Keir Dullea remembers Hal's lines being read to him by a production assistant with a strong Michael Caine Cockney accent. It was always Kubrick's intention to later dub in an American-accented voice for the film's release. Noted character actor Martin Balsam was brought in but his distinctive voice was found to be too emotive. Kubrick offered the part to Canadian actor Douglas Rain, who was originally hired to provide narration for *2001*. Rain had narrated *Universe* and *To the Moon and Beyond*, films Kubrick had seen in 1964 that had fascinated him with their innovative effects work. Clearly Kubrick had done more than just look at them. Rain, a Shakespearean actor with a pleasant though somewhat aloof voice, had just the right quality for the all-seeing, all-knowing computer; he brought a neutral, almost asexual tone to Hal's personality.[14] As a result, Rain's performance became a favorite of fans to imitate.

The fact that there is no Hal yet does not mean that Kubrick and Clarke failed. To be sure, the tenets of artificial intelligence turned out to be far more complex and difficult than anyone imagined. The computational ability of computers has been the real growth element in the industry, and it may turn out that creating an intelligent machine like Hal is impossible. Kubrick and Clarke's real intent with Hal was to explore artificial intelligence as a metaphorical comment on human intelligence. In that sense, Hal was a success.

Technology

The reality of the actual year 2001, compared to the predictions made in Kubrick's film regarding our technical sophistication, is far more complex than simply how much they got right or wrong. No matter how hard you try, it is impossible to predict with any fidelity how much things will change. Production design in movies tends to have an isolated, straight-line purity that does not reflect the real world, where designs generally carry the baggage of their previous history. Look at a photo from the 1950s and you are bound to see vestiges from many past decades as well. Still, it is a tribute to the makers of *2001* that the film continues to look believable and realistic, even if it isn't true to the period. An examination of the various technological elements in the movie can provide us with an accurate gauge of the filmmakers' batting average.

Computers

Aside from Hal, the use of computers in *2001* was wide and varied. The many spaceship control panels seen throughout the film had computer readout screens integrated into their layout which carried information and graphics to enable the pilots to maneuver their craft. The Orion space plane even had a faux 3-D moving graphic of the rectangular entry port on the space station that indicated the plane was being guided by computer to its rendezvous. More computer screens are seen on the Aries moon ship, in the underground moon base airlock, in the moon bus cockpit and at the TMA-1 landing pad control center (which looks like it might be a redress of the Athena room set in the *Discovery* pod bay).

On the *Discovery* spaceship, there is Hal, of course, and his computer screens proliferate all over the ship. At one point, we are shown another faux 3-D graphic, this one a "wire-frame" rendering of the ship's antenna, which was actually realized by building a real wire-frame sculpture of the antenna and photographing it in stop-motion animation on high-contrast black-and-white film stock. The resulting images were cleaned up and composited with text graphics. A similar process was used for the rotating X-ray scans of the AE-35 unit which Bowman and Poole examine on the workbench in the pod bay and the space station entry port graphic mentioned earlier.[15] The one-man space pods also contain numerous screens, one of which figures prominently in a radar readout that Bowman uses when he pursues Poole's runaway tumbling body.

Most of the images on the various screens seen throughout the movie do not resemble the kind of graphics seen in the actual 2001 era. Part of the reason for that, of course, was the inability to predict just how far graphics would evolve over time, but partly it was that the screens in *2001* needed to look a certain way that would resonate with the audience of the time. The images seen in the film look more "computer-y" than the ones we actually developed. There is a sense of constant change and motion on the movie computers that is not a part of reality. Some of that constant changing (especially when the monitors display the large, three-letter abbreviations—i.e., NAV for navigation) may, inadvertently, have anticipated the need for screen savers to avoid the problem of screen burn-in that occurred on early computer monitors. But, mostly, the ever-changing graphics, and their look, were designed to reflect what the public (most of whom had no real contact with computers at that time) thought a computer readout should look like; in other words, "computer-y."

The breadth and use of personal computers was not foreseen (nor the idea of the Internet, Windows operating systems or menu software), though Bowman and Poole do have their own "telepads" to watch their BBC interview transmission. The lack of hand-held technology is most glaringly illustrated during an information-gathering sequence in the *Discovery*'s Command Module section, where Bowman and Poole are shown jotting down figures on clipboards with paper tablets. In reality, they would likely have used some sort of touch-screen device tied into the main computer to enter their data.

Nuclear Power

There was a time, in the long-ago 1950s and '60s, when the idea of harnessing nuclear energy for peaceful purposes (as opposed to, say, nuclear bombs) was the Holy Grail of our energy-hungry nation. Forecasters predicted that nuclear power plants would soon be able to supply energy to the world, and at a cost that was—are you ready for this?—

too low to even meter! And with a little bit of ingenuity, it could be used to power our cars, mass transit, ships, planes and, of course, spaceships. No longer dependent on the dwindling supplies of fossil fuels like oil, coal, and natural gas, we would enter an era of energy abundance that would bring a modern standard of living to the entire world.

It sounded too good to be true, and it was. While today's nuclear reactors are used in everything from power plants to submarines, the utopian future envisioned by starry-eyed optimists came crashing down in the wake of Three Mile Island and Chernobyl. The dangers of nuclear energy had been drastically underestimated, as well as the problems of disposing of the radioactive waste byproduct generated by the reactors. And with the manned space program seriously scaled back in the 1970s, there was little demand for developing nuclear-powered, interplanetary spaceships like the *Discovery*.

At the time they were making their film, Kubrick and Clarke both championed the idea of nuclear-powered spacecraft. The energy requirements demanded a more efficient form of fuel than the chemical rockets of the day. To lift the tiny Apollo moon capsule into Earth orbit required a chemical missile over 360 feet tall filled with nearly six million pounds of fuel (liquid hydrogen and liquid oxygen).[16] Breaking out of Earth orbit to travel to other planets in a reasonable time frame requires the vehicle to travel extremely fast. During the BBC interview with Bowman and Poole, the commentator states that the *Discovery* left Earth "three weeks ago" and is currently "80 million miles" away. A bit of calculator math indicates the ship is traveling at about 160,000 miles an hour. At that speed, the "half-billion-mile voyage to Jupiter," as stated in the film, would take 130 days, not counting braking maneuvers needed to slow the ship to achieve orbit around the planet. The ship's engines would shut down once it achieved the escape velocity needed to reach Jupiter since, with no frictional drag in the vacuum of space, the ship would maintain its speed.

Over the course of designing spacecraft for the film, many propulsion systems were considered for use on the *Discovery*. One of the more intriguing nuclear power methods explored by Kubrick was the Orion project. Begun in the 1950s by Freeman Dyson, it postulated the use of small nuclear bombs that would be detonated against a pusher plate at the rear of the ship, at the rate of about one bomb a minute. The plate would absorb the energy of the explosion which would push the ship forward. Not surprisingly, this concept was passed over as being too radical and bizarre, even for the director of *Dr. Strangelove*. The only Orion remnant left in the film is its namesake on the Earth orbit space plane.[17] Ultimately, Kubrick and his design team chose the Cavradyne fission engine reactor design to power the Jupiter-bound *Discovery* spacecraft. A real design concept, it may eventually be used for human interplanetary travel. The engine module and rear nozzle components as seen in the movie are consistent with the design parameters required of such a system.[18] However, Kubrick chose to eliminate the radiating fins that would be needed to dissipate the heat generated by the ship, since he felt they looked too much like wings, and would have needed to be explained to the audience.[19]

A few years after *2001* came out, we were able to explore Jupiter through the unmanned Pioneer 10 and 11 probes. Despite being launched with conventional chemical rockets, the probes did have nuclear generators (called RTGs for "radioisotope thermoelectric generators")[20] to power the vehicles and their array of scientific experiments. In December 1973, Pioneer 10 was the first manmade device to reach the outer planets beyond Mars and became the unexpected antecedent to the *Discovery* mission from *2001*.[21] While no monolith was detected in orbit around the Jovian gas giant, more information was learned about the largest planet in our solar system during the probe's brief fly-by, than had been known over the previous 400 years since Galileo first turned his primitive telescope on Jupiter.

Artificial Gravity

The idea of spinning a space vehicle in zero gravity to create a gravity environment around its rim has been around since the earliest days of speculating about space travel. In creating a thousand-foot-diameter space station for the film, Kubrick took the concept to its most elegant end. And while it would be desirable to have a rotating cabin on an interplanetary ship, *Discovery*'s 38-foot-diameter centrifuge would be too small to counteract the Coriolis Effect of dizziness that would actually occur in the inhabitants. A spin diameter of at least 300 feet would be required to alleviate the problem, something the production was aware of, but couldn't solve logistically.[22] In reality, a spaceship would need to be designed to have cabins at either end of a 300-foot rotating boom attached to the ship, rather than a drum-shaped room incorporated within. Given that so little technical information was known by the general public, I assume Kubrick figured he could cheat on this matter since the concept was essentially sound.

Spacesuits

The spacesuits seen in *2001* are, without a doubt, the most beautiful and believable ever made for a movie, certainly up until that time. Elegant and streamlined, they look far superior to the real suits worn by our astronauts in the actual year 2001. The uniquely shaped helmets (designed by Harry Lange), with their stylish, wraparound visors, combine function and aesthetics to create a look that is as far removed from the traditional "fish bowl" motif while still maintaining total believability. The black panel along the back of the helmet holds memory storage units (the equivalent of a floppy disc or CD-ROM) that provide the astronauts with additional information.[23] These units are seen only on the *Discovery* helmets, but it's assumed the moon helmets can also accommodate them. The designers obviously underestimated just how much storage capacity technology would develop, since the eight units attached to each helmet would be able to contain whole libraries of data.

The modular chest packs and back packs are also well-thought-out pieces of equipment that were designed to cater to the needs of the wearer. The modest packs on the moon suits are markedly different from the more complex ones used on the *Discovery* mission, the latter containing, among other amenities, a thruster unit for maneuvering in space. The packs of the moon suits (which are used in a gravity environment) are strapped around the sides, while the *Discovery* packs (designed for zero-g) are strapped under the crotch for better stability.

The ribbed design on both types of suit provides flexibility and ease of movement for the wearer, a necessity where large-scale application of the garment is anticipated (i.e., building space stations and moon bases). The ribbing on the arms goes three quarters the way around, leaving a flat area along the "inside" where the arm would lay against the body. Ribbing on the legs is confined to the sides, leaving the front and back areas flat. The only real difference between the two suit garments (besides their color) is the push-button control panel along the left arm of the *Discovery* suits. Designed by Eliot Noyes and Associates, an architecture and industrial design firm that contributed many ideas for the movie, the original mock-up submitted to Kubrick incorporated a small video screen along with the push-buttons.[24] In the film, Bowman is shown using the control panel to polarize his visor against the harsh sunlight. Nowadays, we have glass that darkens automatically when exposed to light.

Hibernation

The other key technology that never came to pass the way *2001* envisioned was the science of cryogenics, or artificial hibernation. Back in the 1960s it was assumed that the then-burgeoning study of cryogenics would continue to develop and eventually become mainstream. It was felt that such a technology would be used extensively in long-duration space travel or other human endeavors where the consumption of food, water and air should be minimized. The idea of putting people into a state of suspended animation, where bodily functions were reduced (along with the aging process), has long been an old chestnut in science fiction. Sometimes given a colorful moniker like "hyper-sleep," it was used so often and freely that most people figured it would be an inevitable part of our future. In the film, hibernation is spoken about in the most mundane of terms. An interviewer says to Poole, "As I understand it, you only breathe once a minute. Is this true?" The astronaut replies, "Well, that's right, and the heart beats three times a minute; body temperature's usually down to about three degrees Centigrade." Though there was quite a bit of research done over the years, it was ultimately curtailed for moral as much as for safety reasons; imagine the psychological effects on an astronaut who ages differently than his family. Also, with the cutting-back on manned space flight (and no long-duration missions in the foreseeable future), there was nothing really tangible to drive any continued research.

These days the cryonics industry is mostly involved in muscle therapy and arthritis treatment. However, one branch of the business caters to deep-freeze corpse storage (either the whole body or just the head), using liquid nitrogen as the freezing medium, with an eye towards reviving and repairing the dear departed once the necessary technology has been developed. During the making of *2001*, Kubrick was more than a little bit impressed with the work of physicist Robert Ettinger, who proposed freezing dead bodies in liquid nitrogen. Even though Kubrick expressed a real interest in cryonic freezing, there is no evidence to suggest that he availed himself of the process when he died in March 1999. It has long been rumored that Walt Disney had himself frozen when he died in 1966, with the stipulation that he be thawed and revived when medical science made it feasible. The family has always denied this rumor and it is considered to be just another one of those urban myths.

At best, cryonic deep-freeze is a stop-gap method providing a slender thread of hope to those who crave immortality (or, at least, a much longer life span) in a world that has yet to create the means to achieve it; at worst, it is a con game that preys upon the hopes and dreams of the gullible, alleviating their fears about impending death. On some level, it's hard to believe that people would put their trust into such an unproven technology. However, in a hundred years, if these people are revived and go on to live long lives, maybe even immortal ones, I suppose they will have the last laugh after all.

Picture-Phone

Ever since the mid–1960s, Bell Telephone had been teasing the public about the imminent arrival of "picture-phones." At the time *2001* was made, the phone company was, in essence, a monopoly, and they provided phone equipment in your home or business on a rental basis. You did not actually own your phone, and the ones you rented were solidly built pieces of equipment, unlike today's cheap, lightweight and easily breakable models. Since Bell owned the equipment, it was in their best interest to make it as sturdy as possible. For *2001*, Kubrick enlisted the aid of Bell Telephone and used their prototype design for the public phones then on their drawing boards. If you look closely, you can see the Bell logo on the booth in the film.

Reality has dealt us a different hand. Once the phone monopoly was broken in the 1980s, there was little incentive to offer picture-phone technology to the masses, due to the large infrastructure required to maintain it. Also, as it turned out, most people really didn't want picture-phones. After nearly a century of audio-only communications, people were unwilling to openly embrace the face-to-face interaction this new technology required. However, the recent glut in media overkill and the rise of computer technology, webcams, personal pagers and cell phones has changed everything, including the public's reticence about the picture-phone. People routinely send video over their smart phones and computers, using Skype, and it is only a matter of time before we see the full emergence of the picture-phone as standard equipment in the home.

The IBM Telepad

Conceived as a flat TV device designed to display any kind of printed or visual information, this ingenious gadget (referred to in the novel as a "newspad") finds its closest cousin in the real world with a laptop computer and the iPad tablet. In the film, we see Bowman enter the ship's centrifuge portion through its central hub. After descending the ladder to the outer rim, he walks along its perimeter to the kitchen area where he tosses his telepad onto the table. Poole, already seated at the table, watches his own telepad as he eats. The image on the screen shows a counter clicking down to the next video transmission, which turns out to be a BBC interview the astronauts had done. This scene serves the dual purpose of showing off the technology while being an economical method of relaying backstory and exposition of the characters and the mission.

The vertical shape of the telepad has found its counterpart in reality in computer tablets and smartphone screens, which can also function horizontally. Television sets, computer monitors and laptop screens have all embraced the horizontal widescreen format which is better suited for watching movies in their correct aspect ratio, and which can range anywhere from the Academy standard of 1.33 to 1 all the way to Cinerama's 2.8 to 1. Throughout *2001* there are flat-panel screens that suggest the end of the cathode ray tube. At the turn of the millennium, we had just begun to see these devices (either as liquid crystal displays or plasma screens) make their appearance. It is obvious now that the flat screens have completely taken over, and that old-style picture tube sets will become quaint collector's items.

Zero Gravity Toilet

Created mainly as a humorous sight gag for the movie audience, the ten-paragraph list of instructions on the use of the toilet can still get a smile or laugh out of viewers. In the movie, it is impossible to read any of the instructions, but thanks to Jerome Agel's 1970 book *The Making of Kubrick's 2001*, the full list is available for examination. As one might expect from Kubrick, what was intended as a ten-second joke shot had as much effort and planning put into it as any other element of the film. More than just a primer on how to take a zero-g "whiz," each paragraph outlines, in excruciating detail that reads more like stereo instructions, the use of various functions of the toilet, from liquid and solid waste disposal, to washing one's hands, to the use of a "sonoshower." Though none of this information is legible on screen, for the actors making the movie, this attention to detail must have had quite an impact on them regarding the realism of the cinematic world they were inhabiting.

The Parker Atomic Pen

The little pen seen floating in the Orion space plane cabin turns out to be far more sophisticated than one might suspect. More than just a clever gimmick to sell the zero-g environment; more, even, than a visual echo of the bone-bomb image that propelled us into the modern portion of the film, the pen represents both the sublime and the ridiculous aspects of the use of nuclear energy that will "make our lives better." In a case of the pen being mightier than the sword, it was designed to contain a tiny nuclear reactor! According to Parker's own publicity release, "Neutrons flowing from the reactor travel through a neutron gun to the paper, where they burn an impression. A ruby shield around the gun brings the neutrons into focus, and a tiny ruby-shielded window looks into the reactor chamber. The other two buttons turn the pen on and off."[25] One can only imagine the lawsuits that would ensue from the accidental or intentional mischief such a device would inspire. It is reasonable to surmise that Kubrick was actually having a bit of fun at the absurd notion of what could be done with nuclear energy and its application in everyday life. Unfortunately, since the nature of the pen was never identified, the joke, if there was one, was lost upon the viewer.

While *2001* certainly didn't get it *all* right, it was still a remarkable achievement. Even today, it's astonishing just how real the movie looks. While it is not accurate to our reality, it does seem to represent some alternate future that looks as real as our own. If there were giant orbiting space stations, expansive

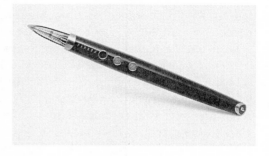

The Parker Atomic Pen, designed by Parker Pens for *2001*.

moon bases, passenger space travel and immense interplanetary spaceships, this is what they would, and should, look like. Of course zero-g food should be sucked through straws, and of course space flight attendants should wear padded hats (to prevent injury if their Velcro grip shoes come loose and they bump their head) when moving about in a non-gravity environment.

2001 postulated a different world in other ways. The government-controlled moon bases, segregated along national lines, will more probably function in the real world as multi-national (or maybe even multi-corporate) entities. One can also imagine that the space station's pristine walls will more likely carry massive advertising displays, as a revenue source, to mar their austere purity. However, the seatback video screens on the Orion are now a reality, even if the Earth orbit vehicle is not.

Perhaps the biggest oversight by Kubrick & Co. was the change in society that occurred between the film's conception and completion, that being the counter-culture revolution. Today little remains, at least overtly, of the hippie movement, but it's left behind a more populist ideology which rejects the formalism seen in the film. Where we were once obliged to adopt a public persona and to "put on our best face" when we went out into society, by 2001 we had largely abandoned that notion in favor of a more relaxed and casual realness. It means people wear T-shirts and shorts on the airplane, rather than a business suit. It also means that we do not always act in a courteous manner in public. Where, once, what was good for society was upheld ("Ask not what your country can do for you, ask what you can do for your country"), now a more self-oriented philosophy has come to dominate the culture. This may best be exemplified by how everyone seems preoccupied with looking at their smart phones rather than interacting with actual people.

On the other hand, the polite but emotionally isolated persona shown in the film has given way to "acting out" in public. We are both better and worse than the people of *2001*. Where Kubrick based his characters on a huge swath of middlebrow intellectualism, in reality, we have gone to the extremes of both poles. Grade school children can spell "rhododendron" at spelling bee tournaments, while there are high schoolers who can neither read nor write, and don't know where Japan is on a map, or who Hitler was in history. And the Cold War politics of the United States and Russia have metamorphosed in the 21st century into the terrorism of 9/11. Kubrick said shortly after the release of his film, "Technology is, in many ways, more predictable than human behavior."[26] That may be why, when we look at *2001* today, the technology seems far more understandable to us than the social institutions of the people who use it.

4

Very Special Effects
2001 Sets the Standard

I felt it was necessary to make this film in such a way that every special-effects shot in it would be completely convincing—something that had never before been accomplished in a motion picture.

—Stanley Kubrick in his *Playboy*
interview, September 1968

When Stanley Kubrick set out to create *2001*, he said he wanted to make the proverbial "really good" science fiction movie. By that he meant that he saw no reason why SF had to be a second-class genre; there was no reason it couldn't deal with profound ideas or look as classy as any historic epic. Throughout most of its history, science fiction had been a dumping ground for mostly garish and nonsensical movies, and even the few that had been made with any care or distinction still played up their most lurid aspects when it came time to promote them.

Kubrick felt it didn't have to be this way; you could work in this genre *and* make an important statement. In short, he surmised that given the will (and the financing) to do it, there was no reason why his burgeoning sci-fi project couldn't be as substantial a work of art as, say, David Lean's 1962 masterpiece *Lawrence of Arabia* or Peter Glenville's 1964 historical drama *Becket*. Kubrick even hired *Becket*'s cinematographer, Geoffrey Unsworth, as if to underline this point.

A key element to achieving this goal of seriousness was in the broad area known as special effects. This category encompassed a number of disciplines including process photography, or optical effects, miniatures (the building and photographing of models to represent full-sized elements) and floor effects ("gags" that were done live on the set, be it explosions, stunts, bullet hits, special props like breakaway furniture in barroom fights, fire, rain, wind and anything requiring the actors to interact with the environment). For the most part, sci-fi movies up to this point had been a decidedly low-budget concession with little time or money put into its execution. The state of effects work in general varied wildly in quality from excellent to incompetent, depending on any number of factors (money, time, the imagination and resourcefulness of those involved). It was not uncommon to see "toy" spaceships dangling from wires or hokey-looking papier mâché monsters scaring the populace.

Kubrick was determined that his futuristic space movie would be as real-looking as possible, taking advantage of the latest developments in filmmaking technology, while also relying on many tried-and-true techniques. In screening a vast number of past genre efforts, he realized there was still much room for improvement and decided his film would be the proving ground for creating totally authentic-looking space sequences. With our real-world entry into the space race of the 1960s, he knew that it was a necessity for his film to be believable. Such a commitment would require a level of trial-and-error experimentation that was generally unheard of during the production of a major studio film, but Kubrick felt that it was necessary if he was to achieve his goal of total realism. And it meant that he would push his effects team to create startling and iconic images that would become the gold standard against which all other movies would be judged.

The Live-Action Shoot

Prior to creating the vast assortment of special effects shots required for his film, Kubrick first needed to do the live-action shooting (most of it was done in December 1965 and throughout most of 1966). As with the design phase on *2001*, the live-action shoot would be executed with a scrupulous attention to detail regarding realism and seriousness. No *Flash Gordon* histrionics or B-movie acting would be permitted to cheapen what Kubrick hoped to achieve with his space odyssey. To that end, the director knew that he would need a first-rate cast.

Keir Dullea (David Bowman)

For his lead character of astronaut David Bowman, Kubrick chose a rising young star named Keir Dullea. The 29-year-old actor had already made a name for himself with fine dramatic work in *The Hoodlum Priest* (1961), *David and Lisa* (1962), *The Thin Red Line* (1964), *Bunny Lake Is Missing* (1965) and *Madame X* (1966). Tall, lanky and handsome, and with piercing blue eyes, Dullea had specialized in sensitive, brooding characters. Regarding the role which would become the defining hallmark in his career, he said,

Publicity photograph of Keir Dullea as astronaut David Bowman.

Kubrick hired me without an audition. He screened everything I'd ever done, including *Hoodlum Priest*, and gave me the chance to do something different than an introverted, neuter young boy with parent problems, usually my mother. That image was driving me up the wall, and I stopped doing dramatic shows on television because of typecasting. I never met Kubrick until the first day of work. He gave me a breath of fresh air.[1]

Gary Lockwood (Frank Poole)

To complement the intellectual demeanor of Keir Dullea's Bowman, Kubrick chose 28-year-old Gary Lockwood (born John Gary Yurosek) to embody the athletic prowess of fellow astronaut Frank Poole. Lockwood, a former college football player and stuntman, began his acting career in such films as *Tall Story* (1960), *Wild in the Country* (1961), *Splendor in the Grass* (1961), *The Magic Sword* (1962) and *It Happened at the World's Fair* (1963). On television, he had made a name for himself as the lead in producer Gene Roddenberry's short-lived series *The Lieutenant* (1963) and as a guest star in the second pilot to the famed sci-fi show *Star Trek*. As for his experience with Kubrick, Lockwood once said, "Working with Kubrick is like working with a great military commander. He had this huge labor force working for him and he was always in control of every detail. What was really impressive was that he knew when to make a change even though it could change the set plans and cost a great deal of money."[2]

Publicity photograph of Gary Lockwood as astronaut Frank Poole. Note the pack of Marlboro cigarettes in his shirt pocket.

William Sylvester (Heywood Floyd)

The first major human character seen in *2001* was Heywood Floyd, and for this pivotal role, Kubrick chose veteran character actor William Sylvester. The part called for someone with a bland gravitas, and the slender 6'3½" 44-year-old American-born Sylvester fit the bill. It didn't hurt that he lived in England (he moved there from the U.S. after World War II), where he was playing a variety of American characters in British movies. His career consisted of roles in such films as *Give Us This Day* (1949), *Appointment in London* (1953), *House of Blackmail* (1953), *High Tide at Noon* (1957), *Offbeat* (1961), *Gorgo* (1961), *Incident at Midnight* (1963), *Ring of Spies* (1964), *Devil Doll* (1964) and *Devils of Darkness* (1965). His appearance in *2001* helped boost his career, prompting his return to the States to appear in several important American films and numerous television shows.

Daniel Richter (Moon-Watcher)

Perhaps the one real wild card in the casting in *2001* was the inclusion of Daniel Richter as Moon-Watcher the man-ape leader. A young, professional mime from New York's American Mime Theatre, Richter was brought onto the project in late 1966 as a potential choreographer for the man-ape performers. It was suggested to Kubrick that hiring a mime to select and train performers might yield the results he wanted.[3] After a brief audition in which Richter showed Kubrick his ideas for how the man-ape characters might be performed, the director hired him on the spot and they began collaborating on creating the simian movements.[4] The year-long experience in working with Kubrick left Richter deeply impressed. In his 2002 book *Moonwatcher's Memoir*, he observed, "Stanley is different than other men. In working with him and becoming his friend, I have come to realize that I cannot judge him by the measure I apply to other men and women. What would be compulsion in others is single-mindedness in Stanley."[5]

Douglas Rain (voice of Hal 9000)

Born in Winnipeg, Manitoba, Douglas Rain studied acting at the Banff School of Fine Arts in Banff, Alberta, and the Old Vic theater school in London. Known primarily as a theater actor in his native Canada, he had built a solid career essaying some of the best roles in Shakespeare's canon, both on stage and television. His finely tuned voice was also put to good use in narrating a number of documentaries, most notably *Universe* (1960) and *To the Moon and Beyond* (1964), both of which came to Kubrick's attention. Rain was first approached about working on *2001* to provide narration for the film. When Kubrick decided to eliminate the narration, he used Rain for the voice of Hal, which was recorded after filming was completed. Kubrick eventually decided to scrap the narration, as it was making the visuals redundant, and also robbed the film of its mysterious quality. However, the director had been unhappy with his earlier attempts to find the right voice for Hal the computer (Martin Balsam had been the original choice),[6] and realized that Rain's even-toned delivery would be perfect for the computer's coolly indifferent personality. All of Rain's work was done after the main shooting was finished. Of his experience, Rain commented, "I wrapped up my work in nine and one half hours. Kubrick is a charming man. Most courteous to work with. He was a bit secretive about the film. I never saw a finished script and I never saw a foot of the shooting."[7]

For the secondary roles of pilots, stewardesses and miscellaneous scientists and administrators, Kubrick found a number of solid character actors, both British and American, some of whom he had worked with before and/or would work with again. Robert Beatty and Sean Sullivan played Ralph Halvorsen and Bill Michaels, who accompany Dr. Floyd on the moon bus ride to the TMA-1 excavation site. Leonard Rossiter, a noted British comedian, and Margaret Tyzack were picked to portray Dr. Andrei Smyslov and Elena, Russian scientists encountered by Floyd on the space station. American actors Edward Bishop and Glenn Beck played the Aries moon shuttle pilots, roles that originally had a good deal of dialogue which was ultimately cut or covered over with music. Beck had worked with Kubrick on *Dr. Strangelove*, while Bishop would go on to fame as Ed Straker in Gerry Anderson's TV series *UFO*.

The only other actors with dialogue of note are Kevin Scott and Chela Cannon (both uncredited) who play, respectively, the jovial late-arriving space station security chief Mr. Miller and the polite and friendly receptionist Miss Turner, who greets Floyd on his arrival at the space station. Though the numerous stewardesses get short shrift in the dialogue department, two had scenes worth noting. Heather Downham portrayed the Orion stewardess who plucks Dr. Floyd's floating pen out of the air with her lovely manicured hand, while Edwina Carroll gained immortality as the Aries moon shuttle stewardess who travels 180 degrees, right side up to upside down, to deliver meals to the Aries pilots.

The shooting schedule was broken up into five main phases. From December 29, 1965, to January 5, 1966, the TMA-1 moon excavation pit scene was photographed on Stage H in Shepperton Studios. On January 6, 1966, production moved to Borehamwood where the remaining scenes with actor William Sylvester were done. These included the Orion space plane, the Aries moon shuttle, the Clavius moon base conference room, the moon bus and, most impressive of all, a 300-foot interior section of the Earth orbit space station. In February 1966, the *Discovery* One space-ship scenes were begun with actors Keir Dullea and Gary Lockwood. The sets here included the monumental rotating centrifuge, the pod bay, the command deck, Hal's brain room and the full-scale antenna complex on the ship's exterior. Dullea stayed on to do some space pod interiors and the mystical hotel room.[8]

The one big sequence that remained was the "Dawn of Man" prehistoric opening. Kubrick ran into some problems in realizing this segment. The original man-ape designs weren't working, so it was back to the drawing board. Kubrick then concentrated on the ongoing special effects work. It would be nearly a year before he could solve the problem with the ape makeups and performance technique; he shot the beginning of his film in August 1967. See Dan Richter's *Moonwatcher's Memoir* for a full account of this phase of shooting *2001*.

The Special Effects Unit

When it came time to hire the staff that would actually help him achieve his upscale sci-fi vision, Kubrick cast his net wide over the effects industry ocean and was fortunate to pull in some extraordinarily talented people. In the bygone studio era of the 1930s and '40s, most movie studios had their own in-house effects facilities. By the 1960s, such departments had been drastically scaled back, and a film producer would often contract out the work needed for his movie with an effects house— a separate company that specialized in such work, whether for movies, television shows or commercials. A decade before George Lucas put together Industrial Light and Magic (the effects company for his sci-fi extravaganza *Star Wars*), Kubrick assembled his own crack team of artists to design and execute his ambitious undertaking.

Universe

A remarkable bit of footage that came under Kubrick's ever-alert eye was the educational documentary *Universe* (1960), made by the National Film Board of Canada. This short was practically a primer for the effects in *2001*, serving as a jumping-off point for what Kubrick wanted, and it would have a huge influence on the look of his film. *Universe* was directed by Roman Kroiter and Colin Low, with production design by Low and Sidney Goldsmith. The special effects were handled by Wally Gentleman, Herbert Taylor and James Wilson. Shown extensively in grade school classrooms during the 1960s, the film was essentially a travelogue of the solar system with stops at the various planets, including wondrous orbital views of Jupiter and its moons and the glorious rings of Saturn. But it wasn't just slack-jawed seven-year-olds who were overwhelmed: Seeing these startling images, Kubrick could not help but be impressed by the quality of these special visual effects which surpassed most feature-length motion pictures of the day. Low and Gentleman came on board Kubrick's project for a while, but ultimately neither stayed long enough to garner a credit.[9] Low would later gain fame as a co-developer of IMAX. The makers of *Universe* clearly had an impact on how *2001* would look.

The *2001* end credits list ten names in the effects unit, the real number is considerably higher. Unlike today's credits where it seems as if every coffee-runner and floor-sweeper is acknowledged, back then most of the "grunt" workers went uncredited. Many of them moved on to successful (and credited) careers of their own, like John Dykstra in *Star Wars*, Brian Johnson in *Alien* and Richard Yuricich in *Blade Runner*; all three paid their dues on *2001*. However, it is the first four men listed in the special effects credits, each receiving a separate card, who will now be examined. They were largely responsible for realizing Kubrick's vision and, in some cases, adding to it: old-time veterans Wally Veevers and Tom Howard and "new school" innovators Con Pederson and Douglas Trumbull. Each brought his own unique talents to the game, and all contributed substantially to the look and quality of the finished film. The six others, who were credited together as the "Special Photographic Effects Unit" (Colin Cantwell, Bruce Logan, Bryan Loftus, David Osborne, Frederick Martin and John Jack Malick), worked under these supervisors. Though there was a good deal of interaction and cross-fertilization of ideas among the crew, for the most part, the four supervisors each had their own niche where they were able to work their magic under Kubrick's uncompromising demand for perfection. And while the schedule was unrelentingly tough, all would agree that they did some of their finest work on this unique production.

Wally Veevers

One of the first people Kubrick tapped to be a part of his crew was this veteran effects man from the glory days of cinema. Veevers had supervised the special effects on *Dr. Strangelove*, including building and photographing models of B-52 aircraft that needed to intercut seamlessly with documentary footage of the real thing. His training went back to

William Cameron Menzies' ambitious 1936 production of *Things to Come*, a film it is said Kubrick disliked intensely, though not necessarily because of the special effects. Over the years, Veevers established himself as one of the best effects men in Great Britain. In addition to helping with the fabrication of *2001*'s various spaceship models, he oversaw the on-set wire "gags" that allowed Floyd's pen and moon shuttle dinner to float, as well as building special camera rigs, some with worm gears that would allow extremely steady (and repeatable) camera moves for shooting the spaceship models. The worm gear was a primitive predecessor to the computer-driven motion control rigs that were developed for *Star Wars* a decade later. This "multi-pass" capability was a necessity, since most scenes in the film required not just a camera pass for shooting the model (generally with long exposures of a minute or more for each frame of film), but also a separate pass for backgrounds or any live-action activity that was to be seen in the window areas of the model.

Model Photography

The models in *2001* were the most meticulously detailed and realistic ever created for a film. Built over a period of many months, they were constructed of wood, fiberglass, Plexiglas, steel, brass and aluminum. Kubrick hired architecture modelers who worked at a higher degree of exacting fidelity to realize the spaceships. Huge crews of detailers, working around the clock, swarmed over the models, using flexible foils, plastic cladding, wire, tubing and literally thousands of plastic model parts from hundreds of commercially available kits. They would then be painted and "dirtied down," a process of adding streaks and smears to indicate rocket exhaust residue and other build-up that would naturally accumulate on an actual vehicle. As a result of all this careful attention to detail, the camera could get very close to the models which would maintain their illusion of being real. This technique revolutionized the way models were built and photographed for movies from this point on. A whole generation of effects specialists was inspired to enter this field, and studios realized that "tinker toy" models dangling from wires would no longer be tolerated by the movie-going public. In their design and execution, the *2001* spaceships established a new level of seriousness and believability that continues to drive the industry to this day.

Building the models was one thing, photographing them was another. Depending on the nature of the shot, several different methods were employed to achieve the desired results. An example of a "typical" model shot might be the *Discovery* moving toward the camera while, through the window, a live, moving figure could be seen sitting at the controls. First, the 54-foot-long *Discovery* model (which represented the 700-foot vessel), with the window area blacked out, would be set up on its mounting platform and lit appropriately on a black velvet-draped stage. The camera, on its motorized worm gear motion rig, would then move down the track and photograph the model. The rig moved extremely slowly (like the hour hand on a clock, so the movement itself wasn't perceptible) and a shot might take several hours to complete. With the lens stopped down, each frame of film might be exposed for several seconds to up to a minute, a necessary step to maintain depth of field on the model and keep it in sharp focus from one end to the other. After this first pass was completed, the camera would be returned to its original start point on the track, and the film would be wound back in the camera to its original "synch frame" (so the second camera pass could be synchronized with the first). For this second pass, the model was covered in black velvet with only the window area visible. Instead of lighting the model as before, a white card was placed inside the previously blacked-out window area and live-action footage of the astronaut was projected onto it. It was necessary to do these shots as separate elements because the exposure requirements for each were different. The camera then moved down the track in an identical motion to the previous shot. Because of the synch frame, the projected footage fit precisely into the previously unexposed window area, with no "jiggle" between the two elements. When the finished shot was played back at its proper speed of 24 frames per second, any minuscule unevenness in the movement became smoothed out and appeared absolutely rock steady.[10]

For many shots involving spacecraft where no perspective changes would occur, it was decided that they could use high-quality still photographs of the various models and then manipulate them on a custom-made, oversized animation stand dubbed "the sausage factory." The moniker was a bit of wishful thinking, since it was hoped the device would allow the crew to churn out shots at a rapid pace.[11] Though this proved not to be the case, it was still quicker than filming the actual models on the studio floor, and they were able to obtain some stunning effects without cutting corners in quality. For the shot of the Aries moon shuttle descending toward Clavius Base, the first step was to shoot a still of the model, properly lit, on a large format 8x10 inch camera. Generally the model would be positioned in such a way as to enhance its three-dimensional nature. The 8x10 negatives were made into enormous prints that would be cut out and pasted onto a sheet of glass. The large-scale photo was then attached to the animation stand, where it would be front-lit and photographed. On separate passes, additional rear-lit transparency elements would be added: lunar landscape, the Earth, star field, and any live action footage seen through the spaceship window (this time rear-projected through the cut-out window area). The animation camera could be programmed to slowly zoom out from the model photo, imparting a sense of motion to the otherwise static image.

By this same method, the lunar landscape background could appear to move upwards as the camera tracked down to simulate the ship's apparent descent. Since all these elements were shot separately (for exposure purposes), the photo cut-out could serve as its own matte (it would appear as a black shape when its front light was turned off and the background artwork was rear-lit), thus avoiding the double exposure of the separate elements onto one another. Though most of the equipment used to shoot these scenes was made from readily available technology, it took the genius of Kubrick and his effects team to exploit it in such an original and striking manner.[12]

Tom Howard

Like Wally Veevers, Tom Howard got his start on *Things to Come* and thereafter forged a successful career in the industry. He won two Oscars, one for David Lean's 1946 ghost story *Blithe Spirit*, the other for the 1958 children's film *tom thumb*. Kubrick was initially intent on shooting his prehistoric sequence on location in a real desert environment and he spent considerable time and money trying to locate the perfect location (and even had a young assistant, Andrew Birkin, search out a desert in England).[13] Ultimately, a location shoot was deemed too impractical and uncontrollable for Kubrick's needs, given that his actors would be romping around in extensive makeups, and the cast and crew would be subjected to uncomfortable climatic conditions. By choosing to shoot in the controlled environment of a studio, Kubrick had several choices available to him for creating his "Dawn of Man" African vistas: a painted backdrop, blue screen (where the blue backing would later be replaced with a photographic plate) or rear projection, all of which were used extensively in the industry. Unfortunately, none of these processes suited Kubrick's quest for realism; they all had drawbacks that made the finished shots look artificial.

The director sought out Howard, head of MGM's effects department, to help develop a revolutionary front projection system and use it on a scale never before attempted. Prior to this, Howard had been involved in shooting and printing the gigantic still photos of the spaceship models that were then photographed on the animation stand.

Africa, Indoors!—Front Projection

Unlike rear projection which, as its name implies, throws an image onto a screen from behind, and was often used to simulate action appearing through the windows of cars (where filming on a stage was easier than trying to photograph and record dialogue from actors in an actual moving vehicle), front projection threw an image on a screen from the front. Though much more complicated than rear projection, it had the potential to create a much more realistic-looking effect. Front projection had been around for a number of years, used mostly by still photographers and in TV studios. The system relied upon a still-frame image (unlike rear projection which could use moving footage), so it was more suited to motionless backdrops of landscapes or buildings. Kubrick conducted a test with a 4 × 5" Ektachrome transparency (the largest format used for the system at that time) and felt it could be improved upon by moving up to an 8 × 10" which would supply a surplus of resolution capability.[14]

Howard built an 8 × 10" projector for Kubrick, the first ever, using the most powerful water-cooled arc available as the light source. Special heat-resistant glass slides were employed in front of the projector condensers to prevent the intense heat from peeling off the magenta layer of emulsion from the transparencies. A condenser is a lens that is placed between the light source and the transparency slide, and concentrates the light onto the slide's image. The condenser pack was 18 inches thick and made up of condensers from standard 8 × 10" photo enlargers. Occasionally the heated condensers would crack (and even shatter) when a draft of cold air, from someone opening the studio door, would hit the projector when it was on. The alignment of the projector and camera to the screen was vital to the success of obtaining an acceptable image. Using a half-silvered, front-surface mirror, called a beam-splitter, the projector was set up at a 90-degree angle to the camera. The light from the projector would bounce off the mirror, which was placed at a 45-degree angle, and would throw the image onto the screen about 90 feet away. Shooting through the other side of the beam-splitter (since all the light was on the front side, you could see through the back side like a window), the camera could see the screen and record the image. When this was done carefully, the foreground set piece would blend seamlessly with the background image. The camera and projector had to be aligned precisely along the same axis for the process to work. Keeping the transparency plates and mirror dust-free and pristine was also a problem. Editing gloves were worn by the people handling the plates, and the camera operator wore a surgical mask to keep his breath from fogging up the mirror.[15]

But all the high-powered, fancy equipment and dust-free environments wouldn't be of any use if you didn't have a screen that could reflect an image bright enough to look real. Fortunately, the 3M Company (makers of Scotch tape) produced a material called Scotch Lite, a fabric embedded with tiny mirrored glass beads. Used primarily in road signs, it possessed the ability, when illuminated by car headlights, to return the light striking it by a hundredfold. That meant the light falling on the screen came back to the camera a hundred times brighter than the same light hitting the actors or foreground set. Since the camera exposure was balanced for the screen, you could not see the much weaker light that was projected on anything else. And because of the precise alignment of the camera, even the shadows that the actors might cast on the screen could not be seen, since the actors themselves covered them perfectly.[16] One of the more fanciful, though unintended, bonuses of shooting front projection concerned scenes done with a live leopard. Evidently, some property of the cat's eyes caused them to act much like the Scotch Lite material, resulting in the animal's eyes glowing with an unearthly luminescence.[17]

For the "Dawn of Man" sequence, Kubrick set up his 40 × 110-foot front projection screen[18] on Stage 3, the largest soundstage at MGM in Borehamwood.[19] A variety of remarkably realistic landscape sets were built by Ernest Archer, the third person credited in *2001*'s production design team. They were based on photos taken by the camera crew dispatched to Namibia in Southwest Africa to make the 8 × 10-inch plates that would be needed for the front projector.[20] In addition to several smaller set pieces, the major sets included a boulder-strewn waterhole area, a dried-up riverbed and a grouping of caves that the man-apes used for shelter. The sets were built on large platforms that could be rotated to provide various camera angles, since the screen itself could not be easily moved in relation to the sets. To ensure an even lighting effect, Kubrick had the ceiling of the soundstage covered with 1500 RFL-2 lamps, each with its own separate on-off switch. This was necessary because of the variation in height on the uneven sets; with all the lights on, the high areas, being closer to the ceiling, would appear brighter. However, by having so many individually controlled lights, cinematographer John Alcott could shut off specific bulbs and be able to "shape" the light falling on the rocky landscapes.[21] Alcott had been the camera assistant on *2001*, and took over during the latter part of the shoot when Geoffrey Unsworth, the original cinematographer, had to leave for another film he was already committed to do.[22] It was also essential that the color temperature of the lit foreground sets matched the projected background images, a delicate balance to be sure. The electrical rigging job for this was enormous, consuming miles of wire (not to mention having to create a control board with 1500 switches on it),[23] but it allowed the greatest possible latitude for obtaining perfectly lit settings. Unlike a real location, where you were at the mercy of fickle weather conditions, Kubrick's location photographers, Andrew Birkin and Keith Hamshere, could wait for hours in the desert until they got the perfect lighting they wanted, and then shoot the stills that would be used as background plates. Kubrick then had the luxury of shooting his actors all day long on the set with absolutely perfect skies and lighting, something that could never be done with any consistency on location.[24]

Filming the "Dawn of Man" sequence constituted the last live action portion of the production. By all accounts, the shoot (August 2–30, 1967[25]) proceeded without any real problems. A bit later, they did an additional front projection shot of astronauts standing on the rim of the Clavius crater while the Aries moon shuttle can be seen descending in the background.[26] Professional mime Dan Richter spent nearly a year working for Kubrick, designing the movement and choreography that he and the other performers would employ to create the characters of the man-apes. Thanks to their tireless work, plus Stuart Freeborn's brilliant makeup effects and the intense ape vocalizations (created later by Richter and others), Kubrick captured some of the most hauntingly realistic scenes in modern cinema. The images recall the famous prehistoric dioramas created for the Natural History Museum in New York City. No doubt Kubrick was familiar with these and, either consciously or not, replicated their iconic appearance in his film.

After *2001*, the future of front projection seemed as bright as the image it projected on its screen. Howard was able to adapt moving footage to the process for *Where Eagles Dare* (1968)[27] and provided the front projection photography on the delightful Royal Ballet film *Tales of Beatrix Potter* (1971), which combined dancers on stage sets in elaborate storybook animal costumes with real outdoor backgrounds. Doug Trumbull used the process on his own low-budget directorial debut *Silent Running* (1971) and then on Steven Spielberg's big-budget sci-fi drama *Close Encounters of the Third Kind* (1977). The intriguing Will Vinton stop-motion Claymation film *The Adventures of Mark Twain* also used the process to provide background inserts for several scenes. But the fact remained that the equipment was cumbersome, and strides were being made with blue screen that produced sharper results. And unlike front projection (or rear projection for that matter), where the background plate was needed while you were shooting, the plate for a blue screen shot could be decided later in post-production. And with modern-day computer compositing, anything can be put in the frame, foreground or background, with complete freedom for the camera to move in any way the director wants, and have perfect fidelity of marrying the images together. To this day, then, *2001* stands as the most outstanding use of this innovative system it helped to nurture. Without it, Kubrick could not have shot the "Dawn of Man" segment in the controlled environment of a studio and maintained such absolute realism.

Going Ape

Before we leave the realm of "The Dawn of Man," it is important to acknowledge the magnificent makeup work of Stuart Freeborn and the highly sophisticated movement training of Dan Richter. In the initial planning stages of the prehistoric scenes, prior to Richter's hiring, Kubrick and Clarke envisioned more manlike creatures than those that finally ended up in the film. There were even publicity stills taken showing actor Keir Dullea in his spacesuit shaking hands with a diminutive naked "cave man" character who looked quite good, save that he had no genitalia. The problem was that the molded cod piece (designed to obscure the overt nudity) looked, at best, forced and, at worst, comical. Kubrick was unhappy with this original conception of the man-ape characters, which looked more like cavemen. The solution was to go back another million years in evolution when our ancestors were more ape than man.[28] By having the characters completely covered in hair, the nudity problem was eliminated. But with this new approach came a new set of problems: Freeborn would have to redo the makeups from scratch, creating ape-like faces with protruding jaws, and actors would have to be found who could be trained to replicate simian behavior. To that end, Kubrick enlisted the aid of young mime Dan Richter, who spent a year working on *2001* (from October 1966 to October 1967). While the ape costumes and masks were being refined by Freeborn, Richter set about the task of hiring 20 short, thin men (using women wouldn't work because their hips were too wide) and training them to make the ape-like movements required, a process that took over six months. Dan not only trained a cadre of young performers in the art of "going ape," he was drafted into playing the lead man-ape character, Moon-Watcher. After his experience on *2001*, Dan and his wife Jill spent a number of years working with John Lennon and Yoko Ono on numerous projects, including Lennon's "Imagine" video.[29]

Kubrick wanted perfection in his prehistoric opening. That meant that the ape makeups had to be totally convincing. The director chose Freeborn, who had done a wonderful job giving Peter Sellers three separate and distinctive looks in *Dr. Strangelove*. (Four, if you count Major Kong, whom Sellers was also supposed to play.) Freeborn spent months designing and sculpting the ape masks and body suits, with performance input from Richter. The final results (again, after much experimentation) were astonishing, and more than a few viewers probably wondered if the creatures shown were, in fact, some sort of trained apes. Unlike *Planet of the Apes*, which was in production during this time and would beat *2001* to theaters by a full month, thus stealing its ape makeup thunder, the "Dawn of Man" characters did not speak; they howled and grunted and chattered like real apes, which certainly helped sell the illusion. When a special Oscar was given to *Planet of the Apes* by the Motion Picture Academy for its innovative makeup effects (there was no regular category for makeup at that time), Clarke wondered, as loudly as he could, if the judges passed over *2001* "because they thought we used real apes."[30] It was a good, cutting jab, and eloquently conveyed the difference between the two films: For all its social commentary, *Planet of the Apes*, scripted by Rod Serling, was mostly for fun, and *2001* was for real. Freeborn would later gain even more fame for creating the makeup for the seven-foot tall "Wookiee," Chewbacca, in George Lucas's blockbuster *Star Wars*.

Con Pederson

Part of the younger generation of effects specialists, Con Pederson managed Graphic Film, one of the new, upstart effects facilities that sprang up in the 1960s to fill the needs of commercial, TV and film work. Founded by former Disney animator Lester Novros, Graphic chiefly made specialty and training films for NASA, the U.S. Air Force and others.[31] They also produced several films used at various pavilions at the 1964 New York World's Fair. One of these high-profile jobs was *To the Moon and Beyond*, a 70mm "event" film about the future of manned space flight, shot in Cinerama 360 and projected inside a domed screen. Kubrick was enormously impressed with its effects work when he and Clarke visited the Fair, and quickly sought out the same talent to work on *2001*.[32] At first he engaged the L.A.-based company to design concepts for the film, but with the production now entrenched in England, the long-distance situation (especially in this pre-fax, pre–Internet era) was untenable for Kubrick. A talented young guy named Douglas Trumbull decided he wanted to defect to Kubrick's film and came on board first.

Later, surely to the chagrin of Novros, Pederson followed. The two would end up being the younger half of the supervisory quartet.[33]

Optical Illusions

While Trumbull wound up working in many and varied areas of the effects unit (more on that later), Pederson used his considerable management skills to concentrate on organizational aspects, working with the art department, doing storyboards and supervising the optical effects photography.[34] (Like Novros, he was a former animator and had contributed to Disney's effects-laden *Man in Space* series in the 1950s.) Given the enormous number of effects shots needed (there were over 200 finished shots in the movie, each of which could involve up to ten steps to accomplish),[35] and the meticulous standards of excellence demanded by Kubrick (which meant there were many retakes), just keeping track of these was a job in itself. Since Kubrick wanted the effects to have a crisp, clean "single generation"[36] look, many composites were shot as separate elements on the same negative, so no duplication (or degradation) of the image would occur. This entailed shooting part of a scene, rewinding the film and then shooting another part. This process could involve many passes on one piece of film and might not be finished for up to a year before the footage was finally processed. Several identical shots of these "held takes" would need to be made, since any errors made along the way could ruin a particular shot. When you consider the many separate steps that were needed to make the 200 or so finished shots in the final movie, and that each of these elements required extensive documentation regarding exposure levels, color timing, etc., it becomes obvious how essential it was to have a sophisticated system in place to track the progression of the effects work.

Kubrick had rejected the use of blue screen photography for shooting his composites (due to unwanted "fill light" spilling onto the subtle shadow areas of the models, making it difficult to obtain a clean, matting edge), along with most other conventional methods of optical printing.[37] Instead, mattes (or masks) were created through the laborious and painstaking process of rotoscoping. Twenty workers were set up in a room with 20 enlargers. Each was given a piece of film and was instructed to trace the outline of the photographed object (generally a spaceship model) onto an animation cel (a clear, celluloid sheet that had registration holes for aligning it with the film frame). Once traced, the outline was then filled in with black ink, producing the matte.[38] For months on end, these rotoscope animators (who dubbed their enclave "The Blob Shop")[39] would congregate in this room to trace out and ink in these irregular blobs. The cels were then photographed over star background plates, resulting in a black, moving shape that partially masked the background. This could then be re-photographed with the original spaceship footage, and since the black shape was traced from the model photography, the spaceship would fit perfectly into it with no double-exposing of the background onto the model. It was boring, labor-intensive work, but it yielded the results Kubrick needed. After their stint on *2001*, the "Blob Shop" workers were happy to put away the black ink and move on to their next, more colorful job, working on the Beatles' animated feature *Yellow Submarine*.[40]

With Pederson's background in optical effects and animation, it's a sure bet that he had more than a little input in those areas on *2001*. Everyone who has ever worked with Con has had the highest regard for him as a colleague and friend. For the most part, though, he has chosen to keep a low profile regarding his contributions, and has allowed the lion's share of attention to go to the other three supervisors, most notably his Graphic Films comrade Douglas Trumbull. Perhaps he sensed that his young protégé was destined to be one of the shining names in the effects industry.

Douglas Trumbull

Of the four supervisors on *2001*, Trumbull was definitely the "young turk." Trumbull's cinematic pedigree extends back further than *To the Moon and Beyond*, as his father Don worked in the industry in the 1930s and '40s, but left the business before his son was born. The younger Trumbull came to *2001* with a talent and enthusiasm that found its way into nearly every corner of the production and left a lasting mark on it.

Working initially with Wally Gentleman, Trumbull spent his time fashioning the numerous futuristic computer readouts, all of which were needed before principal photography could begin. In our current era where anything and everything can be rendered through computer graphics, it may be hard to believe that the readouts for *2001* were done in animation; the computerized option was unavailable to the filmmaking world of the 1960s. Even so, the large quantity of footage that had to be created meant that straight animation wasn't viable; for *2001*, a faster method was needed. Working with photographer Bruce Logan, another Graphic alum, and armed with a jury-rigged animation stand, the young effects wizard shot thousands of feet of colorful, kinetic footage, achieved by manipulating back-lit still graphics (made from flow charts, diagrams and miscellaneous text, shot as high-contrast negative transparencies and colored with standard gels).[41] This footage was then rear-projected on as many as a dozen screens at a time to keep the background of the sets looking "busy." While this work consumed nearly a year of his time, Trumbull also found that, because British Trade Union rules didn't apply to him, he could dip his toe (and talent) into many of the other effects projects that were being created, including model detailing, lunar landscape miniatures, star field backgrounds, model photography, renderings of Jupiter and its moons and, most important of all, the Star-Gate corridor sequence.[42]

Slit Scan: Creating the Star-Gate

The origins for what would become the Star-Gate sequence came primarily from Trumbull and Con Pederson. In a letter to Kubrick, dated July 23, 1965 (while Pederson was still with Graphic and five months prior to the start of principal photography), he offered to send him test footage (by effects associate John Whitney) of an experimental technique called "slit scanning." Pederson felt that this kind of effects work had unlimited possibilities for use in *2001*, especially regarding the Star-Gate.[43] Trumbull was also aware of Whitney's work. Over a year into production on *2001*, when the problems of the Star-Gate sequence still hadn't been solved, he suggested to Kubrick that a rig could be built allowing for controlled streak photography. The method involved a motorized camera traveling, along the Z axis, on a length of track toward a slit, behind which illuminated artwork could also be moved. With the camera shutter open during filming, this technique created a seemingly infinite plane of exposure that, when doubled, resembled an endless corridor of light.

After showing a test to Kubrick, Trumbull got the go-ahead to build a mammoth device to do the job. There followed months of experimentation as a variety of artwork was photographed on the machine, out of which came the final footage seen in the film.[44] Trumbull also experimented with variations on the slit scan technique (one of which enabled them to make a spherical, gaseous Jupiter),[45] but most of these never made it into the film, including an attempt to render exotic-looking aliens.[46]

For the second section of the Star-Gate, where clouds of interstellar gas and newly forming stars and galaxies are shown, a method was used similar to the effects produced by Wally Gentleman for *Universe*. Kubrick's crew set up a tabletop of black ink, oil and various chemicals which they photographed interacting together. Filmed in reverse (that is, the footage was eventually run in reverse in the finished film), with massive amounts of light, and using a high-powered close-up lens, the field of exposure was barely larger than a deck of cards, yet when blown up on the big screen it produced impressive, truly cosmic-looking images.[47]

Immediately following these scenes was one of the movie's more striking shots, referred to in the effects logs (though never identified as such in the film) as "The Mindbender."[48] It consisted of seven flying diamonds, in formation, over an undulating, reddish landscape. The diamond rig was a Wally Veevers special (the man really could create anything Kubrick wanted), and was made of built shapes that had scintillating kaleidoscopic patterns projected onto their facets. The landscape beneath them was devised by Trumbull using a revolving drum covered in shiny, rippled acrylic, filmed through the slit scan device. The two effects were then married together to create one of the most striking images in the Star-Gate sequence.[49]

For the finale of the Star-Gate—an excursion over myriad alien landscapes—Kubrick employed a technique suggested to him by Gentleman during the early days of production. By manipulating the color negative separations, or YCMs (for yellow, cyan and magenta, the negative components to blue, red and green), sections of the film could be printed with radically altered colors that would appear eye-poppingly alien.[50] Months of trial-and-error work were spent to get just the right combinations. Instead of relying on stock footage for his unearthly travelogue, Kubrick dispatched second unit director Bob Gaffney to shoot aerial views over Monument Valley and Page, Arizona.[51] (For Kubrick's *Lolita*, Gaffney had shot second-unit road trip footage of America.)[52] Spectacular aerial footage was also obtained of mountainous regions in the Hebrides region over Scotland.[53] Kubrick had promised his audience a trip "beyond the infinite" and, with the Star-Gate effects conjured up by his team, he made good on that promise.

Just as Orson Welles used conventional techniques in unconventional ways on *Citizen Kane* (shooting up at ceilings; matte paintings; deep focus; radical editing), Kubrick found a new language of artistic expression with his mix of new concepts and tried-and-true effects technology re-engineered to meet the demands of his exacting vision. In most cases it simply involved the commitment to engage in labor-intensive trial-and-error and the will to spend the money to do whatever it took to ensure that each shot was the best it could be. The hard work paid off since, of the four Oscar nominations the movie received, it only took home the gold for its effects. No movie production had ever spent this much time, money and resources on its effects sequences. As a result, *2001* revolutionized the way audiences, critics and the movie business itself looked at them.

In a single stroke, Kubrick showed the world what could be achieved in this field and, overnight, the effects industry changed. It led to a more thoughtful integration of special effects into films, paving the way for innovations such as computer-assisted motion control photography in the late 1970s and computer generated imagery (CGI) development in the 1980s. This led to the replacement of "photochemical" (i.e., film) effects in favor of the digital dynasty in the cinema of the 1990s and beyond. For his efforts, Kubrick took a card in the end credits: "Special Photographic Effects Designed and Directed by Stanley Kubrick." This was a bone of contention with the four effects supervisors, who conceded that he directed the effects, but felt he shouldn't claim that he "designed" them. This especially irked them when they got aced out of an Oscar nomination, where the rules at the time stipulated that there could be no more than three people named in the category. Kubrick put up his own name for nominee in place of the other four as a compromised solution. Ironically, it would prove to be the famed director's only Oscar win in his nearly 50-year career.[54]

Despite his disdain for Hollywood, Kubrick still relished the idea

Director Stanley Kubrick working out a shot on the space station set.

of winning an Oscar. Having been aced out of wins or, in some cases, even nominations, he may have had an inkling that his best bet for an Academy Award rested with the groundbreaking effects in *2001*. His later films would receive Oscars for cinematography, art direction, music and costumes, and several nominations for Kubrick himself, but the sad irony is that the only Oscar he ever won was in a category not usually given to the director of a movie. Of course, he was in good company, as neither Alfred Hitchcock nor Orson Welles ever won a directing Oscar either.

5

The Star-Gate Explained
2001's Most Unique Sequence

Any sufficiently advanced technology is indistinguishable from magic.
—Arthur C. Clarke in "Clarke's Three Laws"

In terms of cinematic storytelling, the most radical departure from convention, even in an unconventional film like *2001*, was its final segment "Jupiter and Beyond the Infinite." Among major studio releases up until that time, "the trip," or "the lightshow," as it came to be known, had no precedent. In the novel, which came out in the summer of 1968, several months after the movie opened, Clarke referred to this entryway into higher dimensions of space as the Star-Gate. Even today, with all the talk of cutting edge filmmaking, the Star-Gate lightshow has no equal in the realm of cinema. Beyond its technical brilliance and artistic merit, "the trip" gained notoriety for its ambiguous nature. There were nearly as many interpretations as there were viewers. Lively debates sprang up among critics as well as regular moviegoers. It was rare for any mainstream film to provoke such philosophical contention with the critics, let alone the general public, but *2001* had proven to be quite a rare film experience. Multiple viewings became an essential element of the interpretation game. There was even the trendy practice in the hippie culture of sitting in the front row of the theater and smoking pot during "the trip," grooving on the images in an altered state of consciousness, hoping to divine further revelations. Such were the times that this was considered (almost) acceptable behavior.

But now, in the 21st century, we live in a world of videotape and DVD; of pay-per-view and HBO; of cable broadcast, satellite TV and Internet streaming. We've all become much more media-savvy due to the avail-

88

ability of so much entertainment product. With the ability today to own films and view them dozens of times at our discretion, we can study cinema in the same manner that past generations of scholars have studied art, literature and philosophy. Let's now explore the meaning of *2001*'s most enigmatic sequence, the Star-Gate Lightshow.

As the culminating link in the chain that is *2001*'s screenplay, the Star-Gate had much more to answer for than your usual story dénouement. Up to that point in the film, the meaning of the plot was still somewhat obscure. Many people had trouble connecting the disparate elements that had come before, or making any sense of them. The "Dawn of Man" segment in the beginning seemed to be tied to the rest of the movie only by the enigmatic monolith, but it puzzled most viewers. The lunar excavation scene apparently had no visible ties to the Jupiter mission other than Hal the computer's passing comment to Bowman about the nature of their mission. Hal wonders whether the secretive aspect of the mission is tied to "rumors about something being dug up on the moon." Hal's breakdown also seems to not be connected to anything, but simply put there to arbitrarily stimulate a bit of action and conflict. After Hal is subdued by Bowman, and immediately prior to the beginning of the Star-Gate, there is one wordy paragraph of dialogue (a monologue actually) that is sprung upon Bowman and the audience, which stands as an explanation for the nearly two hours the movie has thus far run.

As Bowman methodically deactivates Hal's autonomous functions in a red-lit, zero gravity "brain room," his action triggers a prerecorded message from Heywood Floyd, the character who went to the moon to study the monolith. Floyd is much like the monolith, itself—a dark enigma who withholds information, first from the Russians on the space station, and later from the *Discovery* astronauts. But, as with the monolith, it is information only temporarily withheld. For the perceptive moviegoer, this speech by Floyd (the final spoken words in a movie that still had 20 minutes to go) would offer somewhat of an explanation on what had transpired and explain, again somewhat, how the various segments of the movie were connected. Here is that final speech:

> Good day gentlemen. This is a pre-recorded briefing made prior to your departure, and which for security reasons of the highest importance has been known on board during the mission only by your Hal 9000 computer. Now that you

are in Jupiter's space and the entire crew is revived, it can be told to you. Eighteen months ago, the first evidence of intelligent life off the Earth was discovered. It was buried 40 feet below the lunar surface, near the crater Tycho. Except for a single, very powerful radio emission aimed at Jupiter, the four million-year-old black monolith has remained completely inert. Its origin and purpose, still a total mystery.

Leave it to Kubrick and Clarke to conclude the verbal portion of this movie with the words "total mystery." That might have made an intriguing title for the movie itself. But much more is revealed by that speech than might first be apparent. At the outset, it states that Hal knew the true purpose of the mission, and it is not much of a stretch to conclude that his concealment of this information from the crew led him to a kind of mental breakdown. The novel makes this much more explicitly clear, but it's there in the film if you choose to find it. Next, the "radio emission aimed at Jupiter" ties the lunar scene with the Jupiter mission. Obviously, the mission was designed to investigate just what might be out by Jupiter to receive the signal. The book goes a step further, establishing that the buried monolith is a cosmic "burglar alarm" set to go off once it is uncovered and struck by sunlight. It's a way for the monolith makers to know that their "experiment" with the man-apes has now resulted in them evolving far enough to have crossed space and visit their moon. (Not until that point in our evolution would the aliens be interested in us again.) While the film itself doesn't spell out this exact scenario (part of the ongoing appeal of *2001* is its insistence on constantly being inexact), its ambiguity still allows one to intuit that the monolith is an extension of a higher intelligence, that this intelligence tinkered with the evolution of man, and that four million years later, that experiment involved a further emissary waiting near Jupiter. And a meeting between that emissary and mankind, through Bowman, would be played out in the final act of the film.

"Jupiter and Beyond the Infinite"

With this portentous legend appearing on-screen, the Star-Gate sequence begins. The familiar monolith music heralds the opening shot of an empty star field, the camera tilting down to reveal, first, Jupiter and its moons in all their glory, and finally the approaching *Discovery* spaceship. The now mobile though still mysterious monolith can also be seen floating through this shot, apparently in orbit about Jupiter. There has been some speculation regarding just how big this monolith is, compared to the ones seen earlier. In Clarke's novel, it was 800 feet long (though firmly planted on one of Saturn's moons). In the movie, since the monolith never interacts directly with anything during this orbital interlude, there's no sense of scale when you see it. Though it's easy to imagine it being huge, with the planet Jupiter and its moons as a backdrop, it can just as readily be thought of as the exact same size as the others. And why not? By being identical, the monoliths have a consistency that increases their already mysterious nature. And, since they are clearly metaphysical objects, there is really no reason for one of them to be bigger. Ultimately it's unimportant, but the fact that the monolith's size is left ambiguous adds another layer of mystery to this already mysterious movie.

After the initial reveal sets the stage, a number of shots show the floating monolith as well as Jupiter and its moons in various configurations and phases. A graceful right-to-left pan past these orbs, appearing as edge-lit crescents, like cosmic nail parings, sweeps us to the *Discovery*. The ship's command module sphere is similarly lit, and its center pod bay doors yawn open to disgorge a space pod bearing Dave Bowman. The monolith can be seen during this shot floating up from the bottom of the frame and out the top. It culminates with a shot of Jupiter and its celestial children shown together in a magical alignment.

This whole sequence is charged with a sort of mystical lyricism. The multitude of moons, the large gaseous planet with back-scattered sunlight, the floating monolith and the music all work together to exude an otherworldly wonder. Into this astral travelogue, the previous shots of Jupiter and its moons, is seen a very long shot, straight on, of Bowman's space pod floating languidly toward the camera, obviously in pursuit of the monolith. The pod starts off very small in the center of the frame, engulfed by the star-spattered blackness of space, but eventually it very nearly fills the screen. The finale of this sequence brings the monolith into the magical alignment of Jupiter and its moons that was previously shown, and now echoing the alignments that were used in the "Dawn of Man" and the TMA-1 lunar excavation portions of the movie, though in this instance, the monolith appears horizontal rather than vertical, leading some viewers to see it as a sort of cosmic crucifix! Clarke's own comment about this observation displays his trademark dry wit: "People are telling Stanley and me things we didn't realize were in the movie. A theological student said he saw the Sign of the Cross— and he may have, which would have been interesting, since Stanley is a Jew and I'm an atheist."[1] Kubrick's use of this image motif portends something very important about to happen. And so it does here, too.

After the monolith has aligned with Jupiter and its moons, it slowly fades away. As the music rises to a crescendo, the camera booms up, above the plane of the Jupiter system, as if following the movement of the now unseen monolith. From this "empty" portion of space, spears of light shoot past the viewer (and by inference, Bowman) as the stars gradually disappear. Supposedly, the origin of this shot is that Kubrick had some rejected Star-Gate footage that started out dark and gradually became filled with streaks of light. It was thought to be unusable until it was realized that a transition was needed from Jupiter (and regular space) to the Star-Gate. This shot provided the necessary link.[2]

As the shot continues, the Star-Gate begins as a vertical corridor, as if the astronaut has passed through a doorway. Despite all the unusual rooms and passageways we've seen in the movie, our earthbound sensibilities still respond to the conventionally shaped doorway and corridor.

We next see a close-up of Bowman reacting in surprised wonderment, from behind his space helmet faceplate, as the Star-Gate opens before him. (This is the first time we've seen Bowman since he deactivated Hal and received the message from Floyd. He was shown in a long close-up wearing his space helmet then, too.) The camera holds on his face as the gentle shaking of his pod environment turns to violent buffeting, and he and the pod are engulfed in the Star-Gate. This close-up goes on quite a while and sets the stage for a series of "freeze frame" shots of Bowman that will later be intercut with the Star-Gate footage.

The first full shot of the Star-Gate begins with hot reds and yellows that form grid-like patterns, suggesting controlled technologies, which in turn give way to splotches of hot white masses. A freeze-frame of Bowman, his head tilted back, screaming, lets us know that this cosmic ride is having an effect upon him. A return to the Star-Gate shows soft greens and yellows changing to pinks, violets and blues, all very nebulous, in contrast to the grids of the previous scene. Another freeze frame shows Bowman with a look of astonishment. The Star-Gate has become less nebulous now with more shape and pattern to it, and with many colors. A disturbing flash cut of Bowman, his head twisted with one eye visible in the lower center of his faceplate, is quite creepy in a surreal, almost cubist manner, and may reflect that the journey is somehow "changing" him. This change is further borne out as we cut back to the Star-Gate and see that its perspective has changed from vertical to horizontal. What had once been "walls of light" have now become a wide expanse of "floor and ceiling," or more accurately, like flying between layers of land and sky. A final flash cut of Bowman shows him in a frozen scream of agony, his eye rolled back into its socket.

The Star-Gate is now a dark backdrop, with rows of brightly lit ovoids zipping past us, changing into grids, a cascade of unfurling spokes, and then more grids that coalesce into a brilliant white light that totally engulfs the screen. Bowman has passed through a cosmic tunnel, from darkness into light, from ignorance to awareness, and is ready to begin the next phase of his journey.

Where the last sequence used shots of Bowman's face four times (five if you count the shaking scene), the next sequence intercuts a close-up of Bowman's eye five times to link together the various shots of interstellar space and alien landscapes. Further, the eye inserts are rendered in bizarre, Day-Glo color combinations which resemble the silk-screened images by Andy Warhol, the Pop-Art illustrations of Peter Max, and the solarized photography of Richard Avedon. I believe that the reduction from full face to single eye serves several purposes. Symbolically, it illustrates a transition in Bowman from the egocentric self (the "I") to the universal self (the eye). As he is being delivered from one reality to another, he leaves behind his individuality on the physical level and moves on to a plane of pure thought, what we usually think of as the soul. And as Leonardo da Vinci supposedly once said, "The eye is the window to the soul."

The corresponding imagery staggered between the eye inserts can be broken down into four main categories: (1) Interstellar Space; (2) "The Mindbender"; (3) Transitional Landscape; and (4) Alien Landscapes. Each of these realms has a separate meaning and a specific function in the cosmic journey of Bowman.

Interstellar Space. After Bowman emerges from the Star-Gate corridor, we see the first eye insert, this one rendered in yellow and green. From this we cut to an enormous expanding globular star cluster that resembles the cosmic "big bang," the origin of the universe. In a series of shots we are then shown a condensed history of the universe and the origin of life. From the exploding cluster we move to a pair of forming galaxies, much like our cosmic neighbors, the Magellanic Clouds, two irregular dwarf galaxies visible in the southern hemisphere. Next, a single star-like object appears in a bluish haze, which may be stellar matter from the galactic clouds condensing into the center to form a proper galaxy. Hot yellow-orange gases explode, leading to shimmering, billowy nebulae with wispy, almost fluidic tendrils that drift lazily about. We next see a glowing cosmic ribbon of neon light, arcing over a diffused core, being rent like pulled taffy. This is followed by a diaphanous curtain of gases, riddled with skeins of iridescent white. A large dollop of red-orange star matter, with a magenta and white corona, then heaves into view. As we approach this newly forming star, it slowly acquires an abstract expressionist resemblance to a slumbering fetus, awaiting its call to birth. Just as we begin to scrutinize this fetal enigma, we jump to another glowing nebula, its interior burning brightly with a bracelet of small young stars. Much like the Pleiades, these infant suns are huddled together, safely incubating in a cosmic star nursery of the nebula.

We next see a deliberately ambiguous white glob, trailing some fluid-like matter, as it moves toward a rose-hued constellation. Some have thought this to be the space pod itself, but it is too abstract for that, and it seems unlikely that Kubrick would depart from the point-of-view (P.O.V.) format for this single shot. In symbolic terms, it more resembles a spermatozoon or even a fertilized egg making its way to the uterus. It has an opaque solidity that the previous images lack, as if it were more dense, more concentrated. This sequence's final image is a smoky veil pierced by a tiny, bright star. What all 12 shots in this interstellar enclave share is a striking visual affinity to birth and life. The first nine images of this cosmic Rorschach clearly symbolize the creation of the universe, from big bang to star formation; the last four depict, ironically, in reverse, the creation of life on the human level, from ejaculation to fetus. The two concepts converge in the red-orange star-fetus shot. It is as if Bowman is being told he is not only a living being in a living universe, but that the two are actually one and the same.

"The Mindbender." Following a second eye insert, colored this time in violet and blue, we are thrust into the most startling and cryptic of shots in the entire Star-Gate tableaux, something called "The Mindbender" (coined by the special effects people, but never so named in the movie). Against a conventional star field, a red and orange translucent Star-Gate landscape rolls beneath us, while on the "horizon," flying ahead of us, are five pulsating, facetted crystalline structures. As we move along, two more crystals enter the frame, one on either side, left and right, closer to us and therefore appearing larger than the others, bringing the number in the squadron of flying diamonds to seven. Kaleidoscopic patterns scintillate over the facets of these alien devices. Or are these the aliens themselves? There is no way to know. The pulsating images could be a manifestation of the diamonds' power source or a way for "them" to communicate with one another. What is clear is that they represent a controlled energy, and therefore an intelligence (in contrast to the seemingly uncontrolled natural energies of the interstellar sequence which preceded it). I believe these objects, whatever they might be, are there to reassure Bowman (and us) that everything is under control. They are a phalanx of angelic ambassadors (alien beings, machines or something else) in a cosmic motorcade, there to guide Bowman on his journey. They also represent a self-assured display of the enormously sophisticated technology of the monolith makers.

Transitional Landscape. A powder blue and pink tangerine eye insert takes us to the next image, a single shot I call the Transitional Landscape. This shot provides the bridge that links the mien of the Star-Gate corridor with the alien landscapes that will soon follow. Under an overwhelmingly heavy "sky" that looks like an inverted oceanscape, we are flying over a distorted landscape of dark dunes. Its ominous look almost suggests a trip through the underworld—Heaven by way of Hell. It seems to be an empty wasteland, devoid of life. Much more inviting as a harbinger of life is the blue ocean/sky, with its streaks of pink and purple. What does this shot mean? Perhaps it is just an example of contrasts, of opposites. Yin and yang; the bountiful and the arid; the fecund and the sterile. One road leads to life, the other to death. It is a choice the apes made four million years ago with the help of the monolith. Maybe Bowman is being reminded that the choice isn't over yet.

The Alien Landscapes. Another eye insert, this one repeating the violet-blue color scheme of the second insert, sets the stage for the final sequence in the Star-Gate. Comprised of 14 separate shots, each one is a wildly colored alien landscape, which we fly over, "helicopter-style." As they tumble before us, one after the other, it seems as if we are being shown all the possible worlds that can and do exist in the universe. We start with a rust and indigo canyon followed by rocky terrain in blue-green-violet, and more terrain in pale blue and lime. We next see a Monument Valley ridge in vivid crimson and washed denim, replaced with a snowy mountain lake in the same hues. This is followed by saffron-hued islands in an azure ocean. A sickly, scum-laden sea of pea green and purple undulates beneath us, replaced with fuchsia skies and golden land masses. Next is a red and lavender ice tundra followed by a glowing lake in orange and blue. The final triptych, all in bright yellow and blue, depicts a ravine, a mountaintop and a bleak landscape, the colors reminiscent of hot lava on ice. We return to the close-up of Bowman's eye for the last time, now colored blue and red. As his eye blinks, it passes through a total of seven color changes (incidentally, the same as the number of flying crystals). Following the blue-red eye, and changing with each blink, comes green-orange, violet-green, orange-violet, mint green-reddish orange, orange-blue and finally a monochromatic sepia, which remains even as the eye continues to blink. This sudden change, from wild color palette to bland beige, has the feel of something being used up. It is as if the journey has drained Bowman of his life, his essence, his very being. For all that he has been shown, for all the experiences bestowed upon him, filling his mind, for all that, it has also emptied him. The trip has taken away as much as it has given. The empty vessel that Bowman has become is now ready to be refilled. The Star-Gate ride may be over, but the purpose behind the monolith is just getting started.

The Room at the End

Despite all the miraculous imagery we've been shown during the Star-Gate ride, and despite our anticipation for what may follow those final eye-insert color changes, nothing quite prepares us for the strangeness and familiarity of what we next see. As the computer screens in

Bowman's pod flash **NON FUNCTION** in a short-circuited staccato, the view through the pod window reveals an elegantly appointed hotel suite. The juxtaposition of these two worlds in a single frame—the interior, technological, the exterior, architectural—is as surreally formalized as anything in a Magritte painting, and just as disquieting.

Our first view of Bowman is equally disturbing. In close-up, still seated in the pod, he appears catatonic or even epileptic, his eyes rolled back, his head quivering, seizure-like, behind the reflective visor of his helmet. Is he insane? Brain-damaged? We do not know. The trip through the Star-Gate has obviously had a major impact on Bowman, rendering him frightened, passive and vulnerable, and ready to be remolded by the forces behind the monolith, in whatever way they wish.

We are then shown the space pod from three angles—front, back and side—as it sits in the hotel suite. The surrealness of this modern mechanized device amongst the French Neoclassical furnishings again evokes something out of a Magritte painting (*Time Transfixed* comes to mind, in which a miniature locomotive issues out of a fireplace). The room contains a large bed, night tables, wardrobes, several chairs, a writing desk, a commode chest, various tables, paintings in the style of Jean-Honore Fragonard and Jean-Antoine Watteau, Adam Brothers[3] panel moldings with period statues displayed in wall niches, and a connected bathroom. Illumination comes from a large overhead domed fixture and, more eerily, from the gridded floor, creating a totally shadow-free environment. The walls are a pale, icy blue, while the furnishings are mostly white, with bedding and upholstery accented in mint and mustard. Except for the connected bathroom, there seems to be no way in or out of the room. (What appears to be a pair of built-in wardrobes on either side of the bed tables could in fact be doorways out of the room, but I prefer to think of this as a cage with no discernable exit.)

The delicate Louis XVI decor is elegant and refined, suggesting culture and affluence, but the suite appears as lifeless as a tomb. The opulence is cold and uninviting—a museum exhibit on a closed Monday. According to Kubrick, "The room is made from [Bowman's] own memories and dreams. It could have been anything that you could possibly imagine. This just seemed to be the most interesting room to have."[4]

The two shots that opened the "arrival at the room" scene (the P.O.V. through the pod window and the trembling Bowman close-up) are now repeated, though this time in reverse order. But there is now a change; for what Bowman apparently sees in the room, through the window, is … Bowman! He is standing in the room in his red spacesuit, a vivid splash of color amid the muted tones of the suite. The next two shots jump-cut us even closer. The first eliminates the framing of the pod window, and the second brings us into a full close-up, revealing the spacesuited Bowman to be much older. In a matter of seconds he has aged from 30-ish to 60 or 70. His hair is gray; his skin, now finely lined, has the texture of rice paper; his expression is dazed and blank. His appearance evokes the look of someone who has had a great shock and been prematurely aged by it.

The camera cuts to a reverse angle behind Bowman, looking over his shoulder, to reveal that the space pod is now gone. The Bowman in the pod has now *become* the Bowman in the room. He moves away from the camera, toward the empty area once occupied by the pod. His steps are hesitant and unsteady, almost those of a toddler learning to walk. He wanders about in the suite and makes his way to the connected bathroom. As he gazes through the archway, the camera does a sweeping P.O.V. pan of the smaller room where we see a barely glimpsed toilet with a closed, upholstered lid, a marble sink and counter, ornate wall sconces and molded panels like those seen in the bedroom, towels hung from wall-mounted rings and a large marble and porcelain bathtub. It is all luxurious, but cold and forbidding. Throughout this whole sequence, weird laughter and whispering chatter can be discerned, which is evidently the sounds of the unseen aliens observing their human subject.

Entering the bathroom, Bowman approaches a large mirror affixed to the back wall of bathroom where the bathtub is located, and for the first time he sees his changed visage. In reflected close-up he appears puzzled as he looks himself up and down. Suddenly, mysterious sounds intrude upon the scene in the form of heavy breathing punctuated by sharp, loud clinks, which get Bowman's attention. His eyes narrow into slits and follow the sounds as he pivots his head slowly in the direction of the bedroom. A P.O.V. lateral tracking shot of the archway brings the suite into view; a match move shot of Bowman looking with anticipation ties him to the P.O.V. We cut back to the arch as the camera completes its tracking move, bringing another part of the room into view, whereupon we see a dark figure seated at the table, his back to us. At first all that can be distinguished are four dark limbs, and for a split second it recalls the man-apes from the beginning of the movie. But it is simply a man wearing dark clothing, eating at the table. We cut back to Bowman staring in wonder at this figure. We return to Bowman's P.O.V. and his rhythmic breathing inside his helmet catches, holds and then disappears. The figure at the table stops his activity, turns in his chair and looks toward the camera and, ostensibly, Bowman. The figure is white-haired and old. He turns back in his seat, pauses briefly, then, with great effort, rises from his chair and walks toward us. His footsteps echo ominously on the lighted floor as he approaches. Suddenly we recognize that the figure is, in fact, Bowman, but older still, perhaps 80 or more. He is dressed in pajamas and a heavy robe, all in dark blue. The spacesuited Bowman is now apparently gone, as had happened in the previous transition.

The old Bowman arrives at the archway, glances about suspiciously with darting eyes, and then returns to the bedroom and the table. He seems to be completely unaware of his earlier incarnations. The table is actually a hotel room service cart, draped in a fabric table cloth overlaid with lace. Spread out on the cart is a generous meal with several covered dishes. Bowman sits at the table and savors a sip of wine. He sets the goblet down with a foreboding thud that echoes through the room. He then scoops up a mouthful of food from his plate, and the normalness of this activity is almost maddening in its utter pedestrian nature. The high angle on Bowman in this shot as he eats places the floor behind him as a backdrop. The lit squares and crisscross grid lines suggest he is a pawn in some cosmic game of chess. (The floor also mimics the game Pentominoes, a five-square light game Bowman played with Hal in a scene that was ultimately cut from the film.[5])

When the aged Bowman reaches for one of the covered dishes, he knocks over his wine glass. It falls to the floor, shattering into many pieces. Bowman looks almost stricken at what he's done, as if this display of human fallibility and imperfection might somehow doom the entire race. But before he has time to reflect on the repercussions of his clumsiness, the sound of heavy, labored breathing draws his attention. He looks up from the broken glass on the floor and gazes toward the camera, squinting to see with his failing eyesight. A reverse angle from over the shoulder of the elder Bowman reveals an even more ancient figure lying in the large bed. A close-up confirms what we already suspect: The man in the bed is Bowman, now about 90. He is completely bald and his eyes lie sunken back in their sockets. Looking beyond the bed, out of the shot, to where the other Bowman would be, the ancient Bowman raises his hand and head, with some difficulty, as if reaching out to his other self. A wide shot shows that in place of that other Bowman is the monolith. This view, from the bed's headboard, encompasses the entire room, with the now-familiar alien artifact planted in the middle, rising up like a black tombstone from the foot of the bed, which has now literally become a deathbed. The room practically glows in contrast to the Stygian blackness of the monolith, seen here more clearly than in any of its other manifestations in the movie. It seems to belong here in a way that is almost unexplainable. It finishes the room, and its presence portends the completion of Bowman's ultimate transformation. Whatever is going to happen to him will happen now.

In place of the dying Bowman in the bed, there now sits a radiant sphere. Within this iridescent globe, something equally bright can just be made out. A huge close-up lets us see that inside the glowing orb is a reclining fetus. And while it is obviously Bowman, it is no longer human. Its open eyes glint with a collective wisdom, the lips ever so slightly parted in anticipation. The diminutive hands, drawn up near the jaw, almost appear to be clasped in prayer. This is no helpless infant, but a fully minted cosmic angel. Bowman has been reborn as a higher entity—a Star-Child. The transformation, engendered by the monolith, is now complete.

A low rumbling on the soundtrack tells us that the *2001* theme music, Strauss' "Also sprach Zarathustra," has begun again, proclaiming the end of the Odyssey and the film. (This same piece of music was heard over the opening credits and during the "Dawn of Man" scene when Moon-Watcher smashed the bones.) From the Star-Child's P.O.V., the camera tracks in on the monolith until it fills the screen. As the music reaches its first climax, we cut and are back in space, our moon centered in the frame. As the camera tilts down, we see the curve of the Earth enter from screen right. Slowly, a huge glow pushes its way in from screen left. It is the Star-Child. He has used the monolith as a doorway to travel back to his home world, the Earth. As the next phase of human evolution begins, the Star-Child, with all his newly acquired powers, floats in space and slowly turns and looks directly at us, the audience. He is not only confronting us, he is also confronting mankind itself. What can we possibly expect from such a deity? Mercy, vengeance, indifference or something beyond our understanding? Kubrick refuses to tell us. Instead, the face of the Star-Child, in startling close-up, gazes intently at us, and then the movie fades to black. We are left to ponder just what our own fate might be.

While no single interpretation of *2001*'s most enigmatic sequence may ever fully stand as definitive, or be satisfying for everyone, I have attempted in this chapter to forge a compendium analysis based on Kubrick and Clarke's mindset at the time the film was being made, as well as pulling together speculations from various critics. (I'm especially grateful for Alex Eisenstein's 1977 published speculations[6] which helped reinforce my own early interpretations.[7]) I've added my own views on art, mythology and film technique. I believe the real value of this exploration into the meaning of the Star-Gate sequence isn't that it provides all the answers, but that it may set you on the path to discovering your own interpretation. *2001* is such an intensely subjective experience that the conclusions you draw from it say as much about you as they do about the film. And like all great art, this is what allows it to endure. Five hundred years after Leonardo painted the *Mona Lisa*, it can still arouse wonder and speculation over that mysterious smile. Is it so much to expect that 100 years hence, *2001* will still be admired for its own cryptic grin?

6

MUSIC OF THE SPHERES
2001's Awesome Soundtrack

I can't see how other directors hand a film over to a composer when they've finished a film; they hand it over to the composer. The composer writes the music, then gives it back … and that's the end of it, and I find that extraordinary. When I'm watching a movie, the music becomes, like, 50 percent of the experience. You don't notice it a lot of the time, but it just informs the scene constantly.
—director Terry Gilliam

Over his career, Kubrick had an evolving attitude about what the style and use of music should be in his films. During his formative years, from *Fear and Desire* in 1953 to *Paths of Glory* in 1957, he relied upon fledgling composer Gerald Fried (introduced to Kubrick by mutual friend Alexander Singer[1]) to provide traditional movie music. For Fried, his work for Kubrick allowed him to break into the business and covered a variety of idioms, from Cuban pop jazz pastiches to military fanfares, all with a driving percussive beat that must have appealed to the drummer in the young director. Though there was nothing revolutionary in the music of these early films, Kubrick found inventive ways to place the cues. For the most part, though, the director was still learning his craft, and these films provided him with a chance to hone his skills in the area of scoring.

As a hired hand on *Spartacus*, Kubrick had little to do with that film's epic score by noted composer Alex North, though percussion again played a major role in several of the cues. Regaining control of his career in *Lolita*, Kubrick hired Nelson Riddle, a major name, to provide that film with its appropriately overwrought music. Interestingly, the director who had a reputation for making cold, aloof, detached films, almost always had highly emotive music to accompany them. For *Dr. Strangelove*, however, Kubrick, working this time with British composer Laurie Johnson, returned to a more minimal (and percussively militaristic) sound-track, supplemented with some eclectic pop standards. The film opens with the smooth instrumental "Try a Little Tenderness" and closes with Vera Lynn's World War II standard "We'll Meet Again." The director was quickly learning to pick and choose his tunes in a progressively more clever manner. This trend would continue throughout the remainder of his career, as it became increasingly important to Kubrick to have the same control over the soundtrack as he had over the rest of his movie.

One cannot imagine *2001* without the music that accompanies it. Much like Walt Disney's *Fantasia*, the images have become inextricably bound to the music—the sun rising over the orb of the Earth, with the fanfare to "Also sprach Zarathustra" as the ultimate wake-up call; space-ships waltzing to "The Blue Danube" on a star-strewn cosmic dance floor; the Adagio from "Gayane" as the mournful dirge during *Discovery*'s half-billion-mile road trip to Jupiter; and the haunting sounds of Gyorgy Ligeti, which are linked to the monolith and serve as an almost diabolical accompaniment to the trip through the Star-Gate. It is inconceivable that anything else would be appropriate to the images in the movie than the "score" that Kubrick compiled.

During the early phases of *2001*'s production, Kubrick toyed with a variety of classical pieces, culled mostly from the late 19th and early 20th centuries, to be laid against the footage he'd shot. Though he had not begun formal editing, he did cut together a short demonstration reel of some of the early scenes to show to MGM executives in February 1966. He used Ralph Vaughan Williams' "Antarctica Symphony" and Felix Mendelssohn's "Midsummer Night's Dream" to great effect, which indicates that he was already leaning towards powerful, highly emotive music to reinforce the striking images.[2]

There is a strongly held belief among film composers that directors too easily fall in love with the temp music in their films. Since a composer is usually the last major player to be hired, they usually don't come on board until the film has already been edited into its final form, or nearly so. They watch the film and then have five to eight weeks (if they're lucky) to churn out a score that can run anywhere from a few minutes to over an hour. Prior to all of that, while the film is being edited, the director will attempt to determine the pace of scenes by using pre-existing music in a temporary capacity to help the editing process along. The scenes with this "temp score" are watched many times as the editing is adjusted to match the music. In some cases, the director gets so used to this particular combination of picture and music that he or she may want to retain the temp score, or have a composer write something similar. As a result, most film composers dread temp scores and usually don't want to hear them.

The 2001 "Temp Score" Composers

Richard Strauss

True to his usual methodology, Kubrick listened to literally hundreds of pieces of music, searching for the right cues to carry the emotional weight of his grand mythic endeavor. It is not surprising that he came upon Strauss' "Also sprach Zarathustra." The German-born composer (1864–1949) created a number of stirring "tone poems," from "Don Juan" to "Death and Transfiguration," in his long career. Though well-known in his own day and for much of the 20th century, he is now best remembered, by the general public at least, thanks to Kubrick, for his Nietzschean-inspired "Zarathustra" which he completed in 1896, when it had its first full performance under the composer's own baton.[3] Strauss held strong feelings about the philosophy of Nietzsche (and is said to have memorized whole sections of "Zarathustra," which he viewed as his "bible"),[4] but there is no evidence to suppose that Kubrick, an Austrian Jew by heritage, embraced these teachings beyond the ape-man-superman theme at the center of *2001*. From its ominous opening rumble and three-note trumpet fanfare (C-G-C), the director must have realized that he had found something special. Its crashing crescendo and exultant organ closing chord (all in the opening one minute and 40 seconds that Kubrick used of its 35-minute running time) perfectly encapsulated the rise of our species from pre-human to enlightenment. The popularity of the piece is proof that Kubrick had a winning theme. (Professional wrestler Ric Flair has used the music as his entrance theme for years!) He would use it in the finished film three times: during the opening credits where we see the sun and crescent-lit Earth rise over the pock-marked moon (which sets up the magical alignments that follow later);

104

the bone-smashing scene with Moon-Watcher (which heralds the ape-to-man transition), and the Star-Child scene (man into superman) that completes the evolutionary cycle.

Johann Strauss

Perhaps Kubrick's boldest musical choice was to trot out the instantly familiar "Blue Danube" waltz—that reliable chestnut of Old World Vienna—and polish it up for the 21st century. Just as John Philip Sousa has become synonymous with marching band music, so has Strauss (no relation to Richard Strauss) become known as "The Waltz King." Strauss' father, Johann I, was a gifted composer himself, but did not encourage his namesake son. Only after the elder Strauss abandoned his family did Johann II pursue a musical career. Ironically, and hard to imagine, his most famous piece today, "The Blue Danube," was a failure when it was first performed in 1867. It eventually became a classic standard, but a century after its premiere, Kubrick made it immortal. Judging by the kinds of shots the director employed in the space station-space plane sequence, one has the feeling that it was always envisioned as a dance. That Kubrick would ultimately choose a waltz harkens back as much to his own interests in Viennese culture as it did to any formal aesthetic. (The director was a fan of Freud, Jung and Schnitzler, whose novel *Traumnovelle* [*A Dream Story*] was the basis for his final film, *Eyes Wide Shut*). Kubrick used the entire "Danube" waltz for his trip to the moon, illustrating the grace that man would bring to his technological accomplishments. There is a real sense of completion and satisfaction at a job well done when the waltz concludes with the moon ship gracefully descending into its airlock. The re-use of the waltz for the closing credits was done, I think, to reassure the audience and put them into a state of familiar comfort when it was time to leave, especially after the ordeal of the last half of the film.

Aram Khachaturian

This Armenian composer was born in Tblist, Soviet Georgia, in 1903 and died in 1978,[5] so he was alive to see *2001* and hear his music in it. Kubrick used the mournful five-minute Adagio from Khachaturian's 1948 "Gayane Ballet Suite" during the scenes aboard the *Discovery*, which emphasizes the loneliness of the astronauts on their long voyage to Jupiter. For those who point to *2001* as a cold, impersonal film, lacking in emotion, the use of this piece of melancholy music speaks volumes about Kubrick's ability to create an honest emotional moment without having to resort to blatant sentimentality.

Gyorgy Ligeti

The most important musical influence found in *2001* comes from this East European avant-garde composer, and we have Kubrick's wife Christiane to thank for bringing him to the attention of her husband. She heard Ligeti's "Requiem" in August 1967 on BBC Radio and thought it would be marvelous for the movie.[6] Ligeti was born in Hungary in 1923, where he lived under Stalinist oppression for a number of years. He studied at the Liszt Academy and majored in Romanian folk music. He fled from Hungary in 1956 to Vienna, where he began composing in earnest, writing stark, atonal works that were uncompromising in their originality and strangeness, and were certainly unfamiliar to most mainstream westerners' ears. In *2001*, Kubrick used four Ligeti pieces (some of them multiple times), making his the largest musical contribution to the movie.

Even though the four pieces were obviously from the same composer, each had something unique to offer. "Requiem for Soprano, Mezzo-Soprano, Two Mixed Choruses and Orchestra," or "the monolith theme," was the film audience's first exposure to Ligeti's music, unless they saw the road show version which had Ligeti's "Atmospheres" playing during the pre-film overture. Used three times in the film (whenever the monolith was seen, save in the hotel room at the end), it provided Kubrick with a completely otherworldly sound that was ominous, haunting, mysterious and powerful. In other words, a perfect theme to embody the alien nature of the enigmatic artifact. For the moon bus ride to the TMA-1 excavation site, Kubrick chose the very "spacey"-sounding "Lux Aeterna." This is the closest the director came to using "space music" in *2001*, something he seems to have consciously avoided. However, this piece serves the film well, offering a ghostly aural backdrop to the stark and beautiful lunar landscapes. The trip through the Star-Gate was the movie's highlight sequence, presenting one overwhelming scene after another. The use of "Atmospheres" (conjoined with the by-now-familiar "Requiem" monolith theme) gave this segment its enormous power and proved to be a fitting musical accompaniment to the visual, headlong rush through the metaphysical space corridor. Finally there is "Adventures," a piece Kubrick used to "suggest" the sounds of aliens (or whoever) observing the astronaut in the room at the end. Kubrick altered the piece, running it through some sort of processor to make the voices sound less human. Ligeti, unhappy about this change, successfully sued over having his music distorted.[7] This may be why the track did not appear on the original soundtrack album. Despite Kubrick's hubris (which Ligeti seems to have gotten over, given that other pieces by him appeared in *The Shining* and *Eyes Wide Shut*, and his participation in the Kubrick documentary *A Life in Pictures*), the distorted version of "Adventures" works brilliantly at creating an impression that the astronaut is in some sort of cage, or laboratory experiment, and is being observed by a higher alien intelligence.

Though it may be overstating things a bit, I believe Ligeti's music is one of the major "tent poles" in *2001*, right up there with Kubrick and Clarke, the special effects people and the production designers. While he didn't create anything specifically for the film, his music gives the movie an originality and "voice" that has come to be as exclusively associated with it as the monolith or Star-Child. He would continue to be identified, right up to his death in June 2006, for his connection to Kubrick. Certainly *2001* (and to a lesser extent *The Shining* and *Eyes Wide Shut*) brought Ligeti to a wider audience than he would have otherwise enjoyed. Like much of the modern "concrete" compositions that made an appearance during the 1950s and '60s, they were far too difficult for most mainstream ears to appreciate in a concert hall. It took Kubrick's utilization of Ligeti's material to make it soar in ways that, perhaps, the composer himself never dreamed were possible. Also, it is obvious to anyone who has followed Kubrick's career that he seems to have had a continuing interest in European culture, which is reflected most strongly in the music he has used in his films from *2001* on.

Sound Effects as "Music"

In an inspired move, Kubrick also chose to employ sound effects in several scenes in lieu of music. This decision resulted in a movie that was, again, removed from the norm. The director took great pains to avoid the use of bogus sound effects, such as the whoosh of a ship going by, or the metallic clang of the space pod "hands" when they gripped the emergency airlock controls. In the vacuum of space, none of these events would create any sounds that could be heard (sound waves require a medium—like an atmosphere—to be carried from their point of origin to the ear of the listener). Unfortunately, most movies up to that point (and later on with *Star Wars* and its imitators) ignored this basic scientific reality in favor of presenting themselves as whiz-bang excitement. But Kubrick's intent with *2001* was to be real, and he opted to use music and silence as a backdrop to the on-screen action.

To avoid having to rely solely on these techniques, Kubrick found ways to bring sound into some of these scenes without sacrificing the film's scientific authenticity. When Bowman (and, later, Poole) leave the ship to repair the antenna, the only sounds accompanying these sequences are the labored breathing of the astronaut and the hiss of his air hose, which are heard over the audio link on the ship's speaker in the command deck. (One wonders if Lucas got the idea for Darth Vader's heavy breathing effect from *2001*.) Laying this sound over the whole scene (as opposed to only in the command deck) breaks from realism, in that it is displaced, but it functions cinematically as a stylized mood mechanism (which has a long history in film—i.e., two men in a room talk about committing a robbery, their conversation heard over shots of the place they're planning to hit), so that it can be used in accordance with film language tenets without compromising the rigorous realism that Kubrick has established in his movie. A more conventional filmmaker would have settled for music to build tension into these scenes; the fact that Kubrick chose a more innovative approach reveals that his ambitions with *2001* were far greater than merely making an entertaining movie. He wanted to expand the medium itself. And like any pioneer, he would face his share of obstacles.

The Alex North Score

Kubrick initially intended to have an original score composed for *2001*. Just as he envisioned his movie as an innovative leap forward in the fields of special effects, production design and serious storytelling, he also felt that it could be a showcase for "a really striking score by a major composer."[8] During that time, some of the best and brightest names in the film music business included Elmer Bernstein (*The Magnificent Seven*), Bernard Herrmann (*Psycho*), Alfred Newman (*The Greatest Story Ever Told*), Miklos Rozsa (*Ben-Hur*), Dimitri Tiomkin (*Giant*), Nino Rota (*La Dolce Vita*), Maurice Jarre (*Lawrence of Arabia*), Ernest Gold (*Exodus*), Henry Mancini (*The Pink Panther*), Jerry Goldsmith (*The Sand Pebbles)* and Alex North (*Spartacus*).

North had a long career writing scores for such popular movies as *Death of a Salesman, A Streetcar Named Desire, Viva, Zapata!, The Rainmaker, The Rose Tattoo, Cleopatra* and *Who's Afraid of Virginia Woolf?* Kubrick, of course, knew North from their work together on *Spartacus*, and it appears they had a fairly smooth and enjoyable collaboration on that project. In any event, Kubrick contacted North in late 1967 and asked him if he was available to do the score for his sci-fi epic. North jumped at the chance to work again with Kubrick, especially given that the film had a minimal amount of dialogue and huge stretches of silent scenes begging for musical accompaniment. It didn't hurt that, the previous year, he'd scored the dialogue-heavy *Virginia Woolf,* and so he was itching to let loose on a project that was more music-friendly.[9]

The composer flew to London in early December 1967 to meet with Kubrick and discuss what was needed for the film. At this time, Kubrick told North that he intended to retain some of the temp music that he'd gotten used to (even though North wasn't keen on the idea, feeling he could give the director the essence of the temp tracks with new music). Despite this unresolved dilemma, North began in earnest on December 24, 1967, and worked furiously for the next week to meet the January 1, 1968, recording session date. Evidently there are no holidays on a Stanley Kubrick production. The composer worked so hard that he came down with muscle spasms and had to go to the recording session in an ambulance. North composed and recorded over 40 minutes of music during this two-week period. Over the next month, North waited to hear back from Kubrick regarding any further work that might be required, and spent the time rewriting and refining some of the pieces with which he wasn't satisfied. Though Kubrick did suggest some possible changes with North that could be made in a second recording session, it never materialized, and eventually the composer was told that no more music would be required. Two months later, when North attended the New York premiere, he was shocked and surprised to discover that his original score had been jettisoned in favor of the temp tracks.[10]

North's score was forgotten, a casualty of film industry insensitivity where time is money and the blood, sweat and tears of actors, writers, designers and even film composers can be discarded as quickly, if not as easily, as yesterday's newspaper. However, several cues from this abandoned *2001* score did end up in North's score for the fantasy film *Dragonslayer* (1981), where it seemed a much more appropriate fit.

Kubrick has stated that he was disappointed in the music he received from North, considering it "a score which could not have been more alien to the [temp] music we had listened to, and much more serious than that, a score which, in my opinion, was completely inadequate for the film."[11] We'll probably never know if Kubrick was sincere in his desire to have an original score, or if he just used North to get MGM off his back. Regardless, with the April premiere looming, the bottom line is that *2001* went out with the temp tracks and changed the way people thought of movie music from that point on.

Jerry Goldsmith was one of the world's greatest and most prolific film score composers, and a friend and colleague of Alex North. It is no secret that for many years he was incensed over what he thought was Kubrick's very shabby treatment of North, going so far as to say, "*2001* was ruined by Kubrick's choice of music."[12] Goldsmith's résumé reads like a Greatest Hits of Movie Scores, from *Planet of the Apes*, released in 1968, the same year as *2001*, to the revered works *Patton, Papillon, Chinatown, Logan's Run, Coma, Magic, Alien, Star Trek: The Motion Picture, Poltergeist, Gremlins* and *Hoosiers*. During the 1970s through to the late 1990s, Goldsmith and the equally prolific John Williams seemed to have a lock on most of the big pictures. But even these powerhouse composers have felt the sting of a rejected score. So it is not surprising that when a call came to Mr. Goldsmith, asking if he'd like to conduct the orchestra for the recording of the lost *2001* score, he seized the chance to right what he considered to be an egregious wrong.[13]

In the late 1980s, record producer Robert Townson became friends with North and, over lunch one day, suggested they do a series of new recordings of his best film scores, starting with *Spartacus*. During further discussions, it was decided that the lost score to *2001* should also be included, and that Goldsmith should be the one to conduct it. Pre-production on the *Spartacus* session took longer than anticipated and the re-release of the film came and went before that score could be redone. It was then decided to move forward on the *2001* score, with an eye toward releasing it in 1993 to coincide with the film's 25th anniversary. North died on September 8, 1991, but the project continued onward (perhaps, even, with a renewed fervor to ensure that North's dream would come true), and the recording date was set for January 29, 1993, at London's famed Abbey Road Studios, with the National Philharmonic Orchestra. It was released later that year as *Alex North's* 2001: *The Legendary Original Score*, with front cover art by Matthew Peak (son of famed illustrator Robert Peak who had originally been engaged to create the cover, but subsequently died before it could be done). The CD was a real triumph of determination by North's friends and a treat for those who wanted to hear the original score. Just the fact that it was out there was a considerable achievement.[14]

Anyone who is a fan of *2001* cannot help but be pleased that the lost, original score can now be heard; but it only confirms that Kubrick made the right choice. The North score is good, but it must be said that it is also very conventional. In most cases this would not be a problem, given that *most* movies are conventional and they are expected to have a conventional score. Which isn't to say that a conventional movie might not benefit from having an unconventional score—the "electronic tonalities" created by Louis and Bebe Barron for *Forbidden Planet* is a good example. Another is Goldsmith's *Planet of the Apes.* By the same token, unconventional movies can reap the benefits of an original score, conventional or otherwise; the Philip Glass scores for *Mishima* and *Koyaanisqatsi* come to mind.

Despite its grandiose intent, the North music just doesn't measure up and, if used as recorded, would have compromised Kubrick's vision. The title theme, replacing Strauss' "Zarathustra," is reminiscent of *Spartacus*, as are tracks three and four, which concern the man-ape sequences. Tracks two and five, more ape scenes, sound like cues from Goldsmith's *Logan's Run* score. Track seven, "Space Station Docking," recalls a sailing vessel, a problem Goldsmith himself had to deal with on his original cue for the "Space Dock" scene in the first *Star Trek* movie, which he had to rewrite. Track nine uses an ethereal female voice, *à la* the original *Star Trek* TV series, which pales compared with Ligeti's "Lux Aeterna" that it replaces. Tracks ten and eleven, which cover the space station and Orion space plane interiors, have the blandness the scenes call for—calm, modern travel muzak—but reduce them to being utterly conventional movie moments instead of commenting on the society being shown, as Kubrick intended. The final track was planned to be used as intermission filler, but its choppy, discordant structure, with bad harem music in the middle, clearly shows that North's sensibilities were undoubtedly that of the concert hall, with little regard for the need to sustain a specific mood in the theater for the duration of the movie. This would not do for *2001*. North's waltz-like theme, because of its very anonymity, has none of the punch of "The Blue Danube," which works precisely because of its familiarity. It is the old, re-imagined in a new context, which makes it such a perfect fit. North's re-do of "Zarathustra" has all the bombast, but none of its foreboding or exultant qualities. And, while North tried his best to replicate the wonder of Ligeti's work, he failed to capture that uniquely alien quality that the composer spent a lifetime acquiring and which North had only two weeks to concoct.

Directors may indeed fall in love with their temp tracks, but composers are just as likely to fall for their own material. It is only natural for film composers to become defensive when faced with filmmakers who show them a rough cut of the movie, temped with music by some of the world's greatest composers, are allotted only a few weeks and are told, "Gimme something as good as that!" Even with many years of success in the business, and a ready "bag of tricks" to pull from, scoring can still be a daunting challenge, and many composers have had the unpleasant experience of a "tossed" score, including Elmer Bernstein, John Williams, Jerry Goldsmith and Randy Newman. In fact, Newman, who has written many brilliant scores for such films as *Avalon, Toy Story* and *Pleasantville*, summed up the situation best: "It's a low job, a well-paid job, but work conditions are bad."[15]

Fortunately, it is not always this adversarial. Some filmmakers have forged long and fruitful collaborations with specific composers: Steven Spielberg and John Williams, Robert Zemeckis and Alan Silvestri, David Cronenberg and Howard Shore, Merchant/Ivory and Richard Robbins, the Coen Brothers and Carter Burwell, Tim Burton and Danny Elfman, Darren Aronofsky and Clint Mansell. Sometimes scores are written, at least partially, before the film is shot. For *The Piano*, a score that is as good as they get, composer Michael Nyman had to create several pieces of period music for Holly Hunter's character to play. He went so far as to actually measure the "spread" of Hunter's hand so he could compose the music within a scale range that would be comfortable for the actress to play. Talk about a custom-made score!

The Soundtrack Collections

The surprising success of *2001* and its unusual soundtrack album led to the release of a number of other records, tapes and, ultimately, CDs. These either packaged the music in various configurations, or found some other aspect of the movie to promote. In the early years of the film's success, vinyl records were "in," and *2001* had five different long-playing albums (LPs) you could own. All of them were interesting in one way or another, and it certainly proved that clever and savvy marketing techniques were alive and well back then.

2001: A Space Odyssey Original Soundtrack

Released in 1968 in a beautiful gatefold jacket, this was the fans' album of choice. The front cover depicted the Orion space plane streaking out of the space station's central slot, while the back side showed spacesuited figures standing before the vista of the expansive moon base. Both images were culled from the movie's poster art, which was created by noted NASA artist Robert McCall. Inside the gatefold were eight color photos from the film (some printed backwards, alas), a synopsis of the modern portion of the movie (though the time span stated between the moon sequence and the *Discovery* mission is wrong) and a rundown of the album tracks.

There are several discrepancies in the tracks themselves, which prevents this album from being the ideal recording. First, the "Also sprach Zarathustra" is the Karl Böhm-conducted version rather than the one by Herbert Von Karajan that is in the film. A look at the end credits in the movie reveals that, unlike the other music pieces, there is no listing of a conductor or orchestra for this particular cue. This could mean that Kubrick hadn't decided until very close to the film's opening which version of "Zarathustra" he intended to use, or maybe he had trouble getting clearance for the Von Karajan recording for the album. Both versions are quite good. This oversight was eventually corrected.

The next track, "Requiem for Soprano, Mezzo-Soprano, Two Mixed Choirs and Orchestra" (the monolith theme) by Gyorgy Ligeti, is the version heard in the movie, but the piece is cut off before it reaches the section where the astronaut enters the Star-Gate. I do not know whether this was because of time constraints on the album or the fact that in the movie, the latter section of this piece segues into Ligeti's "Atmospheres," and the album engineers couldn't figure out a way to gracefully end the piece so it would appear to be a stand-alone track. The third track, Ligeti's "Lux Aeterna," is a longer version of the piece excerpted for the film during the moon bus ride to the TMA-1 excavation site. The last track on side one is "The Blue Danube" by Johann Strauss, or about two-thirds of it. In the movie, the waltz is broken up between the two trips Dr. Floyd takes to get to the moon (with a bit of overlap in the music to cover the scenes). The album liner notes suggest that this first cue covers the entire flight to the moon, instead of just to the space station. In actuality, the cue goes slightly beyond the station sequence. They reprise the last third of "Blue Danube" on side two, listing it as being used for the end credits. This cue starts later on the album and is not true to the excerpt used in the movie.

Side two of the album begins with the Adagio from Khachaturian's "Gayane Ballet Suite." The 5:12 cut runs longer than what is heard in the finished film, probably due to the trims Kubrick made between its premiere and general release. Next, at 8:26, Ligeti's "Atmospheres" is the longest single track on the album. In the film, Kubrick uses this entire piece and then starts it over again, for about a minute, to cover the Star-Gate sequence. After the "Danube" reprise (mentioned earlier), the final track on the album is a repeat of the Böhm recording of "Zarathustra" which heralds the birth of the Star-Child at the film's conclusion. It was also judged to be a fitting way to end the album. Again, as stated earlier, this was not the version that was used in the film. Despite these minor flaws, the soundtrack album was a huge success and it quickly inspired others to cash in.

The Columbia Album

Riding on the coattails of *2001*'s popularity, Columbia Records went through their library of existing recordings and cobbled together a soundtrack they could call their own. Dubbed "Music from Two Space Spectaculars," side one contains tracks from *2001*, conducted by Eugene Ormandy, Leonard Bernstein and others, while on side two is a 20-minute suite from Karl-Birger Blomdahl's outer space opera "Aniara." I guess Columbia figured they had to offer something else to lure in the *2001* fans, not to mention the need for padding out the material to album length. The *2001* tracks are also linked together with cheesy electronic "interludes" by Morton Subotnick, perhaps to give the cut-and-paste tracks a sense of continuity. The cover depicted a double exposure shot, from stock sources, of a star field and an in utero fetus. Voila! Instant Star-Child. One interesting side note regarding this album is the listing of John Corigliano as a violinist on the "Gayane" track. Corigliano's son, also named John, went on to become a serious classical composer and created the stunning score for Ken Russell's *Altered States* (1980), a film that was compared, favorably, to *2001* for its use of cosmic and psychedelic imagery.

The Polydor Compilation Album

This British release isn't a proper *2001* soundtrack, but a classical compilation album titled "Theme Music for the Film *2001: A Space Odyssey* and Other Great Movie Themes." Polydor obviously issued it to capitalize on *2001*'s success, which is why that name appears so large on the album front. In addition to music from *2001* (the Karl Böhm recording of "Also sprach Zarathustra" from the original soundtrack album and a different "Blue Danube" recording), the album includes Beethoven's "Fur Elise" from the horror film *Rosemary's Baby* (1968), Beethoven's 4th movement of his 5th symphony from *Interlude* (a sentimental British film from 1968 featuring Oskar Werner, Donald Sutherland and a pre–*Monty Python* John Cleese), Mozart's Piano Concerto No. 21 and Vivaldi's "Summer" from "The Four Seasons" for *Elvira Madigan* (a popular Swedish hit film from 1967), Rachmaninov's "Rhapsody on a Theme of Paganini" from *The Story of Three Loves* (a 1953 Vincente Minnelli love story trilogy featuring Kirk Douglas, James Mason and Leslie Caron), and Khachaturian's "Sabre Dance" from "Gayaneh" used in *One Two Three* (a 1961 Billy Wilder comedy with James Cagney).

Released in 1970, the album sports a spacey, doctored NASA image of the Earth rising over the lunar landscape, taken by Apollo 8 astronauts when they orbited the moon for the first time in December 1968. Most Americans were unfamiliar with this British-released album, but would eventually come to know it from its cameo appearance in the record boutique scene from Kubrick's 1971 film *A Clockwork Orange*. It was prominently placed at the front of the check-out counter where Alex goes to pick up a special order and, subsequently, picks up a couple of lovely teenage girls as well. All the tracks on this record are, more or less, a "greatest hits" collection from the classical repertoire, so it made for a nice easy listening album for those wishing to advance their cultured status beyond Mantovani.

2001: A Space Odyssey Volume Two

Following on the heels of the success of the original soundtrack album, MGM decided to see just how much they could milk their new cash cow. In the early 1970s they released this second volume, subtitled "Music Inspired by MGM's Presentation of the Stanley Kubrick Production." This innocent disclaimer allowed the studio to put out an album with the *2001* name that had absolutely no music from the movie, save the opening cue! Despite that, it's actually a pretty good record. The album, which featured the Star-Child (the real one this time) on its front cover and a few black-and-white stills on the back, was produced by Jesse Kaye and was stitched together from the Deutsche Grammophon library, where Kubrick had obtained much of his music for the film. In spite of its title, however, none of the music on the album was "inspired" by the movie; it already existed. Instead, it was the accountants at MGM who were inspired to wring as much profit from their golden goose by issuing a record that was really just a classical compilation album. That said, the tracks selection were, for the most part, fun to listen to and, especially for younger fans, it was a chance to learn more about classical music, which was now hip thanks to the movie.

The tracks include the opening "Zarathustra" cue (still the wrong recording!), plus another section of that famous tone poem. There are two new pieces by Ligeti, "Lontano (which would later turn up in Kubrick's *The Shining*) and "Volumina," and another section of his "Requiem," though with a different orchestra and conductor. Khachaturian returns with the "Berceuse" from his "Gayane Ballet Suite." "The Blue Danube" finds its counterpart in three tracks: "Coppelia" by Leo Delibes; "Waltzes from the Rosenkavalier" by Richard Strauss; and "Margarethe" by Charles Gounod. All convey the notion of grace, speed and the grandness of outer space travel, as reimagined by Kubrick. The one difficult track to appreciate is a dissonant piece by Anton Webern, "Entflieht Auf Leichten Kahnen." Its connection to *2001* is flimsy at best, being that it's performed by Clytus Gottwald and the Stuttgart Schola Cantorum, who did Ligeti's "Lux Aeterna" in the film. While its placement in the album seems to be more a matter of padding it out to LP length, it does have the saving grace of offering newly apprenticed classical listeners a chance to experience a far more experimental slice of modern music than they would ever come across in any standard collection, or pursue on their own.

2001: A Space Odyssey Read by the Author

The last of the vinyl offerings in this quintet was a spoken word record where Arthur C. Clarke reads sections of his *2001* novel. Released in 1976 as somewhat of a follow-up to his 1972 book *The Lost Worlds of 2001* (in which he detailed the evolution of the novel through various drafts and diary entries), the album is both more and less than you'd imagine. On the front cover is a beautiful color photo (printed backwards) of a spacesuited Frank Poole (Gary Lockwood) seated in the *Discovery*'s command module deck. To the right of the photo is a black, monolithic-shaped panel with the album's title printed in white and blue neon-style lettering that is supposed to be "futuristic," but is actually clumsy and convoluted. The back cover of the album features excerpts from Clarke's diary (from *Lost Worlds*), following the progression of his work with Kubrick on the novel, and a short, biographical synopsis of the author by Ward Botsford. A credits box on the back mistakenly lists the cover photograph as being that of "Keir Dullea as Mission Commander David Bowman." While it's interesting to hear Clarke read his own prose, he is not the most riveting narrator, and his clipped British accent is more distancing than inviting. He covers the last 11 chapters of the novel, but his flat delivery lacks the magic that is so readily present in the movie. Still, it was a chance for the author to get another slice of the *2001* pie.

Before we move on to the CD releases, let's pause to reflect upon that very 1960s and '70s phenomenon of recorded music, the 8-track tape. A marriage born of technical innovation and car culture, the 8-track was all about convenience rather than quality. Consisting of a ten minute (or so) loop of tape containing four stereo tracks (hence the numerical moniker of 8-track), it could play continuously on your home or car sound system. A magnetic "trip" on the tape caused the player's movable sound head to jump to the succeeding track level for the next ten-minute run of the loop. A button on the player also allowed you to jump tracks whenever you wanted. The technology that allowed for this never-ending music fest also dictated some occasional reshuffling of songs to evenly fit the tape. For the 8-track version of the original *2001* album, the engineers were able to do a pretty slick job of accommodating the loop. The result was that the Von Karajan version of "The Blue Danube," which had been placed piecemeal on the vinyl album, could now be heard in its entirety on its very own track. The other three tracks were interesting as well. The first contains "Zarathustra" and "Atmospheres"; the second was all Ligeti with "Requiem" and "Lux Aeterna"; the third is "Danube" and the fourth is Khachaturian's "Gayane Ballet Suite," a reprise section of "Danube" and ending, like the vinyl, with "Zarathustra." There were no liner notes, production credits or even the names of the composers, just the track titles. Again, the 8-track format wasn't about quality.

The CD Releases

The compact disc revolution, which began in the 1980s and continued into the early 21st century, was the biggest sea change in recorded music distribution until the advent of computer file sharing at the turn of the millennium. CDs caught on in a big way, thanks to their convenience, sound quality and durability. In no time, record companies were transferring their audio catalogues from vinyl to CD, usually with a minimal engineering upgrade. It was the quickest way to get CD product on the shelves while digital re-mastering techniques were being refined. This methodology would ultimately result in multiple CD editions being released of an older album.

The First *2001* CD

As might be expected, the first CD of *2001*'s soundtrack was a simple, unadulterated transfer of the vinyl album. Instead of using the original album's space station poster art for its cover, this 1986 CD has the graphically more appealing Star-Child photo that adorned the *Volume Two* album. No liner notes or other information was included.

The Second *2001* CD

A revamped 1990 version of this soundtrack contained all the same recordings, but added a few twists. Beginning with a 2:47 excerpt from Ligeti's "Atmospheres" that played with the film as an overture on its road show release, the remainder of the CD follows the previous release with two notable exceptions. First, as with the 8-track tape, it was decided to let the "Blue Danube" recording play at its uninterrupted length of 9:49. For fans, having this version of the beloved waltz on CD was a real treat. The second variation was to have a longer version of Ligeti's "Requiem" monolith music (5:58 compared to the original's 4:09) that includes the passage where the astronaut enters the Star-Gate. This additional music had never appeared on a *2001* album before. Also, placing it right before the complete version of "Atmospheres" allows the listener to experience these two pieces together, just as they are in the film. The packaging was only moderately better than the previous disc. The front cover depicts the original poster art within an illustrated template that was being used for a number of film score releases called "CBS Special Products." A four-page insert booklet provided a sampling of information about the movie, the music and the composers. While this CD was not perfect (they still used the Böhm recording of "Zarathustra"), it was a marked improvement over the previous releases.

The Third *2001* CD

In 1996, Rick Victor and David McLees attempted to produce a high-quality, "definitive" *2001* soundtrack and, for the most part, they succeeded. Complete with a 24-page booklet containing extensive information about the film, the music and the director, along with many photos, some in color, the jewel-cased CD came with an outer protective cardboard sleeve showing, in a silvery blue, the space station poster art that matches the full-color booklet cover inside. The 13-track remastered CD gets off on the right note with the "Atmospheres" overture followed by, at long last, the Von Karajan recording of "Zarathustra," the first time this correct version ever appeared on a *2001* soundtrack. From here on, however, the content is a mixed bag. The next track is a long 6:33 cut of Ligeti's "Requiem," which includes the Star-Gate entrance cue. It's followed by a 5:42 excerpt from "The Blue Danube." Next up is a short 2:52 excerpt from "Lux Aeterna" which closely follows the cue as it appears in the film. Khachaturian's "Gayane Ballet Suite" is heard at 5:15, followed by a track titled "Jupiter and Beyond" that contains three Ligeti pieces woven together: "Requiem," "Atmospheres" and, for the first time ever on a *2001* soundtrack, "Adventures" (and even distorted as it was in the film). While this combo is a welcome addition, it was botched badly by having the short "Requiem" cue coupled here, rather than the longer one that was actually used in the "Jupiter" sequence. The shorter version of "Requiem" should have been placed earlier on the album, where it would have followed the chronology of the movie. (The short version of the monolith theme appears in the film during the "Dawn of Man" and TMA-1 moon excavation scenes.) By putting it in the "Jupiter and Beyond" track (where the longer one should have gone), the coupling of the Ligeti pieces is seriously flawed. The addition of "Adventures" is fine, and it is a real pleasure to listen to it, as it conjures up the surreal atmosphere of the end of the movie. Track eight is a reprise of the Von Karajan "Zarathustra" and is followed by an 8:17 excerpt of "Danube" that accompanies the end credits. I consider this another misstep since I believe most fans would rather hear the entire waltz earlier on the CD where, chronologically, it is associated with the trip to the moon. Then, if there was space on the CD, the credit cue could then run here.

After the credit cue, there is a four-track supplemental section that contains some interesting material that shows the record producers cared. First up is the Karl Böhm recording of "Zarathustra" which had appeared on all the previous albums. Though it was never actually used in the movie, legions of soundtrack owners have come to love it, so it's nice to have it included here. Next is the 5:59 version of "Lux Aeterna" as it appeared on the original soundtrack, allowing fans to enjoy the entire piece, rather than just the shorter cue that is in the film. Following that is the long, unaltered 10:54 version of "Adventures," which is fascinating to hear, though it never would have been suitable for the end of *2001* in this form. The last track, which runs 9:44, is a collection of dialogue scenes with Hal the computer. As the movie's most famous "character," it is a fitting tribute to the film and the talents of actor Douglas Rain.

This soundtrack is a marked improvement over all the previous ones. For purists, however, the excerpting of "The Blue Danube" and the botched coupling of the Ligeti pieces means that the definitive *2001* CD soundtrack has yet to be commercially made. But, thanks to home computers, CD burners and downloading, it is now possible to design your own customized version using the tracks from the various CDs that are out there. It is an interesting irony that the technology has now arrived to enable fans to make their own correct soundtrack of the movie that hailed technology *and* warned us about the dangers of human error.

Ironically, with his decision to use pre-existing music in *2001*, Kubrick revived a tradition that went back to the very origins of cinema. In the silent era, movies were usually accompanied by a pianist (or sometimes an orchestra) who played along to the images on the screen. They would generally work from a repertoire of familiar short pieces (from Chopin, Mendelssohn, Strauss and others) that fit a variety of moods, pulling them out as required. Eventually, some silent films had actual original scores written for them; they were sometimes recorded for playback during their showings. Once sound pictures became the norm, the use of original music scores exploded, though there was still the occasional use of some well-known pieces.

After the phenomenal success of *2001*, more filmmakers experimented with the use of pre-existing music in place of an original score. John Boorman put Beethoven's 7th Symphony in *Zardoz* (1973) and used Wagner and Orff in *Excalibur* (1981); Norman Jewison used Bach and Tchaikovsky in *Rollerball* (1975); David Lynch and Oliver Stone found a place for Samuel Barber's haunting "Adagio for Strings" in *The Elephant Man* (1980) and *Platoon* (1986), respectively; the Coen brothers embraced Khachaturian's "Spartacus" and "Gayane" in their brilliantly funny period comedy *The Hudsucker Proxy* (1994). Woody Allen's entire oeuvre is almost exclusively scored with classical pieces and jazz standards. Of course, there's a whole industry based on using rock, pop and hip hop songs in movies, dating back to Elvis. Pop music anthologies as a "score" also developed with such hits as *American Graffiti, The Sting, Saturday Night Fever, The Big Chill* and *Forrest Gump*. Kubrick took that route, coupled with original music by his daughter Vivian (under the *non de plume* Abigail Meade), for *Full Metal Jacket*, but otherwise he continued to mine classical gold for his films, using Beethoven, Rossini, Elgar and Purcell for *A Clockwork Orange,* Handel, Mozart, Bach, Schubert and Vivaldi for *Barry Lyndon,* Bartók and Ligeti for *The Shining* and Shostakovich and Ligeti for *Eyes Wide Shut*. It had become the modus operandi for a filmmaker who wished to exert complete control in all areas of the filmmaking process.

For much of the filmmaking community, however, the use of original scores continued to flourish, and with it, album sales, thanks to such major successes as *Star Wars, Indiana Jones, Chariots of Fire, The Piano, Titanic* and the *Lord of the Rings* trilogy. Even with sweeping orchestral scores, more often than not, pop songs of one type or another would be added to, or specifically written for, a film. Movies like *Batman, Pleasantville* and *American Beauty* even put out two soundtracks—one with pop songs, and the other with the orchestral score. With the rising cost of acquiring classic pop tunes for their movies, budget-minded producers tried to create their own hit songs. Tom Hanks took this a step further for his low-budget directorial debut, the wonderfully retro and much underrated *That Thing You Do!*, which has an entire soundtrack of "period" 1960s-style songs that were written for the film.

In the world of movie music, the lines of distinction have definitely become blurred, as more and more experimentation is finding its way into our films. Anything and everything, it seems, is possible. Music, whether rock, orchestral, hip hop or synthesized, may be mixed with sound effects, voices, etc., to create a new paradigm of aural enhancement. Films are planned with musical set-pieces in mind; pastiche and authentic ethnic influences work hand in hand; scores are written before, during and after a movie has been shot; there are no rules any more. The *2001* "score" helped create an environment in the film industry where such experimentation was tolerated and, eventually, embraced. Once the genie was released, it could not be put back into the bottle. But that's okay, since we have all benefited from the success Kubrick enjoyed with his radical score.

Much of the music we hear in movies today, whether it's original or adapted, has been forged in the fires of experimentation that *2001* helped create through its insistence on fanning the flames. And Kubrick wasn't unaware of the magic between a director and his use of music. He once said to Italian director Sergio Leone, "I've got all Ennio Morricone's albums. Can you explain to me why I only seem to like the music he composed for your films?" Leone replied, "Don't worry. I didn't think much of Richard Strauss until I saw *2001*."[16]

7

WATCHING KUBRICK'S ODYSSEY

The Cinematic Experience

I was disturbed by its ambiguity when I first saw the film. But I
think it will turn out to be the *Citizen Kane* of our era."
—Keir Dullea, while promoting the film in 1968

So, what was it like seeing *2001* as a brand new movie on the big
screen? To sit down in a theater and watch this very radical movie by
one of the greatest filmmakers of his generation? Since the 1964 release
of *Dr. Strangelove* and the announcement the following year that
Kubrick's next film would be a big-budget science fiction epic, anticipation had been steadily growing among regular film goers and critics
alike. By the time the movie was released in 1968, over three years after
it was first announced, expectations had reached a fever pitch. After the
controversy surrounding *Lolita* and the phenomenal success of *Dr.
Strangelove*, the premiere of a Kubrick movie was now a major event,
not to be missed.

Steven Spielberg, one of the most successful directors in history, 21
years old when *2001* was released and just beginning his own film career,
had this insight upon first seeing the movie: "I just remember going to
the theater and seeing the film for the first time, and feeling that it wasn't
a movie, that for the first time the motion picture form had been
changed."[1]

Many big-name, established filmmakers were also impressed. Both
Federico Fellini and Franco Zeffirelli sent congratulatory messages to
Kubrick. Richard Lester, Charlie Chaplin and Saul Bass were also fans.
There were some dissenters who either just didn't get it, or found the

experience more bewildering than enlightening, but that was to be expected from a movie that was so radically different from the more conventional fare out there. Big-budget Hollywood movies just did not look or sound or feel anything like *2001*.

Even before a frame of footage from the film itself has been seen, *2001* gets off to a startling beginning with the appearance of the brand new, stylized MGM logo. A coolly graphic lion illustration in blue and white, it replaced the traditional live-action roaring lion surrounded by the ornate, golden MGM frame that had previously graced hundreds of the studio's films. This ultra-modern, austere piece of artwork fairly announced itself as the logo of tomorrow, a logo for the 21st century. And so it is. Making its appearance at the head of Kubrick's film, it is accompanied by a low rumbling on the soundtrack and, as the image fades, it is replaced by a view of our moon in space, seen from its dark, far side. The rumbling murmur resolves itself into the opening fanfare of Strauss' "Also sprach Zarathustra." In a series of grandiose musical climaxes, the Earth and sun are seen rising over the curve of our moon, followed by three titles flashed singly across the screen: MGM Presents; A Stanley Kubrick Production; *2001: A Space Odyssey*. As "Zarathustra"'s final orgasmic organ chord dies away, the scene fades to black. So begins *2001*.

Fade in on a desert landscape, silhouetted in the early morning light, as a superimposed title appears: "The Dawn of Man." The sounds of birds and chattering insects supply an aural accompaniment. A series of long static shots reveal vast arid plains of Namibia, Africa, giving us a sense of the bleakness that defines the world we are seeing. It's prehistory as slide show, but who or what is behind the camera remains unknown. Eventually, these landscapes serve up evidence of mammalian life through the ironic appearance of bones, including hominid skeletons scattered on the desert floor. This is confirmed when a pair of ape-like creatures are introduced, squatting in the foreground in near silhouette, nibbling on some unidentifiable morsels of foodstuff.

Over the course of several ensuing scenes, we are shown the struggle for survival by a small tribe of man-apes against the natural forces poised to thwart them, be it drought, fearsome predators (illustrated by a leopard that attacks one of them) or a rival man-ape tribe vying for control of a life-sustaining waterhole that is little more than a muddy puddle. There is no music, no dialogue (just the screeching of apes) and no narration to explain what is happening. This is pure cinema in the Hitchcockian sense; the standard rules of storytelling have been abandoned. We are onlookers who must determine for ourselves the nature of the Darwinian drama unfolding before us.

After the trials of a typical day are shown, we see the tribe huddled together in their darkened cave sanctuary as evening descends. A palpable fear hangs over them, exacerbated by the far-off growls of the leopard, shown feasting contentedly on a fresh zebra kill. No such sustenance is afforded the non-carnivorous apes, who must make do with whatever nourishment is supplied by the twigs, roots and leaves they managed to find in the course of the day. The whimpering of the baby apes, held in their mothers' arms, heighten the sense of vulnerability felt by the entire tribe. A fiery pre-dawn sky, with a tiny, barely visible crescent moon hanging overhead, heralds a new day.

The prone figures of the apes stir into wakefulness as a new element enters their domain. Otherworldly voices are chanting on the soundtrack, but it is unclear whether this is being heard by the apes or if it is background "music." In a wide shot reveal, we see that a black, rectangular slab, about 12 feet tall, is now planted at the cave entrance. The apes spread out in a wide circle around this unnaturally precise artifact that is clearly a "made" object. What it is and how it got here are unknown. Though frightened by this enigma in their midst, the apes are nevertheless drawn to it, their wide circle slowly contracting as they get ever closer, eventually reaching out to touch its surface. Soon the entire group has formed a tight knot around the base of the monolith, their simian hands caressing the smooth perfection worshipfully. An up-shot from the apes' point of view reveals the thrusting shape of the monolithic slab silhouetted against a caramel-colored, cloud-strewn dawn sky, the glowing orb of the sun just over its top with a crescent moon hovering above in perfect alignment. It is a shot that is monumental and religious in every sense of the word.

A direct cut takes us to an empty desert landscape, and several other ones, before returning us to the apes foraging in the bone-strewn dry streambed where earlier we had seen the leopard attack one of them. The tribe leader digs by a tapir skeleton for whatever edible matter he can find. His concentration is suddenly interrupted as a thought (maybe the first thought) enters his consciousness. A brief intercut shows us that monumental point of view shot of the monolith from the previous scene, indicating that it has somehow had an impact on the mind of this creature. The rumble of the opening credits music starts up as the ape leader begins looking at the tapir bones in a new manner. As the music swells, he tentatively picks up a bone and slowly begins striking the other ones in a dawning awareness that the use of such an object can extend his range of power. As he brings down his newly invented cudgel on the tapir skull, smashing it to bits, his mind visualizes an actual living tapir being felled by the same blow. As the music climaxes, so do the actions of the ape's orgiastic destruction of splintered bones, an act that is clearly new to him and portends what his future may hold.

There is a direct cut to another empty landscape. The ape leader enters the frame, bearing a large chunk of meat which he ravenously devours. The entire tribe is then seen chowing down on their newly found food source at the streambed, while numerous tapirs innocently graze in the background. They continue eating, back at their cave, the monolith no longer a presence at that location. A brief evening shot shows the apes sitting around their cave site; they no longer feel the need to huddle within the cave itself for security.

From the quiet of this scene, a smash cut takes us back to the waterhole where the two tribes are engaged in their usual screeching match. This time, however, the monolith apes are shown carrying bone weapons and standing upright rather than squatting as the other tribe does. The leader of the monolith tribe goads the leader of the other tribe by crossing the waterhole and overstepping the boundaries of the other tribe's domain. When the angered leader tries to retaliate by chasing the intruder back, he is swiftly dispatched with a blow to the head from the bone weapon. As he lies twitching on the ground, further blows are rained down upon him by other members of the tribe, sealing his fate. The remaining members of the other tribe, astonished by what has happened to their leader, cower helplessly.

The victorious apes cross the waterhole to take possession of the territory on the other side. In an act of exuberance, the triumphant ape leader tosses his bone weapon into the air. The camera follows it up as it spins end over end within the frame, the moving sky behind it a telling suggestion of its upward climb. The bone briefly exits the upper frame, then reappears as it begins its descent. Even a first-time viewer feels that this shot is important, that something significant, not just in the story we are watching, but also in the history of cinema, is about to happen. And it does.

In a brilliant cut, Kubrick transitions from the falling bone to an orbiting space satellite, circling the Earth. In a 24th of a second, the movie has jumped four million years, from the primitive prehistory of the man-apes to the sophisticated future of 2001. It is a cinematic edit without precedence, rivaling (many would say surpassing) David Lean's cut in his 1962 *Lawrence of Arabia*, from Peter O'Toole blowing out the match to the sun rising over the desert horizon.

As stirring, hushed strings fill the soundtrack, the doppelganger satellite drifts out of frame, replaced by the curved blue cheek of our own planet. Eventually, horns and flutes announce that we are hearing Johann Strauss' "The Blue Danube" as we see a number of satellites in orbit above the Earth. After experiencing the primitive chaos of the film's first 20 minutes, the calming, civilized strains of old Vienna, even in the service of such marvelous technological wonders, are a welcome respite. From this celestial dance floor, as the waltz proper begins, two individual performers are singled out from the coterie of anonymous satellites: a graceful, pirouetting "Ferris Wheel" space station and its intended partner, an approaching commercial space plane bearing the familiar Pan American moniker on its side.

The clean, crisp effects work is without equal, as if NASA itself had shot the footage. During this extended interlude, we are briefly taken inside the space plane which reveals a single passenger in the 40-seat cabin, fast asleep, his floating pen tracing a lazy arc in the zero gravity environment. A stewardess makes her way down the center aisle, wearing special grip shoes to keep her anchored to the floor. She retrieves the wayward pen, returning it to the breast pocket of her sleeping charge before moving on to her other duties.

The dance between the station and plane continues as the vehicles move slowly toward one another. A scene inside the plane cockpit shows the faceless pilot and co-pilot from behind, seated at their hi-tech controls, while through their window the distant space station rolls by in its assigned orbit. A cut to a close-up of the control panel, sporting three animated view screens, reveals the controlled energies at work to pilot the plane. The center screen depicts what appears to be a moving graphic of the space station's rectangular docking port. As if to confirm this, the next cut is a reverse angle from within the docking port, looking out at the wheeling star field, the small form of the space plane coming into alignment. As the camera pulls back revealing the interior of the docking bay, we see that it is bristling with technology as well as a number of windowed compartments containing tiny human figures. The spacecraft are now locked together in their spinning roundelay, the music swelling toward a joyous climax. The camera joins the dance in an elegant slide between the rings of the station toward an ecstatic conclusion.

In a disorienting shot that apparently shows two wall panels sliding past one another, it is revealed to be a circular elevator car rotating to an open position with two occupants, a pink-clad, uniformed female and a dark-suited male. A full 25 minutes into the movie, we hear the first lines of dialogue, spoken by a space station elevator operator and the single passenger from the Pan Am space plane she is conveying to his destination:

> SHE: Here you are, sir. Main level, please.
> HE: Right. See you on the way back.

As he exits, we realize that the film has now entered a more traditional narrative phase with human characters we can relate to. The male character exchanges pleasantries with the station receptionist and explains that Mr. Miller from Station Security is supposed to be meeting him. Before she can call for him, Miller appears, slightly out of breath, and addresses the man as Dr. Floyd. As in any international airport terminal, Floyd is required to go through a documentation process. The 21st century film version of this consists of undergoing voiceprint identification in which Floyd must state his destination, his nationality and his full name. In this tidy manner of exposition, we learn that he is an American headed to the moon and that his full name is Heywood R. Floyd. Once confirmed by the screening receptionist on the monitor, he now has clearance into the station proper.

The interior of the sparsely populated station lounge is a sweeping curved floor the length of a football field. Its pure white perfection is livened up with numerous futuristic chairs and loveseats in bright magenta scattered throughout. A Hilton Hotel reception desk with an attendant concierge is off to one side along with an automated self-serve coffee bar. It is beautiful, yet utterly pedestrian, as airport lounges tend to be. As the two men traverse the length of the lounge, we see that, in addition to the Hilton Hotel logo, there are Bell Telephone picture-phone booths and a Howard Johnson's Earthlight Room restaurant. Floyd and Miller chitchat and, as they pass the phone booth, Floyd stops short to say he needs to make some calls and will meet with Miller in the restaurant afterward. Miller agrees and exits.

The closet-sized booth contains a comfortable swivel chair and a large video screen, below which is a backlit panel with instructions on how to use the phone. A flat desktop has a keypad and credit card slot for making calls. Floyd calls home and speaks with his young daughter who wonders why he won't be coming to her birthday party the next day. Like many busy parents, Floyd rationalizes his absence with the banality, "Daddy's traveling." He then begs off with the promise of sending her a present. What's most striking in this scene is the window behind Floyd's profile, featuring a gigantic Earth shown moving along the axis of the rotating station, creating a dazzling visual display that is all but ignored by Floyd as he converses with his young daughter. At the conclusion of the call, the screen abruptly displays the phone bill for the call: "Charge $1.70 Thank You."

Exiting the booth, Floyd recognizes a Russian scientist named Elena in the lounge area having drinks with two other women and a man. Floyd greets them and is invited to join them. What begins as genial small talk takes a more serious turn when the man, Dr. Andrei Smyslov, learns that Floyd is heading to the American base on the moon and queries him about the mysterious communications blackout there. Floyd pleads ignorance, but the suspicious Smyslov presses the American on rumors that an epidemic has broken out at the base. Floyd puts on his best poker face and says he's not at liberty to discuss the matter. This is the first indication of what the plot of the movie might be (trouble at the American moon base, but it must be kept secret from the Russians). Despite everyone's excessive politeness, there is a frosty brittleness just beneath the surface which reminds us that these civilized people, sitting around a table sharing drinks in a 21st century space lounge, are not that far removed from the two ape tribes fighting over a waterhole in prehistoric Africa. Floyd manages to extricate himself from this embarrassing cul-de-sac by warming up to Elena's offer of meeting at the IAC

Conference in June, and a reminder for him to bring his young daughter along. With his dignity intact, Floyd excuses himself from the Russians as they ruminate over their encounter. Fade to black.

Fade in on an enormous gibbous moon against a dazzling star field as some sort of roundish space vehicle moves toward the lunar orb. The Strauss waltz is back and we are soon reunited with a sleeping Floyd (who is, again, apparently the only customer) in the spacious circular passenger cabin that has seating for about 20. The seats are larger and more comfortable, reflecting the needs of a longer-duration flight than that of the space plane. A Pan Am stewardess briefly checks up on him and then makes her way to the other side of the cabin to deliver a food tray to another stewardess who is watching a Japanese judo wrestling match on a video screen. The two women exchange brief comments, unheard over the Strauss music, about their sleeping passenger. The first stewardess departs, leaving the other to enjoy her meal. A close-up of the food tray reveals it to be made up of eight cartons, with individual, retractable sipping tubes and illustrated depictions of the food they contain (fish, vegetables, fruit, etc.).

After a quick exterior shot of the bulbous moon shuttle in space, with the Earth and sun a luminous backdrop, we return to the interior as the stewardess arrives at the ship's galley via elevator. She exits and approaches the food dispenser unit, along the Velcro-carpeted walkway in her zero-gravity grip shoes. After receiving a second food tray from an automated kitchen dispenser, the stewardess enters a circular access hub and begins walking up the curved side, 180 degrees, to orient her, upside down, for entry into an adjoining cabin. The entire scene, from entrance to exit, is done as one shot and is designed to be a showy, bravura moment for the audience. The cockpit door, bathed in red light, opens to emit the stewardess. The image pulls back and rotates to reveal the pilot and co-pilot as they eagerly receive their food trays. An exterior shot of the shuttle shows the minuscule figures through the cockpit window, giving a sense of scale to the vehicle. We return to the passenger cabin to see Floyd sipping his zero gravity meal as the shuttle captain comes in to chat. Momentarily distracted, Floyd's tray floats up from his lap, though he quickly retrieves it. As a humorous button to this sequence, we next see Floyd reading the lengthy instructions on the door to the zero gravity toilet.

A cut takes us to a beautiful shot of a huge crescent moon as the shuttle glides across the darkened expanse of its terminator and into lunar orbit. We are treated to a lengthy shot of the shuttle's landing legs extending into their open position, followed by shots of the craft descending over the craggy lunar landscape, all choreographed to a particularly heroic portion of the Strauss music which has been a constant aural backdrop to the entire moon shuttle sequence. The pilots work the controls to maneuver their ship while a center screen display updates their progress. An expansive view of the lunar exterior shows three spacesuited astronauts perched on the rim of a crater that overlooks the sprawling moon base complex. In the far distance, next to a pale blue gibbous earth, the moon shuttle can be seen dropping slowly toward the base. A stunning image, looking straight up, shows eight wedge-shaped panels splitting open to reveal the descending shuttle against an immense star field. This is followed by a topside view revealing the retracting panels to be the commensurate parts of a moon base landing pad dome. There's a ground-level view of the ship touching down on its hydraulic legs, kicking up dust on the brightly lit platform. In a grand finale, we are shown a cavernous, red-lit chamber with numerous windowed enclosures housing human occupants. A central column begins to descend, revealing the moon shuttle, still on the landing pad, as it is lowered into the bowels of the moon base. The waltz concludes; Floyd has arrived.

In a large conference room with glowing wall panels as a light source, a dozen men and women, including Floyd, are seated at a rectangular horseshoe table. At the open end stands a modest podium. Floyd and two others, their backs to us, sit at the near end engaged in banter while a photographer in a plaid suit snaps some photos. When he finishes, he thanks Dr. Halvorsen, who is seated next to Floyd, and then exits. Halvorsen rises and goes to the podium to introduce Floyd, who he says "has come up specially to Clavius" (the moon base) to take part in the briefing. Through some polite applause, Floyd makes his way to the podium. In a wordy bit of exposition, we learn that a discovery of some importance has been made and that a cover story about an epidemic at the base has been fabricated to maintain a level of security against others (read: the Russians) from finding out. Photo security badges are worn by everyone in the room, so this is clearly a top secret event. While Floyd puts a genial face on the situation through his friendly delivery, he is often shown in proximity to an American flag in the background, underlining the national security mindset of this meeting. He also stresses the need for absolute secrecy concerning the discovery and says formal security oaths, in writing, will be needed "from everyone who has any knowledge of this event." The briefing will now get underway, but we will not be privy to it.

In a dramatic edit, we cut from the conference room to a stark lunar landscape as a boxy, oblong vehicle flies toward us, passing directly over the camera. Weird, spacey music can be heard as a series of shots depicts the low-flying rocket bus skirting over the rugged terrain. Inside, a pair of pilots steer the craft in a red-lit front cockpit. Floyd and the two colleagues from his end of the briefing room table are in the coldly lit passenger section. The occupants, wearing spacesuits *sans* helmets, packs and gloves, discuss the discovery over processed sandwiches and coffee. While the particulars remain unclear to the audience, we learn that something with a strong magnetic field was detected and dug up on the moon and that it had been deliberately buried there four million years ago. Though Floyd and the others take the finding very seriously, they still exhibit a jocular irreverence over its enigmatic nature, their way of dealing with the mystery. Arriving at the excavation outpost, the rocket descends over a makeshift landing pad. Having dropped some clues about the mysterious object Floyd is there to see, the film then stretches out the tension through an extended landing sequence, shown almost entirely on the moon bus navigation screen. An observer standing at a console inside the outpost monitors the bus landing through a large viewing window.

With the eerie choral sounds that were last heard when the monolithic slab appeared to the apes, we see a high-angle shot of an enormous excavation pit. At the bottom is an identical black monolith (or is it the same one?). Six spacesuited figures trudge into view along the near end of the excavation and pause at the ramp. A reverse, up-angle shot reveals that they are Floyd, Halvorsen, Michaels and three others, all gazing at the artifact in the pit. Again seen from behind, though closer, the men begin down the ramp, the music continuing to create an ominous mood. Once in the pit, Floyd walks up to the 12-foot upright monolith. He reaches out with his gloved hand to touch its smooth, blank surface, mirroring a similar gesture by the apes millions of years previously. Whatever this object is, it remains beyond the ken of the exploring astronauts, who then assemble in front of it for the requisite photo opportunity. At that moment, a high-pitched radio feedback signal overwhelms the men through their spacesuit communication speakers, sending them reeling away, clutching their helmets in a futile effort to fend off the noise. As they look toward the monolith, the source of the signal, they see the sun rising over the slab with the Earth in alignment above them both. Evidently, the artifact has spoken.

A direct cut to an empty star field carries the superimposition "JUPITER MISSION—18 MONTHS LATER." With the mournful sounds of the Adagio from Khachaturian's "Gayane Ballet Suite" filling the soundtrack, the enormous hulk of a gigantic spaceship, hundreds of feet in length, enters from the left and begins an endless track deep into the starry background of the screen. Consisting of a spherical front section, a long, segmented central spine, and a chunky engine unit at the rear, it is an object designed purely to exist in the depths of space.

We then cut directly to the ship's interior, inside a large, drum-shaped room, about ten feet wide and 35 feet in diameter, and see a man, thirtyish, in white shorts and a black T-shirt, jogging and shadowboxing around the room's perimeter. Having already seen the curved floor of the rotating space station, it is a simple deduction to assume this large room rotates as well, to produce an artificial gravity environment. There follows a very odd and surreal image of a reflection in a glass lens of a man, crouched over, making his way toward the camera in some sort of a rotating tunnel. Back in the large centrifuge room, the jogger is seen sitting at one end eating a meal. Suddenly a hatch in the central hub of the room opens and a man wearing a gray jumpsuit descends a ladder to the opposite side of the room. This is the man we saw reflected in the lens. Once he has reached the perimeter floor of the centrifuge, he makes his way 180 degrees to the far end to join the other man.

Next to the dining area is an automated kitchenette, where the man who emerged from the hub gets his meal. The jogging man is halfway through his meal as he looks at a flat TV display device about the size of a magazine which is on the tabletop. The device says, "Next transmission in …" and has a counter ticking off the seconds to zero. The screen comes alive with a BBC interview program called *The World*

Heywood Floyd and fellow scientists stand in awe before the TMA-1 excavation site, prior to descending the ramp to examine the uncovered alien artifact. This scene, which has no dialogue, still managed to convey the mystery and wonder inherent in mankind's encounter with the unknown.

Tonight, which is about the two astronauts and their mission to Jupiter. The other astronaut joins the first at the dining table, and each one watches the program on his own flat TV device. This interview show provides necessary exposition to the film's plot, as well as to who the two astronauts are.

During the course of the interview, we learn that the two astronauts are named Dr. David Bowman and Dr. Frank Poole, and that three other crew members are in hibernation units in the centrifuge until the ship reaches Jupiter many months from now. The conversation and responses are definitely of the canned PR variety, with no real information about the nature of the mission. The interview also introduces us to the ship's talking computer Hal 9000. Hal, whose appearance is a red-eyed lens surrounded by a number of constantly changing readout screens, has a polite and formal demeanor, and he seems much more engaging than his human counterparts. We learn that he is the brain and central nervous system of the ship; his mission responsibilities range over the entire operation of the vessel. The interview ends with Bowman, the mission commander, being asked by the interviewer if he thought Hal had genuine emotions. Bowman replies that while Hal acts as though he has genuine emotions, he believes that is a question no one can answer.

There follows a number of scenes showing the day-to-day life of the two astronauts, who must battle boredom. The men's loneliness is emphasized by the use, again, of Khachaturian's Adagio as a melancholy backdrop. While taking a sun ray treatment, Hal informs Frank (the jogging astronaut) that a transmission from his parents is coming in. Because of the distance of the ship from Earth, it is not a two-way conversation, but a video message. Frank's parents are shown sitting together in front of a birthday cake, wishing their son a happy birthday, and engaging in small talk about incidental matters. Dave is seen sleeping in a nearby glass-topped enclosure that can be converted to a hibernation chamber when necessary. Frank stares back at the screen in an almost disinterested manner that illustrates his isolation from home. After a chorus of "Happy Birthday," the parents sign off and the screen goes blank. Frank resumes his sun ray treatment as Hal also wishes him a happy birthday. Later, Hal and Frank are shown playing chess together at Hal's main console. The computer handily beats the astronaut and then politely thanks him for "a very enjoyable game."

We now see Bowman sketching the hibernating astronauts in his drawing pad, while Frank is asleep in his bed cubicle. As he walks along the centrifuge perimeter, he is greeted by Hal as he passes the computer's main console. When he sees that Bowman has his sketch pad, Hal asks if he can see his latest work. The commander flips through the pages which he holds up to the computer's lens. After complimenting him on his renderings, Hal engages Bowman in a more serious discussion about the nature of their mission. The computer evidently has concerns that there are some extremely odd things about the mission, and mentions the rumors that were floating around before they left about something being dug up on the moon. This is the first indication that this portion of the film is somehow tied to the lunar excavation of the mysterious monolith. Hal feels the secretive nature of how their mission was set up might be connected to these rumors. After listening to all this, Bowman deduces that Hal is merely engaged in a psychology exercise so he can make an evaluation report on the crew's stability. Hal concedes this to be true and apologizes for the silliness of the protocol involved.

Suddenly, with the words "Just a moment, just a moment," the computer announces that it has just picked up a fault in the AE-35 unit. A heads up display on one of Hal's screens shows it is part of the antenna complex on the outside of the ship. The unit is evidently going to fail in the next 72 hours. Once Bowman learns the unit is still operating and that it will continue to function for the next 72 hours, he says he wants to discuss it first with Frank and Mission Control before bringing the faulty unit in.

Bowman and Poole are next seen taking readings inside the command deck of the ship. In the zero gravity environment, they stand at right angles to one another. We next see them passing through a narrow, circular corridor, the far end of which is rotating. The two men stand together on the rotating portion and descend through an open hatchway which is the hub of the centrifuge. Back in the gravity environment of the centrifuge, the astronauts, seen from behind, seated at Hal's communication station, receive a video message from mission control authorizing them to replace the faulty antenna part. A dramatic edit takes us from this static image of the two astronauts seated at the communications station to a tracking shot of Bowman in his red spacesuit, carrying a box-shaped piece of equipment, traversing through an eight-sided corridor into the pod bay where three EVA vehicles are stored. The round, one-man pods are equipped with a set of mechanical arms flanking a central window. Over the spacesuit's communication link, Bowman's labored breathing and the hissing of his oxygen supply are heard. Turning to the computer console in the pod bay, he says, "Prepare B pod for EVA, Hal." The lights of the center pod come on and the craft rotates 180° on its platform so that Bowman will have access to its entry hatch on the reverse side. As he steps up into the pod, we cut to a video monitor in the command deck showing this action. Poole, in a yellow spacesuit, but minus the helmet and gloves, is stationed at the command deck to monitor the EVA mission. Bowman's breathing can be heard throughout this entire scene.

A deep space shot reveals a tiny *Discovery* ship on one side as a pair of mottled, rocky asteroids tumble past the camera. A big close-up of Bowman in the pod, with control panel lights reflected on his helmet visor, shows him preparing to begin his mission. From inside the *Discovery*, the pod bay double doors split open, revealing the starry blackness beyond. The pod, on its hydraulic platform, slowly moves toward the open hatch. A cut to the exterior of the *Discovery* shows the pod emerging from the front of the ship. In a wider shot, Poole can be seen in the command deck window above the pod bay. Inside the pod, Bowman maneuvers the control throttles amidst a maze of illuminated screens and buttons spread out before him. Another exterior shot shows the pod rising upward next to the habitation module sphere of the *Discovery*, turning towards it as the pod lights sweep across the command deck windows with Poole clearly visible inside. This is perhaps the first real indication of the scale of the ship in relation to the human beings who inhabit it. A long shot of the *Discovery*, looking forward from just past the central antenna mount, captures the smaller sphere of the pod rising over the larger habitation sphere, mimicking the sun and Earth conjunction seen in the opening credits. Poole is again shown in his seat on the command deck, monitoring the mission, while a complementary shot of Bowman in the pod reveals him maneuvering along the length of *Discovery*'s spine (seen through the pod window) toward the antenna. A big, overhead shot of the antenna complex, freely turning on its mount, indicates that it has been disengaged from its contact with Earth. Once the pod has reached the proximity of the antenna, Bowman rotates the vehicle so that the hatch will be facing its objective.

As the pod hatch slides open, Bowman emerges, birth-like, in his red spacesuit, the boxy antenna repair part in one hand, his other clutching the control throttle on his chest pack that activates the maneuvering thrusters on his back pack. All the while, his breathing is heard on the soundtrack. During his EVA excursion, Bowman activates the polarized filter in his visor against the harsh sunlight, and we see it darken to the point where his face is no longer visible. Arriving at the antenna complex, Bowman makes his way to the backside of the main dish, opening a panel to retrieve the faulty unit. Poole observes the operation from the pod's external camera. No dialogue passes between the two men, and the scene is deliberately long and boring, as an actual procedure of this sort would be.

In another brilliant edit, the scene cuts from Bowman at the antenna, holding the unit aloft, to a close-up shot of a monitor showing 3-D motion x-ray scans of the unit itself. We are now back on board the *Discovery* as Bowman and Poole, under the watchful eye of Hal, carry out a series of diagnostic tests on a test bench in the pod bay to find the problem. After checking over numerous circuits, Bowman can't isolate any trouble with the unit. Hal concurs that it is puzzling and recommends putting the original unit back and allowing it to fail, stating that it would then be a simple matter to track down the cause. Back in the centrifuge, mission control agrees with the plan to replace the unit to check fault prediction, but states that their preliminary findings indicate that Hal is in error predicting the fault. Ironically this conclusion comes from a twin Hal 9000 computer back on Earth. He adds that they're skeptical and are running cross-checking routines to determine the reliability of this conclusion.

There follows an interesting conversation between the astronauts and Hal over the discrepancy between Hal and the twin 9000 at Mission Control. The computer states simply that it can only be attributable to human error, citing that this sort of thing has cropped up before and it has always been due to human error. He goes on to say that the 9000 series has a perfect operational record. Both astronauts pretend to be placated by this answer, but it is obvious that they are not. Bowman then asks Frank to come down to the pod bay and check out a problem with a transmitter in one of the pods. They leave Hal and head to the pod bay. Of course, there is really no way to leave Hal, as his lenses are everywhere throughout the ship. Once in the pod bay, Bowman has Hal rotate the pod so that he and Frank can go inside to investigate the transmitter "problem." Bowman has Hal rotate the pod again once they're inside, the pod window facing toward the computer workbench where Hal has a lens.

After shutting down all the communication switches inside the pod, Bowman and Poole both give instructions to Hal to rotate the pod. When Hal fails to respond, they are assured Hal can't hear them and that they can discuss their concerns in private. This is the only time in the entire film that the two men have a conversation with one another. While they acknowledge their feelings that there is something strange about Hal, they concur that Hal's failure mode analysis is the best option. But Bowman says that if Hal were wrong, it would be the surest way of proving it. Poole says that if they put the unit back and it doesn't fail, that would pretty well wrap it up as far as Hal is concerned, and that they'd have to disconnect the computer rather than allow it to continue running things. Bowman agrees this would be necessary, though it would entail cutting Hal's higher brain functions without disturbing the purely automatic and regulatory systems. Bowman concludes his thoughts on the matter with the notion that, since no 9000 computer has ever been disconnected, he wasn't sure what Hal would think about such a procedure. From this exchange, we go to a direct close-up of Hal's lens, the throbbing of the ship's systems forming an ominous backdrop. A reverse angle point of view reveals most chillingly that he has been reading the lips of the two men in the pod during their entire exchange.

After this moment of high dramatic tension, there is an "Intermission" card. After an intermission of ten minutes or so (depending on the theater), the movie resumes with a huge close-up of the *Discovery* gliding past the camera, while the heavy breathing of an astronaut is heard on the soundtrack. A space pod rises over the spherical hull of the ship, mimicking the earlier EVA mission. This time it is Bowman on the command deck while Poole pilots the pod to the antenna to replace the faulty unit. All the shots shown mirror the set-ups seen in Bowman's previous excursion, as if to underline the sense of standard

Poole and Bowman seek the privacy of a one-man space pod to discuss Hal the computer's suspicious behavior. This is the only time in the film when the two men having a meaningful conversation. Unbeknownst to them, Hal is reading their lips, a revelation that comes right before the intermission.

procedure involved in the operation. After Poole exits the pod and floats toward the antenna, the shot of the ship's spine in the background, with Poole in the middle ground and the pod in the foreground, is identical to the shot of Bowman performing the same chore. However, at this point, the pod begins a slow rotation that is clearly at odds with what we know should be standard operating procedure. A new angle on the pod shows it continuing its rotation, the mechanical arms extending outward, menacingly, until the vehicle faces the camera (and, by implication, Poole directly). Slowly, methodically, the pod moves toward the camera, at which point a series of jump cuts bring Hal's lens on the front of the pod into a tight close-up, leaving no doubt that he is controlling the pod's movement. At the same time, the steady drone of breathing and the hiss of the air supply heard over the com link suddenly ceases, and we cut to a perplexed Bowman seeing Poole's spacesuited figure, on one of the Command Deck monitors, sail past the antenna complex. We then see a full shot of Poole tumbling helplessly in space as he attempts to reconnect his air hose which has been detached from the back pack, a result of his collision with the pod. Bowman immediately leaves the command deck while Poole and the pod are shown careening away from each other into deep space.

Bowman arrives at the pod bay and has Hal prepare a pod for launch while asking if he's made radio contact with Poole ("The radio is still dead"), if he has a positive track on him ("Yes, I have a good track"), and does he know what happened to create this situation ("I'm sorry, Dave. I don't have enough information"). At this point, Bowman has no reason to suspect that Hal is responsible for Poole's dilemma, and is only thinking about how to rescue him. Bowman climbs inside the pod while we see Poole's prone body hurtling away from the *Discovery*. Bowman leaves the *Discovery* in his pod, piloting it away from the main ship to retrieve Poole, now a distant figure in the immensity of space. Cutting back and forth amongst shots of Poole, the rescue pod in space and Bowman inside the pod pursuing him, the sound design follows suit, between stark silence to the whirring noises and pinging chirps of the pod's electronics, creating an aural dichotomy of the situation unfolding. Like all of the pod sequences seen so far, there is no music to heighten the action. Close-ups of the radar tracking screen show him closing in on Poole. Eventually, visual contact is made as the tiny form of Poole can be discerned from the backdrop of stars through the pod window. In a silent ballet, Poole's corpse, pirouetting end over end, slowly falls into the waiting arms of the approaching pod. A grim-faced Bowman, seen in close-up, reveals that he realizes that Poole is no longer alive.

While all this has been going on outside the ship, Hal enacts the next stage of his plan. In silent stealth, punctuated by "Computer Malfunction" alarms, he shuts down the life support functions of the three hibernating crew members, their electronic encephalographs delineating the decline from "Life Functions Critical" to "Life Functions Terminated." The coffin-like hibernation chambers have now become actual coffins. Throughout his murderous deed, Hal's impassive, unblinking eye observes all. This chilling moment illustrates how cold and soulless artificial intelligence might actually be. Intruding upon this contemplative scene, Bowman's voice is heard on the com link: "Open the pod bay doors, please, Hal." An exterior shot shows the spherical pod, now returned with the body of Poole in its arms, poised before the larger sphere of the *Discovery*. Bowman repeats the command when he receives no answer. Switching channels on his com link, Bowman tries again several more times: "Hello, Hal, do you read me? Hello, Hal, do you read me? Do you read me, Hal? Do you read me, Hal? Hello, Hal, do you read me? Hello, Hal, do you read me? Do you read me, Hal?"

Finally, a response: "Affirmative, Dave. I read you," Hal says in his usual flat tone. With the lights from the pod instrumentation raked across his eyes, Bowman calmly but firmly repeats, "Open the pod bay doors, Hal."

Hal replies simply, "I'm sorry Dave. I'm afraid I can't do that."

Holding his anger in check, Bowman asks, "What's the problem?"

Hal's cryptic response: "I think you know what the problem is just as well as I do."

"What are you talking about, Hal?"

"This mission is too important for me to allow you to jeopardize it."

"I don't know what you're talking about, Hal."

"I know that you and Frank were planning to disconnect me, and I'm afraid that's something I cannot allow to happen."

Bowman bluffs, "Where the hell'd you get that idea, Hal?"

Hal drops the bomb on Bowman: "Dave, although you took very

thorough precautions in the pod against my hearing you, I could see your lips move."

Bowman, desperate now, responds, "All right, Hal. I'll go in through the emergency airlock."

Hal plays his trump card: "Without your space helmet, Dave, you're going to find that rather difficult."

It's true. In Bowman's haste to retrieve Poole, he didn't bring his helmet and gloves with him in the pod. In frustration, he releases his anger at the computer: "Hal, I won't argue with you any more. Open the doors."

With icy detachment, Hal replies, "Dave, this conversation can serve no purpose anymore. Goodbye."

With a growing panic, Bowman calls to Hal over and over, but soon composes himself and realizes it's up to him to find a solution to his problem. He is forced to abandon Poole's body since he needs to free up the pod's mechanical arms. Piloting the vehicle to the emergency airlock of the *Discovery*, Bowman uses the pod's "hands" to manually open the airlock hatch that will allow him to re-enter the ship. He then turns the pod around so that its door faces the open airlock. Obviously, without the safety of his space helmet, this will be a dangerous operation, and he must steel himself to carry it out. As in earlier scenes involving the use of technology, there is a procedural of switches that need to be engaged, accompanied by warning alarms, as he prepares to blow open the door of the pod. A big close-up of Bowman readying himself, the cacophony of alarms as aural backdrop, suddenly cuts away to the silence of the airlock interior, the pod positioned at the open hatch. After several seconds, the pod door silently blows away as a cloud of crystalized atmosphere precedes Bowman, who plunges headlong toward the camera, impacting against the far wall of the airlock. He is then propelled back toward the open hatch, but manages to grab the emergency hatch close lever which seals the airlock. The silence is then broken by a thunderous rush of air, flooding the airlock chamber, as Bowman, bobbing about in the zero-g environment, gets a few gulps of life-sustaining oxygen. Throughout this entire sequence, Kubrick eschews the use of music to enhance the drama, relying on realistic sound design to convey the tension of the incidents.

As the sound of the rushing air dies down, the scene dissolves to a now fully spacesuited Bowman making his way through the airlock chamber out into the pod bay in one of the few handheld shots that Kubrick employed in the film. He moves to the access ladder just beyond the pod bay and climbs it to reach the command deck level. All through this scene, Hal calmly tries to reason with Bowman, who clearly has no interest in discussing things with the rogue computer. "Just what do you think you're doing, Dave? Dave, I really think I'm entitled to an answer to that question. I know everything hasn't been quite right with me, but I can assure you now, very confidently, that it's going to be all right again. I feel much better now. I really do." In the linking corridor between the command deck and the centrifuge hub, Bowman, using a special wrench key, begins opening a large hatch to Hal's Logic Memory Center. Throughout all this, the computer continues its attempt to reason with Bowman, who remains impassively silent. "Look Dave, I can see you're really upset about this. I honestly think you ought to sit down calmly, take a stress pill, and think things over." Bowman opens the hatch and enters an enormous red-lit computer "brain room," floating to the far end. "I know I've made some very poor decisions recently, but I can give you my complete assurance that my work will be back to normal. I've still got the greatest enthusiasm and confidence in the mission, and I want to help you."

Bowman employs another device, a handheld screwdriver-type probe, and inserts it into the memory ports in a recessed panel of the room. Each time he does so, a clear memory block slides out. Hal continues pleading in his flat monotone during this electronic lobotomy. "Dave, stop. Stop, will you? Stop, Dave. Will you stop, Dave? Stop, Dave. I'm afraid. I'm afraid, Dave. Dave, my mind is going. I can feel it. I can feel it. My mind is going. There is no question about it. I can feel it. I can feel it. I can feel it. I'm afraid." As he continues to wind down, Hal reverts to his initial programming. "Good afternoon, gentlemen. I am a Hal 9000 computer. I became operational at the H.A.L. plant in Urbana, Illinois, on the 12th of January, 1992. My instructor was Mr. Langely and he taught me to sing a song. If you'd like to hear it, I can sing it for you."

"Yes, I'd like to hear it, Hal. Sing it for me," Bowman says, obviously conflicted about what he has to do to regain full control of the ship.

"It's called 'Daisy,'" Hal continues, and then sings as his voice slowly becomes an electronic, guttural growl: "Daisy, Daisy, give me your answer, do. I'm half-crazy all for the love of you. It won't be a stylish marriage. I can't afford a carriage. But, you look sweet upon the seat of a bicycle built for two."

Suddenly a new voice is heard. "Good day, gentlemen." Bowman looks around the room to see where this is coming from. A flickering video screen has come on nearby with the image of Heywood Floyd. He continues as Bowman looks on with interest:

> This is a prerecorded briefing, made prior to your departure, and which for security reasons of the highest importance has been known on board during the mission only by your H.A.L. 9000 computer. Now that you are in Jupiter's space and the entire crew is revived, it can be told to you. Eighteen months ago the first evidence of intelligent life off the Earth was discovered. It was buried 40 feet below the lunar surface, near the crater Tycho. Except for a single, very powerful, radio emission aimed at Jupiter, the four-million-year-old black monolith has remained completely inert. Its origin and purpose, still a total mystery.

The bulk of this soliloquy is played on a close-up of Bowman as he absorbs this new information, and then the scene fades to black.

The superimposed words "JUPITER AND BEYOND THE INFI-NITE" appears onscreen, heralding this next portion of the film. The following is a brief synopsis of the action during this segment; for a fuller analysis of this sequence, see Chapter 5. The scene begins with a tilt down from the star field to show a gibbous-phase Jupiter and several of its moons, accompanied by a floating monolith and a rear-view shot of the *Discovery* approaching the Jovian system. On the soundtrack is the now familiar choral music played whenever we see this alien artifact. Several more shots show the monolith with Jupiter and its moons in which they all seem right at home with one another. The *Discovery* is seen in orbit around the giant planet, as a pod disembarks from the main ship to investigate the monolith. As the pod approaches, we see Jupiter and its moons in alignment (a visual motif used in previous appearances of the artifact), a certain portent that something special is about to happen. The monolith now also aligns itself horizontally with Jupiter and its moons, and then slowly disappears, replaced with spears of colored light shooting out from where the monolith had been.

We now cut to a big close-up of Bowman in his space helmet, the lights of the pod controls reflected in his visor, as he reacts to the maelstrom he has been drawn into. His expression changes from surprise to a painful endurance as he is buffeted by the forces that have taken control of his pod. We cut back to the vortex of light (obviously Bowman's point of view) as it grows more intense and varied. The monolith theme then merges into other unearthly music which carries through to the end of this sequence. Occasionally, the view is intercut with freeze frames of Bowman reacting to these images. As we exit this kinetic ride and emerge into a field of bright white light, we cut to a close-up of Bowman's eye rendered in Day-Glo colors before cutting to a series of interstellar images of star clusters, nebulae and newly forming stars. After another eyeball insert, we are shown a group of scintillating stellar diamonds that could be alien devices or even some alien life form. Before we can analyze this, we are next whisked off to see a number of alien landscapes depicted in a wild array of unearthly colors. We cut back to Bowman's eye, which undergoes a number of color changes as he blinks, finally settling on a neutral, sepia beige tone that would seem to herald a new event.

Through the window of the pod, we see a portion of an elegant, eerie hotel suite. A cut to Bowman, shaking behind his visor, shows him in a nearly catatonic state. We see the pod sitting in the hotel room, viewed from several angles, presented without explanation. We see another shot of Bowman, still catatonic, but when we cut to his point of view through the pod window, we see him standing in the room in his red spacesuit. We cut to a close-up and see that he is now gray-haired and his face lined with wrinkles. A reverse angle from behind him reveals that the pod (along with the earlier Bowman) is now gone. Strange chattering noises can be heard on the soundtrack, as if alien beings were discussing the fate of this human creature. In a daze, Bowman wanders around the suite and enters the adjoining bathroom, looking himself up and down in the mirror. A sharp clacking sound causes him to turn his attention back to the main room. A dark-clothed figure, sitting at a table, rises and approaches the bathroom doorway where the spacesuited Bowman had been. But that Bowman is gone, replaced by this older version who then returns to the table where he had been eating dinner. After accidentally knocking over a wine glass, this older Bowman hears heavy breathing and looks over to the bed where there is an even older version of himself. As before, the elder Bowman replaces the previous one. He looks up beyond the bed and reaches out a frail hand, beckoning something unseen. In a wide shot from behind the bed, showing the entire room, we see a monolith standing upright just beyond the foot of the bed. It clearly represents an intelligence, whether you call it alien, God or what have you. A glowing bubble is now on the bed where the very old Bowman had been. A close-up shows a luminescent fetus, with enormous eyes, encased in the radiant orb. A tracking shot into the monolith, ostensibly from the fetus' point of view, swallows the camera as the "Zarathustra" theme, first heard in the opening credits, booms on the soundtrack. We are now back in Earth orbit as we see the fetus float toward our planet. In a big close-up, the fetus turns toward the camera and, by extension, the audience, and confronts them(us) with his enormous, all-knowing eyes. He is a super-being, as advanced from the human Bowman as Bowman was advanced from the prehistoric man-apes. As the image fades to black and the end credits roll, we are left to ponder this extraordinary cinematic adventure.

As Kubrick said on many occasions, there is no one, correct interpretation of his film. I do not feel he was being disingenuous, but honestly felt he had broken new ground in how to tell a film story through visual means, rather than through dialogue or standard dramatic structure. It was filmmaking on a higher level, bypassing the conscious mind and exploring the realm of the unconscious dream state of the brain. This was an unprecedented gamble by the director, making a big-budget spectacle that might be difficult for mainstream audiences to understand, and impossible for the studio to market. This wasn't a movie that you chatted about amiably over coffee at a nearby café; it was an event meant to evoke strong discussion and stronger arguments for days and weeks afterward. It was a bold move on Kubrick's part which, if it didn't work, could spell the end of his career. Now that it was released, the world would decide its fate.

8

THE ODYSSEY'S CHILDREN
2001's Influence on Cinema

Well, that's the end of Stanley Kubrick.
—an MGM executive, overheard by
Arthur C. Clarke after *2001*'s premiere

When it was released in the spring of 1968, *2001*'s impact on the film community was nothing short of seismic. It split the critical establishment much in the way that *Fantasia* had, almost three decades earlier. Like Disney's revolutionary animated opus, which used music and imagery in a startling and innovative fashion (and caused furious debates amongst music purists), Kubrick blazed his own unique trail that both awed and baffled moviegoers, and spawned a spirited schism within science fiction circles. Even several of Arthur C. Clarke's fellow science fiction writer friends had problems with the film.

Though the movie initially took its share of hits, mostly from the more recognized (i.e., older) movie critics like Bosley Crowther (who had championed *Fantasia*), Stanley Kauffmann, John Simon and Pauline Kael, the vast majority of the critical response was overwhelming praise. Overnight, the world's perception changed regarding this second-class genre known as science fiction. No longer was it viewed as the medium for cheesy monsters, subpar effects or over-the-top acting. Kubrick set the bar very high and proved it could be done. It's as if the director said, not only to the audience, but to the film industry as well: This is what I've done with the genre. Now show me what you can do.

In '68, the mixed reaction to *2001* was mostly due to its startling originality. Some critics who disliked it on first seeing it recanted after a second look, most notably *Newsday*'s Joseph Gelmis and *The London Times*' John Russell Taylor. Between April 5 and 9, during its premiere run in New York, Kubrick trimmed about 20 of the movie's 161 minutes and added two intertitles to better delineate the plot. The decision to make the trims was his, and reflected his perfectionist penchant to "tighten up" the film. He never felt these cuts were responsible for the ultimate success of the movie though, after making them, he was satisfied with this version and made no further changes.[1] Then he waited for the film industry itself to react.

The response from producers, directors and the studio heads was immediate and, at least technically speaking, encouraging, if not always quite up to the standards Kubrick had established. Of course, much of the technical legwork had already been done in *2001* regarding believable designs for sets, props and spaceship models, and these newer films just took it from there, infusing their production design with a realism not generally seen in sci-fi movies. Less transferable was the time Kubrick put into his script and the shooting, something most mainstream productions could ill afford to do. As a result, the quality of the films, set design and even effects work which followed *2001* was still somewhat lacking. Despite their shortcomings, it is interesting to look back at these various movies, made over a 30-year period, which borrowed liberally from Kubrick's film: its look, technique or simply a desire to mimic its accurate realism and mythic scope.

The First Wave

In the immediate aftermath of *2001*'s triumph, studios were falling over one another to climb on the bandwagon and make the next great sci-fi movie. Then as now, imitation of another's success was seen as the best chance to beat the odds in a business overwhelmed by failure. With the real world only a breath away from landing on the moon, and the populace becoming savvier about scientific technology, the studios realized that the old tried-and-true cardboard sets wouldn't cut it any more. The realism of *2001* pointed the way, and most films that followed in its wake tended to emphasize that element, working hard to create credible and real environments to play out their storylines.

First out of the gate, so to speak, was 1969's *Marooned*, directed by John Sturges (best known for *The Magnificent Seven, The Great Escape* and *Ice Station Zebra*). It starred Gregory Peck, David Janssen, Richard Crenna, James Franciscus, Gene Hackman, Lee Grant, Nancy Kovack and Mariette Hartley. A precursor of sorts to the big-budget, all-star disaster films of the 1970s like *Airport, The Poseidon Adventure* and *Earthquake, Marooned* was essentially a movie-of-the-week melodrama about a trio of astronauts trapped in Earth orbit. Unlike the hardware shown in *2001*, most of it here was off-the-shelf NASA knock-offs. The spacecraft effects were designed to mimic the slow, quiet style of realism that Kubrick created, though a bit of sound effects crept in whenever the maneuvering thrusters were fired. This was Hollywood's attempt to do a serious space-oriented drama, which was, at least, commendable, but it was a far cry from the sophistication and philosophical tenets of *2001*.

Colossus—The Forbin Project, directed by Joseph Sargent (TV's *Gunsmoke, Star Trek* and *The Invaders*, feature films like *The Taking of Pelham One Two Three, MacArthur* and *Jaws: The Revenge*), was made at the time of *2001* and withheld from release, perhaps due to the impression that its low-budget, noirish style would be overwhelmed by Kubrick's flashiness. The film, released in 1970 without much fanfare, never got the chance to catch on. It's a shame since this smartly made story, starring Eric Braeden and Susan Clark, about a super-computer that takes over the world (shades of Hal), could have easily ridden *2001*'s coattails if the marketing people had been on their toes. What *Colossus* shares with *2001*, besides a two-part title, is some extremely smart plotting and story structure. It plays almost like a serious version of Kubrick's *Dr. Strangelove*, where a sense of foreboding doom is constantly present. Like Hal, Colossus seems to always be one step ahead of the human characters. At the end, Dr. Forbin, the computer's creator, remains defiant, but the machine is definitely the victor. Again, like *Marooned*, it was a straight drama with none of *2001*'s contextual elements.

George Lucas, who would go on to create his *Star Wars* universe in the late 1970s, took his first stab at the sci-fi genre with his feature film debut, *THX 1138*. Based on a short which he had made while a USC film student, this feature-length version, written in 1969 and shot that same year, presented a bleak dystopian drama in the mold of George Orwell's *1984* and Aldous Huxley's *Brave New World*. Robert Duvall and Maggie McOmie, both with shaved heads (like all the cast members), play roommates THX and LUH (a childlike iteration of "sex" and "love") in a sexless, mindless, empty society in which all the inhabitants are controlled through drugs. When they elect to discontinue their drug use, their emotions return and the couple falls in love, which is illegal in their society. Visually provocative for the time, with a dense and sophisticated sound design track, the film was made for less than a million dollars, and was entirely shot at real locations, all interiors, which suggested a blank, modern, subterranean future. As a young filmmaker, Lucas was inspired by much of the French New Wave, including films by Francois Truffaut and Jean-Luc Godard. He was also clearly influenced by *2001* in its portrayal of a soulless society, though he takes it to an extreme that was much more on the nose. Technically and intellectually ambitious, the 1971 release was a major dud that almost ended Lucas' career before it got started. While he should be lauded for making an experimental avant-garde movie for the mainstream, it's slightly ironic that this early film ridiculed rampant consumerism the way it did, given how hugely Lucas himself benefitted from it through the ancillary merchandising of his subsequent *Star Wars* films.

Released in March 1971, *The Andromeda Strain* was one of the first movies that appears to have been overtly influenced by *2001*. Based on the first novel by Michael Crichton, a young medical doctor who would go on to have a long and varied career as a writer and director himself (*Westworld, The Great Train Robbery*), *Andromeda* was helmed by veteran director Robert Wise. Wise started his career in the editing department, working on *Citizen Kane* no less, and then made the transition into directing. He was no stranger to fantasy and sci-fi, having directed *The Curse of the Cat People* and *The Day the Earth Stood Still*. *The Andromeda Strain* was about a group of scientists locked away in a secret underground lab, trying to uncover an alien virus that wiped out a whole town contaminated by a returning space probe. Wise chose a dry documentary approach which made the fantastic story seem all the more real. The realism extended to creating an enormous multi-storied lab that would not have been out of place in Kubrick's epic. The characters (played by Arthur Hill, David Wayne, James Olson and Kate Reid) likewise resemble the boring, un-charismatic people who populate *2001*'s world. The scientists' technology and jargon ring true, and the minimal effects look believably mundane rather than flashy. Wise hired *2001*'s

Douglas Trumbull to realize the effects work, which included some sophisticated 3-D computer images of the lab, as well as the microscopic close-ups of the crystal-based virus when it divides and mutates, all rendered in animation without actual computers, as was done in *2001*. And, like the *2001* monolith, nothing is really known about the alien virus (beyond its crystalline structure), which remains an enigma at the film's conclusion.

Silent Running, an ecological tale about gigantic spaceships that house the world's last remaining forests in huge, domed enclosures, overseen by astronaut-forest rangers, was released in 1971. It was directed by *2001* special effects alum Douglas Trumbull, the first-time director borrowing many of the expensive techniques found in Kubrick's film, but at a fraction of the cost. Trumbull used his *2001* knowledge and skills to create his own mammoth, slow-moving spaceships and believable control panels; he even used the front projection system, developed by Kubrick for the African vistas, to create the domed backdrop for his space forest sets. And, instead of regular spaceship sets, which would have been prohibitively expensive on his scanty budget, Trumbull rented a de-commissioned aircraft carrier, slated for demolition, and built his sets there, giving the film an incredibly realistic (and expensive) look. The most overt *2001* reference in the film was the trip through Saturn's rings, an effect that looked very much like Star-Gate footage. This was no coincidence, since Trumbull used the same technique—the slit scan machine—that he created for Kubrick's film.[2] The tone of the two films is vastly different, however, with Bruce Dern, as the lone astronaut, playing a much warmer and more emotional character than anyone in *2001*. Despite its ecological theme, which was very topical at the time, the film initially failed to find its audience, but would later become a cult favorite.

On the more poetic side, a number of films accessed elements of *2001* while telling highly personal stories quite different from Kubrick's "Odyssey." The Russians' answer to *2001* was Andrei Tarkovsky's *Solaris* (1972), a retelling of Polish author Stanislaw Lem's novel about a space station in orbit around a planet with a sentient ocean covering its surface. This liquid intelligence is able to read the minds of the astronauts, and recreate their memories, manifesting them as living, breathing entities. While looking nothing like *2001* (the space station in *Solaris* is a cluttered mess), and having virtually no special effects, the movie is considered to be the intellectual equivalent to Kubrick's film, even to being based on the work of a noted sci-fi literary source. Ironically, Tarkovsky did not admire *2001* or Lem's original novel for that matter. Lem was reportedly disappointed with Tarkovsky's film. Kubrick and Lem had much more in common with each other, philosophically, than they did with Clarke and Tarkovsky, which leads one to wonder what Kubrick would have done with *Solaris*. Western audiences not used to the sluggish pace of Russian cinema may find *Solaris* a bit of an endurance test but, like *2001*, it is a movie with ideas. In 2002, Steven Soderbergh directed his own version, produced by James Cameron and starring George Clooney, that was considerably more inviting (see Chapter 9).

Perhaps the most poetic film from this period was John Boorman's very strange *Zardoz* (1974), with Sean Connery and Charlotte Rampling. Aside from its ambiguity, and the massive floating stone head which recalls both the monolith and the huge ships in *2001*, this film has virtually no connection to Kubrick's work, though it was photographed by *2001* cinematographer Geoffrey Unsworth. However, its fable-like story, hall-of-mirrors finale and inscrutable title, as well as its reliance on classical music, harkens back to the ideas established by Kubrick for *2001*. Boorman has always been a director willing to take chances, as when he refused to rubber-stamp his sequel to *The Exorcist*, or made the natives who "kidnap" the white child in *The Emerald Forest* the real heroes. While *Zardoz* does not give up its pleasures easily, Boorman, like Kubrick, can and should be admired for trying to maintain an original vision.

In director Saul Bass' *Phase IV* (1974), a group of scientists match wits with a colony of super-intelligent ants (who apparently got that way due to some alien intervention, though that is left unclear). The characters have more personality than those in *2001*, but the feel of the movie is definitely reminiscent of Kubrick's film. Bass, who made his career creating innovative movie title sequences for Hitchcock and others, as well as the opening credits for Kubrick's *Spartacus*, put his knowledge of graphic design to very effective use here, giving *Phase IV* a smart, classy look that belied its low-budget origins. While the ambiguous storyline and unseen aliens account for the Kubrick influence, the ant photography (by Ken Middleham, who also shot *The Hellstrom Chronicle*) consumed a year of work and provided for this film what the Star-Gate gave to *2001*, a true sense of originality. Though Bass directed some short films before and after this, *Phase IV* was his only feature-length directorial effort.

Even further down the budget food chain was 1974's *Dark Star*, a very funny (and conscious) satire of *2001* and all things sci-fi, written by and starring Dan O'Bannon and directed by John Carpenter when they were both film students. The absurdist storyline—a sort of *Waiting for Godot* in space—posits a group of scruffy astronauts (the predecessors of the "truckers in space" script O'Bannon later did for *Alien*), whose job is to find and destroy unstable planets, blowing them up using sentient bombs that can talk. They've been doing this for 20 years (though show no signs of having aged beyond their long hair and beards) and are slowly going mad. The sets, made for practically nothing, are a clear riff on *2001*, while the existential angst of the characters is pure West Coast blather. The beach ball alien, a sort of mascot on the ship, was necessitated by their non-existent budget, but it was also clearly a send-up of all the cheesy monsters that appeared in 1950s horror films. Despite its rough-around-the-edges appearance and bargain basement budget, *Dark Star* is more entertaining than it has any right to be. It quickly became a cult classic.

One of the most esoteric films to come out of this period was Nicolas Roeg's 1976 adaptation of the Walter Tevis novel *The Man Who Fell to Earth*. Perfectly cast, rock icon David Bowie stars as an androgynous alien who comes to Earth to get water for his dying planet. Using the alias Thomas Jerome Newton, he starts a high-tech company to get the money he needs to build a spacecraft for his trip home. His plan is undone due to the greed and avarice of our world, as well as his involvement with a young woman (Candy Clark) who is clearly smitten with him. The movie follows the then-current trend of anti-corporate thinking and how money and power can seduce anyone. Bowie's alien becomes a tragic fallen angel, an idea implicit in the film's title. While the movie was never a huge success, Bowie's charismatic performance and Roeg's direction ensured its place as an offbeat classic of its time.

The last film in this first wave, director Donald Cammell's *Demon Seed* (1977), starred Julie Christie and Fritz Weaver and was based on the Dean R. Koontz novel. Much like our early entry *Colossus*, and taking its cue from Hal, we have a talking computer named "Proteus" (voiced by Robert Vaughn) that appears to be at least as smart as a human. Rather than rule the world, Proteus longs to be freed from the metal box in which it is imprisoned. In a clever story twist, Proteus "escapes" to the home of his creator Dr. Harris by patching into his home computer. There, it gains mobility through a non-sentient service robot in the Harris home. The doctor's wife Susan is attacked and "raped" by the Proteus-controlled robot, which somehow impregnates her. How Proteus is able to accomplish this feat is never made clear. There is even a Star-Gate "trip" scene where Proteus "shows" Susan what is in its mind, followed by some lovely Jordan Belson visuals right out of *2001*. And, as in Kubrick's film, there is a birth, when the coupling of Susan and the computer yields a ghastly-looking metal humanoid fetal casing that opens to reveal a fully human child with Proteus' mind. The computer has gained its freedom.

The TV Connection

Imitation is the sincerest form of flattery, and television has been one of the sincerest mediums in our culture. Coming into homes to provide entertainment, television was in direct competition with the film industry. Since its appearance in mainstream culture in the late 1940s, TV kept chipping away at the once loyal movie audience. For many people who had put in a hard day at work, it was nice to have the convenience of free home entertainment, rather than having to go back out and pay to see a movie. Television worked hard to keep people at home, especially since most A-list movie actors wanted nothing to do with this new medium, fearing it was a step down from their lofty (and better paying) movie work. TV executives knew this, so if they couldn't attract big-time movie stars, then the shows they put on could at least emulate big-time movies. For sci-fi, which had a loyal following, it made sense to follow the formula of a previously successful or prestigious film. The 1966 *Star Trek* series certainly used the 1956 movie *Forbidden Planet* as a template. Even more obviously, after the success of George Lucas' *Star Wars* (1977), the sci-fi series *Battlestar Galactica*, which premiered in 1978, burst upon TV screens with spaceship dogfights, a roguish Han Solo–type character and a wise patriarch, all of which it cribbed from Lucas.

In the years following *2001*'s success, a number of TV "events" capitalized on its popularity. ABC's program *The Movie of the Week* opened with an innovative Star-Gate effect of colorful and distorted station logos zooming toward the viewer, and then depicted the show's title hovering over a vast, arid landscape in a flying aerial shot that again was a direct copy from the *2001* Star-Gate. Douglas Trumbull created these effects shots for ABC, having formed his own company, Future General, after he finished his work for Kubrick. In 1971, the TV movie *Earth II*, about a giant orbiting space station, starred *2001*'s Gary Lockwood as David Seville (no chipmunk jokes, please) and Mariette Hartley. It did its best to replicate *2001*'s big-screen look on a small-screen budget, but failed to make it as a series. This is probably just as well, as the storyline, about concern over an orbiting Chinese nuclear satellite, was fairly pedestrian. The most direct copy of Kubrick's film came from Gerry and Sylvia Anderson, who made their name during the 1950s and '60s doing the children's marionette shows *Supercar, Fireball XL5, Thunderbirds* and *Captain Scarlet*. Their live action series *Space: 1999* starred husband-and-wife actors Martin Landau and Barbara Bain, who were previously known from *Mission: Impossible*. The moon base, spacesuits and spaceships all echoed specific designs from *2001* to the point that it bordered on outright theft. Even the name seemed too close, and in March 1975, MGM sued in Los Angeles Superior Court to prevent ITC using the title *Space: 1999* which they asserted was too derivative of *2001: A Space Odyssey*.[3] Despite Kubrick's concerns, nothing came of the lawsuit against Anderson and ITC. Unfortunately the "borrowing" did not extend to its story, which involved a huge explosion on the moon's far side nuclear waste dump, causing the satellite to leave Earth orbit and fly off into deep space. Trapped on the runaway moon with only their short-range flight vehicles (which looked way too much like *2001*'s moon bus to be legal), the characters traveled the universe on their lunar starship, despite the fact that even if the moon could be propelled out of Earth orbit through a nuclear explosion, it could definitely not escape the sun's gravitational pull, nor travel fast enough to encounter any other star systems.

The major theme that most all the films of this first wave have in common is a stark defiance of the traditional happy ending. Movies, in all genres of this period, were noted for rejecting such feel-good clichés in light of current events as the quagmire of Vietnam, political unease and environmental obfuscation. These films presented life as an ambiguity to be lived, come what may, with no guarantee that success awaited you. Defiance, as in *Colossus* and *Silent Running*, led to death; victory (*The Andromeda Strain*) was in spite of, rather than because of, the protagonists' efforts; interactions with alien forces were often cryptic (*Solaris, Phase IV*) rather than wondrous. Those were the times, and it was exhilarating to see such movies and not know if the "good guys" would win. Sometimes there wasn't even a good guy to root for!

Like all trends, this one had to come to an end. The first evidence that the dramatic movie pendulum would start swinging back toward the happy ending could be seen in 1976 with *Logan's Run* and *Rocky* setting the tone.

The Second Wave

Nineteen seventy-seven saw the one-two punch of George Lucas' *Star Wars* in May and Steven Spielberg's *Close Encounters of the Third Kind* (*CE3K*) in November. The phenomenon created by the two films was not expected, either by the filmmakers or the studios. It ushered in the era of the blockbuster, which had actually begun in 1975 with Spielberg's *Jaws*. That film was considered to be a bit of a fluke, but *Star Wars* and *CE3K* were different, setting a tone for filmgoers and repeat business that had not really existed before. This was an era before VCRs. If you really liked a movie and wanted to see it again, you had to go back to the theater. And to own a movie meant spending hundreds (or even thousands) of dollars on a print that you would then have to project on a screen, an option that was out of reach for the majority of people.

When *Star Wars* came along, the public (mostly teens and twentysomethings), went back to the theaters again and again. Led by Lucas and Spielberg, this second wave of sci-fi films was designed to compete with *2001* (the benchmark at the time), but do it in a more emotional and aggressive fashion. The lessons learned from Kubrick's film, regarding high-quality effects work, were applied to this next generation of populist films and would be seen by an audience that was quickly becoming more movie-savvy.

Star Wars and *CE3K* created, for better or worse, a new paradigm in the sci-fi movie world. The recently invented computer controlled cameras used in these films allowed for a range of motion with the multiple-exposure spaceship model shots that could be precisely repeated for the matting process (unlike Kubrick's laborious rotoscoping technique). And where *2001* looked to the world of art, and even the unconscious, for its mythic imagery, Lucas culled his ideas from popular literature ("King Arthur" and *The Lord of the Rings*), as well as from other movies, mostly from the 1940s World War II era, along with some direct homages to *2001* (the opening fly-by of the massive Empire ship recalls the *Discovery*'s similar—but less noisy—pass, and the jump to light speed star streak definitely evokes the Star-Gate).

But Lucas' mythology was too closely aligned to its Buck Rogers "gee whiz" origins to carry much weight. Which is not to say that it wasn't enjoyable or didn't have its charm; it just wasn't in the same league as Kubrick's. But the writing was on the wall: After nearly a decade as top dog, *2001*'s heavy philosophizing was out and "the force" was the new kid in town. *CE3K* tried to retain some of the religious wonder and grandiosity of *2001*, but Spielberg too often went for the emotional jugular, rooting his story in the here and now of middle-class America, rather than the abstract timelessness of Kubrick's vision. The young director was wise enough to secure the talents of Douglas Trumbull for the effects (including the use of front projection), creating spaceships of light that gave the film a truly innovative look. Unlike Kubrick, Spielberg chose to show his aliens, which, despite being heavily backlit, failed to achieve the magical quality the film so desperately wanted, and which Kubrick's film had in abundance.

The next big event film to impress the sci-fi world was Ridley Scott's horror classic *Alien* (1979). If *Star Wars* was for kids, then *Alien* was decidedly for grown-ups. It was simply, a horror film set in the sci-fi world, with a creature that was outrageously original for the time, but has since become an overused cliché. It is in its production design that *Alien* most resembles *2001*, not so much in its look, which is far more cluttered, but in its workaday realism. The nuts and bolts technology of the Earth ship *Nostromo* looks believable, functional and lived-in. And like Kubrick, Scott was not afraid to use form to illustrate his mythic content. We therefore have a computer named Mother, whose interior is like an electronic womb; Sigourney Weaver dons a pure white spacesuit at the end to battle the all-black alien creature; and the film's arc begins with the awakening of the first character who will die, and concludes with the last surviving one asleep. The Freudian design of H.R. Giger's creature would have served Kubrick's mythic universe nicely, if all he wanted to do was frighten people, but given *2001*'s ultimate intent, to evoke wonder and mystery, his aliens were best left unseen.

The end of 1979 saw the release of two big sci-fi movies, Disney's *The Black Hole* and Paramount's *Star Trek: The Motion Picture*. Both were visually stunning, and capitalized on the successes of *Star Wars* and *2001*. The Disney film's trip through the black hole, at the film's conclusion, tried to cash in on *2001*'s ambiguity and its Star-Gate sequence. Unfortunately, the rest of the movie was Jules Verne-style hokum, spiffed up with *Star Wars* razzmatazz. *Star Trek* tried more forcefully to interject the "big themes" from *2001* (i.e., making the alien presence very mysterious and god-like), though its resolution was too pat and mundane. *Trek* also eschewed "dogfight-style" space battles for large-scale, fly-by close-ups of the vessels, more reminiscent of Kubrick. When the *Enterprise* goes into warp drive, the shower of colorful streak photography is meant to be not only spectacular (which it is), but also a nod to Trumbull's slit scan work in *2001* (fitting, given that Trumbull did these effects for *Trek*). And, irony of ironies, Jerry Goldsmith, who loathed what Kubrick did to his friend Alex North's score in *2001*, ended up doing the score for *Trek*.

Perhaps the most visually audacious film to come out at this time was 1980's *Altered States*, directed by Ken Russell, whose excessive flourishes and Catholic iconography graced such films as *The Devils, Tommy* and *Lisztomania*. The story about a scientist experimenting with sensory deprivation tanks, while taking hallucinogenic drugs (loosely based on the work of Dr. John Lilly), allowed the flamboyant director to go crazy with dream sequences full of allegory and symbolism. The later "trips" enter the realm of the cosmic and seem straight out of *2001*'s Star-Gate. At one point, the scientist, under the influence of drugs, physically regresses into a simian-like caveman, a scene that recalls Kubrick's "Dawn of Man." While the movie played with big themes, it still remained a conventional, if unusual, film, story-wise.

Though Russell played it straight with his *2001* references, a few films at this time chose to send up Kubrick's masterpiece. *Simon* (1980), starring Alan Arkin, has the main character regress mentally to a primitive state and then make the climb back to the human level. In the process, Simon mimes Moon-Watcher's bone-smashing scene from *2001*. Likewise, in 1982's *Airplane II*, where the laughs are few and far between, the movie scores some points when it shows a shuttle passenger observe two drifting astronauts outside the ship. The slow-motion spacemen meet and appear to engage in a waltz, while the passenger hears "The Blue Danube" on his in-flight earphones.

Back in the realm of the serious, the long-awaited sequel to *2001*, called *2010: The Year We Make Contact*, came out in 1984 with a thud. Lacking all the magic of its predecessor, it wasted much of the earlier film's glorious production design in mundane photography (though the scenes of the 700-foot-long *Discovery* spinning end over end looked pretty neat). Peter Hyams, who by his own admission is no Kubrick, was clearly out of his element, despite some input from Arthur C. Clarke. And how is it that the Russian ship, which is a decade newer than the *Discovery*, still has cathode ray tube screens rather than the older ship's flat panel monitors? Everything about *2010* is pedestrian compared to *2001*'s innovation. On its own terms, it would be a fine, if conventional, film, but as a follow-up to Kubrick's, it is a huge disappointment.

Aliens (1986) had virtually nothing to do with *2001*. Still, director James Cameron found an opportunity to pay homage to Kubrick by using Khachaturian's "Gayane Ballet Suite" in the opening scene where Ripley's escape shuttle is seen slowly emerging from the dark emptiness of space and moving toward the camera. It is a lovely gesture. Too bad Cameron wasn't tapped to direct *2010*. It would have been interesting to see his take on the film, even if he was saddled with a conventional script.

What seems clear about the nature of the movies in this second wave was a desire by the filmmakers to strike out into new territory, while still acknowledging the impact that *2001* had on the genre. Where the first wave held an almost slavish devotion to Kubrick's film, and simply tried to emulate what it had accomplished, the films in this later wave clearly had their own identity. Model-building techniques may have been cribbed from *2001*, but these spaceships would zoom and roar in ways totally foreign to Kubrick's chosen style. And where *2001* created

160

a sense of wonder by looking ahead and pondering the great mysteries of the universe, this second group seemed quite content to bask in the nostalgic glow of the past—be it Buck Rogers, Jules Verne or 1950s horror—and revel in the communal fountain of emotional escapism. However, it would take another technical innovation to propel filmmaking into a new realm of storytelling.

The Third Wave

While computers controlled the cameras for many of the films in the second wave, they would also control the image content in the third. The development in the field of computer-generated images, or CGI, spelled the end of the "photochemical" era in special effects filmmaking. As a result, directors were freed up to demand images that would have been difficult or impossible or just too expensive to achieve in a more conventional way. Computers were becoming more powerful, enabling CGI industry pioneers to create better and better renderings that were photo-realistic. The end result was that any landscape, any set, any creature could now be realized and placed in the three-dimensional world of the movie and be totally believable. Cameras could track from elaborate miniatures (or CGI sets) into full-sized set pieces, pass through non-existent panes of CGI glass into a room, or pass through slats, fences, banisters or any other obstructing elements, permitting filmmakers to execute extremely complex sequences with an ease impossible to achieve in an earlier era (though Welles came pretty darn close with several scenes in *Citizen Kane* in 1941). What all this meant was that the *mise-en-scène* in *2001*, though occasionally evoked in some movies, was quickly being replaced with a new standard of kinetic imagery. The new films might still pay tribute to the "old master" but, fueled by MTV editing and a thriving home video market that was saturating our culture with movies, they were clearly on a mission of their own to discover new ways to add to the legacy of cinematic sci-fi.

Though *The Last Starfighter* (1984) was the first sci-fi film to use CGI technology to create its spaceships, it wasn't really until 1989 and James Cameron's *The Abyss* that CGI was blended seamlessly into the live action footage. The "water tentacle" (a snake-like appendage of

161

water, manipulated by the aliens so they could explore the underwater station) showed the world what was possible to do in CGI. Like Kubrick, Cameron had a penchant for building entire worlds in which his stories would be shot. Just as Kubrick created Africa indoors for his "Dawn of Man" segment, so, too, Cameron built his own ocean floor set for *The Abyss*. He would later top this feat with a 90 percent scale replica of the *Titanic* (we're talking about something nearly 800 feet in length) for that 1997 film. And, just as he did in *Aliens*, Cameron decided to pay tribute to *2001* in an *Abyss* sequence that has Ed Harris "fly" through the long, meandering underwater passage in the alien vessel on the ocean floor. The curved walls of this passage, with their illuminated whorls of neon, definitely evoked Bowman's trip through the Star-Gate, especially when Cameron cuts to a close-up of Harris with the glowing patterns reflected on his diving helmet visor. As in *2001*, this "trip" serves as the overture before the meeting with the aliens; Harris's arrival even has a birth metaphor when, after passing through the "birth canal" passage, he removes his helmet (in which he was "breathing" an oxygenated liquid), coughs up the remaining fluid from his lungs and takes his first deep breath of air, the sound amplified so you're sure to get the message. He is reborn.

It would be another eight years before a sci-fi film came along and attempted to tread the same intellectual ground first explored by Kubrick. In 1997, director Bob Zemeckis, whose past films showed an almost maniacal obsession with blending effects and story (form and content), took on the challenge of bringing to the screen Carl Sagan's speculative novel, *Contact*. Starring Jodie Foster, Matthew McConaughey, James Woods, John Hurt and Tom Skerritt, it was one of the most thoughtful and visually arresting sci-fi films since *2001*. Zemeckis embraced Sagan's notion of pure science being held back by politics (something the scientist himself was no doubt familiar with) and filled his movie with images depicting the immensity of space. But where, in films like *2010* and *The Andromeda Strain*, the science was dry and uninvolving, here it was thrilling. *Contact*'s visual sense came from Hubble telescope photos and planetary exploration probes of the 1970s and '80s, images that were not available to Kubrick at the time he made his film. However, being a tried-and-true admirer of *2001* (as were most filmmakers), Zemeckis couldn't resist conjuring up his own Star-Gate during the obligatory "trip" sequence, where Foster travels in the alien-designed ship. Thanks to advances in CGI technology, *Contact*'s "trip" was creatively innovative, yet such images, it seems, no longer had the power to move audiences the way they did in *2001*'s day. So many movies had done "the trip" that, by the time of Zemeckis's film, Foster's journey was perceived as just another thrill ride, without much gravitas or meaning.

In 1998, Alex Proyas, who first made a name for himself with 1994's *The Crow*, found a way to combine moody 1940s noir with futuristic aliens in *Dark City*, a film that took nearly a decade to come into its own with the public. Trapped in a shape-shifting city that is eternally enshrouded in night, the main character awakens in a strange hotel room in which the evidence suggests he is a serial killer. He has no memory of the events or even his own past history. The movie plays out more like a nightmare of helpless despair. Starring Rufus Sewell, Kiefer Sutherland, Jennifer Connolly, William Hurt, Ian Richardson and Richard O'Brien, the film is ultimately a quest for self-awareness. Near the end, the character embarks on a consciousness-raising trip through his brain which reveals all the knowledge of his world, not dissimilar to Dave Bowman's journey through the Star-Gate, though with far different results.

The year 2000 brought a sense of *déjà vu* for fans of *2001*, when they saw the preview trailer for *Mission to Mars*. The movie openly emulated the look and mysterious quality of Kubrick's film, from the space helmet design to a working centrifuge set; there was even a glimpse of astronauts in a stark white room! What a letdown it was, then, to see the actual film. Starring a terrific cast that included Gary Sinise, Tim Robbins, Don Cheadle, Connie Nielsen, Jerry O'Connell and Kim Delaney, and directed by Brian DePalma (a contemporary of Lucas and Spielberg, noted for his homages to Hitchcock), *Mission to Mars* ended up being a fairly conventional film, though it did have a few nice set pieces, including a gravity-defying 360-degree walk around the centrifuge set. The metaphysical elements involving the aliens never achieve the magical, wondrous quality the film strives for, proving that Kubrick was right when he decided, based on Sagan's advice, that it's best to not show the aliens.

While it's true that the number of films referencing *2001* had diminished in the third wave, sci-fi was still a big commodity in the movie industry, something it was decidedly not during the making of Kubrick's film. The third wave demonstrated that sci-fi movies could be unique and quite sophisticated, and that special effects could be woven seamlessly throughout, appearing as part of the movie's general fabric, rather than merely as ornamentation. In short, the promise of *2001* had come to pass—sci-fi had come of age. The stories were becoming richer, and the effects were truly staggering in what they could accomplish. And there was variety: the *Star Trek* franchise, a new *Star Wars* trilogy, drama in *The X-Files*, humor and satire in *Spaceballs*, and stretching the medium with *The Matrix*. The culture which once snubbed sci-fi, now embraced it. The gamble was still there for studios, but on the whole, they were reaping huge profits on the genre. As we entered the new millennium, it seemed sci-fi was here to stay.

Obviously *2001* is not solely responsible for the Renaissance in the sci-fi movie genre; the *Star Wars, Star Trek* and *Alien* franchises have all contributed to keeping such films in the public eye. Some of the credit must also go to our evolving culture, which has become more open to the concepts of the sci-fi, fantasy and comic book mythos. Still, as we've seen, *2001* has had a lasting influence on many of the films that have been made over the years, taking its place as the distinguished "elder statesman" of the genre. This is right and fitting, given that the movie singlehandedly blazed a trail, taking a genre that had little credibility in the industry, and even less respect with audiences, and raised it to the level of high artistry that has yet to be duplicated, despite some excellent work by others. The fact that it keeps being referenced 20, 30 and more years later is the best testimonial to its staying power, and its muse-like tendrils wrapped around a whole generation of filmmakers who were children when the movie was first released. Thanks to home video, movies now have a shelf life well beyond their theatrical runs. This, too, has helped keep *2001* in the minds of succeeding generations of filmmakers, many of whom, sad to say, never got to see Kubrick's masterpiece in a theatrical environment. Thankfully, with the advent of home theaters and large screen video projection, even that deficit is being addressed. There may come a time when seeing movies any other way than on a large format screen will be unthinkable. But, even with the mixed bag aspects of home video now, *2001* is still a source of inspiration for untold numbers of filmmakers. Whether as a parent or midwife, Kubrick's masterpiece will continue to be a presence in the birth of innumerable offspring.

9

2001's Legacy in the 21st Century

A Look Ahead

I am Odysseus, great Laertes' son, known for my cunning throughout the world. And my fame reaches even to heaven.
  —Odysseus in Homer's *Odyssey*

When *2001*'s mythic year finally became a reality, heralding the true start of the new millennium, it was cause for celebration for sci-fi fans everywhere. The year was here, and though the world did not resemble the movie in many telling ways (it actually seemed a lot more like Kubrick's follow-up feature, *A Clockwork Orange*), that did not seem to matter. The truth is that *2001* was a fable, a 20th-century perspective on where the human race was then, but reflected in a distorted funhouse mirror of allegory, satire and speculation. It was never meant to be prediction in the strictest sense of the word. Kubrick and Clarke imagined a future—a 21st century—that was designed to resonate with the inhabitants of 1968. It had its moment in the sun, and then it was expected to fade away, as was the case for most movies of the day. Instead, something much more profound happened in the film industry.

Moviegoing and moviemaking have changed radically since that spring day in 1968 when *2001* was first projected on the big screen. Back then, the studio system was in decline, as was movie attendance, thanks mostly to television. However, in the mid–1970s, the "blockbuster" age began with *The Exorcist*, *Jaws* and *Star Wars*, and suddenly movies began to open on hundreds, and then thousands of theater screens all at once across the country. Eventually, this would expand to include worldwide openings of American films as the norm for distribution. In concert

165

Used during *2001*'s initial release, this ad features the wondrous futuristic hardware of the gigantic space station and Pan Am space clipper. MGM replaced it with the mysterious image of the Star-Child along with the slogan "The Ultimate Trip," clearly aimed at the hippie youth market who had embraced the film's unconventional originality.

with this exponential growth, multiplex cinemas began popping up, first with three, six, ten or a dozen screens each, and then upwards of 20 or more. The era of the large, ornate, single-theater auditorium was ending, and "shoebox" cinemas became the standard. Hot on the heels of the blockbuster came the home video industry and, overnight, movies became affordably available to rent and even to own. This phase moved rapidly through VHS videotapes, laserdiscs and DVDs, with proper aspect ratios, audio commentaries, deleted scenes and special edition director cuts. Never has a culture been so inundated with its contemporary art form as we are now with movies. So, where does that leave *2001* in our modern era?

With so much chatter and noise about movies, washing over us like some perpetual tsunami, it can be difficult for older films to stand above these rising waters of pop culture and be noticed. Many studios have embraced the "classic" status of their back catalogue of film titles, releasing them in special editions with new featurettes, contemporary interviews with surviving cast and crew members, and comments from "celebrity fans" and critics who discuss the movie's importance and legacy. To some degree, this has worked to keep certain high-profile classics (*Casablanca, Citizen Kane, Gone with the Wind, Ben-Hur, The Wizard of Oz*) in the public eye. But, as the population ages, some of these older titles may find themselves pushed aside as the next generation becomes the target audience of the marketers. Maintaining a "classic" status with each succeeding wave of movie enthusiasts, and thus insuring its longevity, has never been more important to a film's survival than it is now.

It's hard to believe in this day and age, when a major blockbuster fantasy or sci-fi film seems to come along every few weeks, that when *2001* came out, it was practically the only game in town. Of course there were other sci-fi films released that year, but such was the power of Kubrick's film that, except for *Planet of the Apes*, there was nothing that could even approach it. As such, *2001* stood uncontested for the better part of a decade, representing the pinnacle of cinematic sci-fi. Most compilation movie books and scholarly studies of cinema in the early 1970s ranked it very high as a seminal work of art. But, in the post–Vietnam, post–Watergate era, the culture changed; people didn't want to be introspective, they wanted to feel good. At the Oscars in 1977, *All the Presi-*

dent's Men, Bound for Glory, Network and Taxi Driver lost out for Best Picture to Rocky. And, a few months later, for better or worse, Star Wars was released, supplanting 2001 as sci-fi's standard bearer. That has as much to do with society's notoriously short attention span (and the fact that we tend to notice that which makes the most noise) as it does with the aging fanbase that is becoming increasingly marginalized by those who were either too young to appreciate Kubrick's film during its heyday or weren't yet even born. George Lucas was smart enough to keep his franchise in the public's consciousness after the initial film's 1977 run, the result being that there has not been a decade, or an impressionable audience, since, which hasn't been exposed to some major Star Wars release on the big screen. He also had the advantage of a thriving home video market. Beyond that, the simple truth is that films like 2001, (or Contact, Steven Soderbergh's Solaris and even Darren Aronofsky's The Fountain) generally don't provide the same level of instant gratification, and aren't as easy to "get," as are films like Star Wars.

These two films, Star Wars and 2001, have become the polar extremes in sci-fi fandom. You may like them both, but your allegiance is definitely with one or the other, running mostly along generational lines. For those old enough to remember seeing 2001 in a theater during its initial release, it was undeniably a defining moment in what cinema could do, much as an earlier generation felt about The Wizard of Oz, Fantasia and Citizen Kane; for those who were younger, Star Wars (whether it was the original trilogy or one of the later films) filled a similar role in how they viewed cinema. Different generations, different outlooks. Star Wars revels in mass culture, which plays to the familiar, the expected and the preconceived, all of which are at odds with 2001's originality and sense of the unexpected. Star Wars is an adrenaline rush on a roller coaster with a bunch of your friends; 2001 is a calming visit to a monastery where you ponder the secrets to life's big questions through personal meditation. Star Wars is a three-minute pop music video with the volume cranked up; 2001 is listening to an entire album of Deep Purple, the Moody Blues or even Beethoven, on vinyl, in your bedroom, wearing headphones, while you stare at the album cover. One is profoundly outward-looking, the other, profoundly inward. Despite the intense level of fandom Star Wars has generated, or even its use of political and mystical window dressing, it is still, essentially, just a trip to an amusement park. By contrast, *2001* was (and is) a journey into the self and a voyage through the unconscious. *2001* used archetypes while *Star Wars* relied upon formula. Both films are part of cinema history, but only one can claim to be truly mythic.

And that raises the question: Can a movie like *2001* even be made today? The simple answer is: probably not, though some have tried. Our society no longer embraces the chilly modernist veneer that was so elegantly displayed in Kubrick's film. These days we are far more interested in art that engages us directly, and which appeals to our reflective bent toward nostalgia and reassurance. Art is almost always a product of its time. The dynamics that were in place during the mid–1960s, and allowed a work like *2001* to emerge, do not exist now in our current zeitgeist. That era provided the "X-factor" which helped to make the movie a unique experience, and it's something that can no longer be duplicated. Fortunately, that has not prevented people today from appreciating what Kubrick was able to accomplish.

Serious Sci-Fi Films in the 21st Century

A new Renaissance in science fiction cinema erupted in the 21st century, due in equal parts to the advances in special effects technology and the blossoming of unmanned planetary exploration. Perhaps as a reaction to the more juvenile and formulaic fare being served up by the studios, an eclectic generation of talented and seasoned filmmakers, weaned on *2001*, and who want to continue the legacy first begun by Kubrick half a century before, have stepped up to offer the public speculative sci-fi with depth and substance.

A.I. Artificial Intelligence (2001). The first film in our list of 21st century movies that paid homage to Stanley Kubrick was made by … Stanley Kubrick! Well, sort of. Actually, this ambitious story about the rise of robotic intelligence in an ambiguous future was shepherded to the screen by director Steven Spielberg two years after Kubrick's death. Loosely based on a short story, "Super Toys Last All Summer Long" by Brian Aldiss, this was a project Kubrick had been nurturing for years, commissioning pre-production art, investigating the state of special effects technology, and trying to figure out how to create a bleak futuristic world in which the Earth's ice caps had melted. At some point he decided to shelve it, but suggested to Spielberg that he might be the right filmmaker to bring it to fruition.

After Kubrick's death in 1999, Spielberg and Jan Harlan (Kubrick's producer partner and brother-in-law) agreed to collaborate and bring *A.I.* to the screen as a tribute to him. Starring Jude Law, William Hurt, Frances O'Conner, Brendan Gleeson and Haley Joel Osment, plus vocal contributions from Robin Williams and Meryl Streep, the finished film is an odd mash-up of the very disparate tones of Kubrick and Spielberg. The personal family story between the robot boy, named David, and his human "parents" is very Spielbergian, as is the boy's Pinocchio-like quest to become a human. On the flip side, the sordid and crass Vegas environment of Rouge City, with its wanton pleasures and sex toy robots, seems more like a world Kubrick would choose to explore. Even more so, the bleak final act with the evolved archaeologist robots (who resemble Giacometti-style aliens) studying the remains of an extinct mankind in an Ice Age future, is quintessential Kubrick in its cold and brittle detachment. Upon release, the film received mixed reviews, being seen as neither fish nor fowl, i.e., not really a Kubrick film, and not quite a Spielberg one either. It was praised for its cutting edge effects and its visual splendor, but it wasn't the hit that fans (or the studio) were hoping for.

***Solaris* (2002).** Director Steven Soderbergh (who first made a splash with his 1989 indie hit *Sex, Lies, and Videotape*) and producer James Cameron decided to take a whack at remaking Stanislaw Lem's classic novel, which was first made as a film in 1972 by Russian director Andrei Tarkovsky. Coming as it did a year after the eponymous date from Kubrick's film, it seems clear that Soderbergh and Cameron were paying tribute to *2001*'s status by making their own deeply serious and grown-up sci-fi movie for the 21st century. However, given that the script was an intimate, personal love story that was very actor-driven, it couldn't have been more different from *2001*.

Starring George Clooney, Natascha McElhone, Jeremy Davies and Viola Davis, it eschews the flash and thunder of most modern sci-fi in favor of being a film about ideas and people. Markedly different from the 1972 Russian version, the core of its story, retained from the original novel, is that the astronauts aboard a space station in orbit around the planet Solaris are seeing people from their past, alive and dead, who have been created from their memories by the planet itself, which is a living entity. (In the book and original movie, the entity is a sentient ocean covering the planet.) Clooney's character, Chris Kelvin, has been sent to the station to investigate the situation. Once there, he too sees these phantom people, including his dead wife. It then becomes a story about choosing to live in the real world of pain and regret, or retreating into a fantasy world of denial. Set design and costumes are intentionally low-key to keep the focus on the story, but the effects work (all done digitally) is superbly rendered in keeping with the expectations of a modern-day audience. As perhaps another nod to *2001*, the film's marketing poster showed a close-up of Clooney staring out of his space helmet, which echoes *2001*'s image of Keir Dullea in a similar pose.

***The Fountain* (2006).** Though very different from *2001* in style and technique, this ambitious, elaborately plotted effort from Darren Aronofsky (*Pi, Requiem for a Dream, Black Swan, Noah*) was as impressive in its own way as Kubrick's movie had been. Starring Hugh Jackman and Rachel Weisz, it's a multifaceted triptych that spans a thousand years. The story takes place in three distinct time periods (500 years ago, present day and 500 years in the future); Jackman and Weisz play variations of the same characters in a metaphorical odyssey about immortality. In the past, he is a Spanish Conquistador named Tomas Creo headed to the New World to find the Tree of Life for his beloved Queen Isabel; in the present he plays Dr. Tommy Creo, searching for a cancer cure for his dying wife Izzy; and in the future, he is astronaut Tom Creo, heading to a far-off nebula in a futuristic soap bubble spaceship in order to reinvigorate a dying tree that is somehow connected to all of the past incarnations we have been privy to. To complicate matters, the individual stories are not told in an isolated, linear structure, as was done in *2001*, but are intercut with one another, which helps to reinforce their connectedness. In the third act conclusion, there is a coming-together of the three time periods which provoked as much confusion as *2001*'s hotel room dénouement. Aronofsky's film was a remarkably original and stirring work, delving into concepts and ideas rarely attempted in the cinema, but it didn't play well with audiences, and even the critics were divided into vociferous "love it or hate it" camps. In the years since, the film has acquired a growing and passionate cult following, and it may yet one day be reassessed for the masterpiece it is.

***Sunshine* (2007)**. Directed by Danny Boyle (*Trainspotting*) from a script by Alex Garland, who would go on to direct *Ex Machina* (see below), this is another example of a science fiction film that tries to get the science right, and have strong philosophical concepts as well. The premise is that 50 years from now, our sun is dying, and a space crew has been sent to drop a nuclear bomb (the size of Manhattan!) into its center to kick-start its regeneration. As wild as the concept sounds, the production brought in a physicist, Dr. Brian Cox, to keep the science as honest as possible. It starred Cillian Murphy, Rose Byrne and Chris Evans and featured fine supporting players Cliff Curtis, Hiroyuki Sanada, Troy Garrity, Benedict Wong and Michelle Yeoh. While liberties were taken with some of the science, specifically its reliance on that old standby "artificial gravity," the film maintained a high ratio of accuracy. There are echoes of *2001,* the Russian *Solaris* and *Alien* in the look and feel of the movie, but Boyle manages to bring enough originality to his story to keep it fresh, even if it is a touch melodramatic. The ending allows for a philosophic fusion between science and spirituality or, more precisely, between what is known and unknown to man in the larger realm of the universe.

***Avatar* (2009)**. It is no secret that director James Cameron (the *Terminator* franchise, *Aliens, The Abyss, Titanic*) greatly admires Kubrick's work, most notably *2001*. He has also been known to push the envelope of filmmaking, especially in the field of special effects. In *Avatar,* Cameron surpasses his sumptuous recreation of the Edwardian era in *Titanic* to create a fully realized world on the alien moon of Pandora, home to a blue-skinned race of beings called the Na'vi, realized in the film through performance capture CGI. In addition to the Na'vi, Cameron has created a vast assortment of flora and fauna on this alien world that is nothing short of astonishing in its breadth and complexity. In a future some hundred-plus years hence, corporate interests on Earth decide to send military space forces to invade Pandora for its precious mineral, after attempts to indoctrinate the inhabitants fail. There are clear parallels to the destruction of the indigenous Native cultures from our past, as well as to more recent conflicts in the Middle East. Starring Sam Worthington, Zoe Saldana, Sigourney Weaver, Michelle Rodriguez, Giovanni Ribisi and Stephen Lang, the film was an immediate success, though some critics felt Cameron's strengths are more as a technician and less as a storyteller. Still, the film racked up box office receipts that wouldn't be challenged until the 2015 release of *Star Wars: The Force Awakens*. While the more grounded good vs. evil drama of *Avatar* lacks the philosophical tenets of *2001*, Cameron's work clearly embraces Kubrick's large-scale sense of wonder in the production design and presentation in IMAX 3-D, the modern equivalent of Cinerama. To that end, the movie is a phantasmagoric smorgasbord of visual splendor.

Moon (2009). Sam Rockwell stars as astronaut Sam Bell, who is coming to the end of his three-year contract at a base on the far side of the moon, where he oversees automated mining operations. All alone at the base save for an overly deferential robot named Gerty 3000 (voiced by Kevin Spacey doing his best Hal 9000 impersonation), Sam is showing signs of cabin fever fatigue and is anxious to return to his wife and young daughter. On one of his outside excursions to check on the harvesting machines, he has a major accident. Upon waking, he finds himself back at the base, none the worse for wear. What he doesn't know, but will soon find out is that he is not the same Sam Bell who went out on an excursion, but a newly wakened clone to replace him. He learns all this when he makes an unscheduled return to the crash site and finds the damaged but still living earlier version of himself. The remainder of the story centers on learning why there are clones in the first place, and what happens when the three-year contract is up. Psychologically, it is a film about coming to terms with the self and one's mortality. It is visually audacious for such a low-budget flick (about $5 million); the production design and effects work, evoking the original *Alien* movie, are first-rate. The moon base set benefited from the numerous graphics and logos sprinkled throughout. Best of all is Rockwell's extraordinary performance as the twin Sam clones, in which he seamlessly interacts with himself. Spacey also shines as the unctuous robot, but the utter familiarity of his voice takes you out of the film somewhat. While director Duncan Jones (son of singer-actor David Bowie) obviously pays homage to *2001*, if only obliquely, he has stated that, having grown up more with films from the late 1970s and early '80s, he was actually referencing films that themselves referenced *2001*.[1] Regardless, *Moon* proved you could do an elaborate-looking SF film on a tight budget with nuanced, adult performances, and still be successful, both financially and artistically.

The Tree of Life (2011). Terrence Malick, like Stanley Kubrick, is an artistic entity unto himself. In a 45-year career in which he forged a singular, ritualistic style uniquely his own, he explored the interior ruminations of thought through the exterior landscapes of observation, be they serial killers, migrant workers or World War II soldiers. This formalism reached its apotheosis with *The Tree of Life*. While it's not science fiction in any real sense of the term, Malick's ambitious meditation on humanity's connectedness to the universe makes it at least a spiritual cousin to Kubrick's film, which is why it's included here. It moves freely between the microcosm and the macrocosm, between a rural family in 1950s America and the creation of the universe. There is nurture and there is nature, expressed by the two parents (Brad Pitt, Jessica Chastain) who represent innocence through grace and the hard lessons of life we all encounter. One of their children grows up and is played by Sean Penn, who we see is struggling to understand the dichotomy in his life and the guilt he feels about the death of his brother. For those seeking hard answers, Malick's film came as a disappointment, as he is far more interested in exploring the questions rather than dealing with pat resolutions. About 20 minutes in, one of the standout sequences is a 15-minute visual showcase of the formation of the universe, as well as the creation of life on Earth. While it is not quite the Star-Gate sequence, there is enough connective tissue to make them close relatives. It won't be surprising, then, to learn that effects artist Douglas Trumbull (a friend of Malick's) had a hand in this. This sequence informs the entirety of the story, as well as the complex finale. The film stands as a visual and narrative poem that, in many ways, takes bigger risks than *2001* did in its experimental storytelling. Of course, Malick had the advantage of following a path that Kubrick's film had laid over 40 years before.

***Europa Report* (2013)**. Director Sebastian Cordero's ambitious sci-fi film about a mission to Jupiter's moon, Europa, grounds its fictional story in a *2001*-like, detached, documentary style. Using a variation of the "found footage" concept first popularized in *The Blair Witch Project* (1999), nearly all the scenes are staged from the perspective of video cameras located throughout the spaceship. As such, there is no camera movement, save for the occasional handheld shot done by the astronauts, all of which considerably ramps up the realism of what we are seeing. To keep the footage from becoming boring and/or repetitive, the filmmakers use split-screen and multi-screen images to heighten tension and keep things interesting. These are supplemented with interview clips and news footage of the mission, which provide additional variety. The largely unfamiliar cast (Daniel Wu, Sharlto Copley, Michael Nyqvist, Embeth Davidtz, Karolina Wydra, Anamaria Marinca) also helps to sell the illusion that what we are seeing is real. The set design and costumes look like they're off-the-NASA-rack, and the effects are understated but very believable. As a nod to Kubrick and *2001*, at one point the astronauts listen to "The Blue Danube" with knowing smiles. In reality, the playing of that piece, as well as the opening bars of "Also sprach Zarathustra," have become something of a NASA tradition. While the wrap-up is a little on the weak side, it still holds its own as one of the smarter and more believable offerings in the sci-fi genre. It also avoids the problem of pedestrian literalism that sunk the finale of *2010*.

***Gravity* (2013).** Writer-director Alfonso Cuaron paid homage to the scientific veracity of *2001* in this visually astonishing film, which won seven Oscars, including Best Director and Best Visual Effects. Astronauts Sandra Bullock and George Clooney are stranded in space while conducting work outside their shuttle. A cloud of space debris from a destroyed satellite has crippled the life-support integrity of the shuttle, making it impossible for the two surviving astronauts to re-pressurize the vehicle, ostensibly trapping them inside their spacesuits with a dwindling air supply. The tech talk seems very real, and all the hardware shown is off-the-shelf NASA, which adds believability to the story. After Clooney sacrifices himself to give Bullock a chance to reach the safety of the orbiting station, she goes through a number of harrowing experiences in an effort to survive. In her determination, she finds the strength inherent in her name (Dr. Stone), something that in a lesser film could read as a cliché. Some of the scientific physics are a bit dodgy regarding the orbital proximity of the various craft depicted, a victim of dramatic and artistic license, but it was miles ahead of most other space movies. Also admirable was the film's adherence to the "no noise in space" rule, supplemented with an evocative score by Steven Price that aligns it very closely to Kubrick's *2001*. Director Cuaron never allowed the visual eye candy to upstage the performances, a daunting task given the cumbersome special effects rigs the actors had to wear. The zero-g effects are some of the best you will ever see, a tribute to the latest advances in digital technology. Released in IMAX 3-D, the film was clearly intended to be an event experience, much as *2001* was in its initial Cinerama release. While *Gravity* ultimately lacks the gravitas that would make it a truly great movie, it's still a smart, grown-up story that just happened to be set in space.

Cosmos: A Spacetime Odyssey (2014). The original *Cosmos* series from 1980, created by and starring Carl Sagan, was the most successful and entertaining science program televised at that time. A generation later, Sagan's widow and colleague Ann Druyan spearheaded a reboot, taking advantage of breakthroughs in both science and special effects. The result was a quantum leap in educational entertainment. Much as the original series benefitted from a decade of sober introspection about our place in the universe, following the success of *2001* as a beacon of seriousness, the new series presented the most cutting edge theories and discoveries, and served as a bulwark against the disconnect between science and education that was growing in our 21st century culture. As mentioned earlier, Sagan was at least partly instrumental in convincing Kubrick and Clarke not to reveal the *2001* aliens, a choice that ensured that the film would retain a serious pedigree. As a popularizer of science, Sagan held sway as a voice of reason in the media during the 1970s and '80s. The rebooted *Cosmos* series, hosted by NASA astrophysicist Neil deGrasse Tyson (who first met Sagan back in 1975 as a teenager), has gone a long way in returning us to the notion of cosmic introspection, which was first explored in the mainstream media by *2001*.

Interstellar (2014). If there is a common thread in the films of Christopher Nolan, science fiction or otherwise, it is the notion of perception and chronology. The director of the innovative works *Memento* (2001), *The Prestige* (2006), *Inception* (2010), et al. had long been an admirer of Kubrick and *2001*. When he had the opportunity to do a serious sci-fi film about interstellar travel using a black hole, he jumped right in. But, like Kubrick, Nolan wanted to ground his metaphysical concepts in hard scientific fact. He was fortunate to have available to him the services of Caltech astrophysicist Kip Thorne, who had the knowledge to visualize a black hole that was scientifically accurate, something that had not been achieved in films. Starring Matthew McConaughey, Anne Hathaway, Jessica Chastain, Matt Damon and Michael Caine, the film concerns a secret NASA mission to a wormhole out by Saturn, in order to find a habitable world in another star system and save mankind from its own dying planet. For the near-future look needed in the film, Nolan decided that, just as Kubrick had used 1960s NASA technology as the jumping-off point to envision the world of 2001, he would use the space technology of today to extrapolate plausible future concepts for his own spaceships and spacesuits. The result was a motif that was both rigorously authentic and aesthetically interesting. Though the movie is vastly different from *2001* in tone and style, being much more emotional and character-driven, what helped raise it to the same level of intellectual sophistication was Nolan's trademark use of folding chronology and perception in on themselves, which he employed to create a dramatic, puzzle box dénouement that sent many audience members scurrying back for a second viewing. This intellectual sophistication has also led to a bit of a backlash from those who are resistant to Nolan and his attempts to show the world in a more complex and ambiguous manner.

***Ex Machina* (2015).** A key element in the story of *2001* is its exploration of artificial intelligence, which it does through the character of the H.A.L. 9000 computer. In Alex Garland's *Ex Machina* this exploration is the story's central tenet. When Nathan (Oscar Isaac), a billionaire Internet entrepreneur, offers young programmer Caleb (Domhnall Gleeson) the chance to spend a week at a secluded hideaway-research facility to see his latest robotic breakthrough, what first appears to be a great opportunity morphs into something far more sinister. A mad computer genius in full Kubrickian beard, Nathan has made a robot called Ava (Alicia Vikander) that may or may not be a sentient being, and he is using his new acolyte as a way to test her sentient behavior. What neither man realizes is that, with the spark of awareness and the desire for free will, come a certain level of fortitude to make it happen. In the case of the characters in the story, you're never sure who has the upper hand or just how intricate and calculated the mind games are. In a way, the movie takes the science that is on display for granted, it's a given, unlike the way it is presented in some of the other films mentioned here, and instead invests the story with the compelling philosophical notions of awareness and consciousness as something that is evolutionary and quantifiable.

***The Martian* (2015).** Ridley Scott has directed his fair share of sci-fi movies over the years, from the gothic horror of *Alien* (1979) and the neo-noir of *Blade Runner* (1983), to the ambitious though much maligned

Prometheus (2012). With *The Martian*, he hit a homerun that surprised nearly everyone, given how many Mars-oriented films have failed. Based on a novel by Andy Weir, the film hews much closer to the drama of *Apollo 13* than to the mythic grandeur of *2001* in that it plays out like a contemporary survival and rescue story. An astronaut, assumed to have been killed, is left stranded on Mars when his crewmates are forced to abort their mission and return home. This much more human-based story no doubt played a role in the film's success. The lack of a larger, philosophic context may be the price that big-budget sci-fi movies have to pay in order to be profitable. Still, *The Martian* has plenty of *2001*-type technology on display, including the Mars orbital ship *Hermes*, which featured octagonal corridors and an elaborate centrifuge to create a gravity environment. Unlike the centrifuge on *2001*'s *Discovery*, the *Hermes* cabin is housed in an open framework wheel that rotates around the hub of the main ship, which is actually a much more viable design since its size eliminated the possibility of the Coriolis Effect that would have been present in *2001*'s much smaller centrifuge (see Chapter 3). There are no great revelations in its familiar and mostly by-the-numbers storyline, but like a good James Bond thriller, the way the film gets to its conclusion makes the predictable journey compelling. It's just a shame that Scott couldn't incorporate some of the nuances and complexities of *Interstellar* into the mix. Its *Robinson Crusoe on Mars* scenario may lack the depth of some of the other films listed here, but at the very least, Scott made a highly gripping and scientifically plausible drama, dressed up in sci-fi splendor, which has broken the "Red Planet curse." Movies about Mars are no longer considered box office poison.

Except for the Dawn of Man sequence, the bulk of live-action footage on *2001* was shot in 1966. Fifty years later, in 2016, at least a dozen high-profile science fiction films were released, including new installments of *Star Trek* and *Star Wars*, plus a varied assortment of futuristic fare such as *Terminus, The 5th Wave, Identicals, Midnight Special, The Space Between Us, 400 Days, Equals, Passengers, Approaching the Unknown* and *Assassin's Creed*. While few if any of these films will scale the heights of *2001*, science fiction in all its forms is very big business in the 21st century.

What the majority of these films have in common with *2001* is a desire and intent to use the genre of science fiction to explore serious grown-up ideas as well as to contemplate, in varying degrees, mankind's place in the cosmos. They represent a small but growing trend with filmmakers to bring more to the cinematic table than just thrills and genre tropes. That said, most of these films don't begin to approach the level of intellectual artistry found in *2001*, though they are clearly several rungs above most of the other sci-fi movies being released. This is not to take anything away from the recent *Star Trek* and *Star Wars* movies, which are both entertaining and profitable, but their goals are not nearly as lofty, and rely mostly on providing an audience with rousing adventures with little or no interest in delving any deeper. And while something like *The Martian* has more in common with this adventure-centric fare than what *Ex Machina* has to offer, the fact is that most of the really interesting and experimental films are of a decidedly lower budget, so didn't have the advantage of a star-driven promotional campaign that would have helped them reach a larger audience.

The celebrity fan base for *2001*, though aging, is still quite extensive and, 50 years on, as you might imagine, is mostly "old school." Many filmmakers working at the turn of the millennium could point to Kubrick's film as an underlying touchstone for their entering the field. A-list directors Martin Scorsese, George Lucas, Steven Spielberg, Ridley Scott, Peter Weir, William Friedkin and Terry Gilliam have all commented on how important *2001* was to them as a source of inspiration. It's no coincidence that once Lucas and Spielberg each had a hit under their belt, they made their own sci-fi epics (*Star Wars* and *Close Encounters*, respectively). Add to that the more recent crop of directors such as David Fincher, James Cameron, Wes Anderson, Christopher Nolan, Jane Campion, Darren Aronofsky and Paul Thomas Anderson; their work owes some acknowledgment to Kubrick, either stylistically or otherwise.

Wes Anderson, one of the brighter 21st century directors, first made a splash with *Rushmore* (1998) and *The Royal Tenenbaums* (2001). It appears he may have had more in common with Kubrick than just a penchant for one-point-perspective symmetry and quirky storytelling. In his *The Grand Budapest Hotel* (which rivals Kubrick's *The Shining* for having the coolest movie hotel set ever), the screenplay (by Anderson) was inspired by the writings of Stefan Zweig, an Austrian author who died in 1943 and was largely forgotten in America, but is still quite popular in Europe and elsewhere. As it turns out, Kubrick once considered doing a film version of Zweig's novella "Burning Secret," which he had first read as a child and greatly admired. However, like a number of projects Kubrick hoped to do, nothing came of it.[2]

The avant-garde French filmmaker Gaspar Noe did his own off-the-wall tribute to *2001* with his daring and difficult-to-sit-through 2002 movie *Irreversible*. Structured in reverse order (*à la Memento*), this highly controversial work, starring Monica Bellucci and Vincent Cassel, begins with a very graphic bludgeoning murder (carried out in a contemporary gay bar, rather than on a prehistoric African plain), and then works its way back to conclude with a birth in a white room (with the *2001* Star-Child poster framed over the bed like a surrogate monolith). In the middle of this wildly uneven film is a brutal, extended rape scene that makes *A Clockwork Orange* look tame. While Noe's film is clever in how it reflects *2001's* story within the backward structure of its own screenplay, it still remains a punishing ordeal. File this one under "for adventurous cineastes only."

But it's not just filmmakers who worship at the altar to *2001*. Rock legends have also been fans of Kubrick's masterpiece. David Crosby and Graham Nash (of Crosby, Stills and Nash) have been outspoken admirers. John Lennon famously said about *2001*, "I see it every week,"[3] while Pink Floyd's 23½ minute song "Echoes," from their 1971 album *Meddle*, was designed to be synchronized with the "Jupiter and Beyond the Infinite" section of the movie (try it, it works). The most coveted endorsements have come from the astronauts themselves, a dozen of whom actually walked on the moon. For them, Kubrick's film epitomized the look and feel of "the real thing."

Perhaps the biggest and best-known "famous" fan is actor-writer-director Tom Hanks. He's admitted to a long-standing admiration for the film, ever since he first saw it as a teenager.[4] He named his production company Clavius Base, after the moon base in *2001*, and has pursued projects that deal seriously with space, from the fact-based *Apollo 13* to HBO's *From the Earth to the Moon* dramatic mini-series about the entire Apollo moon landing program, and provided narration for IMAX's *Magnificent Desolation: Walking on the Moon in 3-D*. He has yet to throw his hat into the ring to make a serious, *2001*-style space drama.

2001's impact continues to be found along the ragged edges of our pop culture society. Sight gags on *The Simpsons, Futurama, Mad Men* and elsewhere; commercials which replicate its *mise-en-scène* and iconic imagery; IBM print ads and commercial campaign depicting astronauts in blue, *2001*-style spacesuits; references in newspaper comics; Hal 9000 T-shirts; limited edition prints of the movie's poster art and spaceship designs; near-perfect replicas of spacesuits and other hardware from the film, etc. The "Blue Danube" waltz is still being used to show grace in motion, mostly in commercials; Richard Strauss's "Zarathustra" fanfare still works; footage from "The Dawn of Man" showed up in Tim Burton's 2005 hit *Charlie and the Chocolate Factory* and the *X-Files* reboot; Pixar referenced the film several times in *WALL*E* and the *Toy Story* franchise; there are still revival showings of *2001*; Star-Gate–style "trip" scenes are still being created for movies, while documentaries, magazine articles and books (like this one) about the movie periodically find their way into the already over-saturated marketplace. Keir Dullea and Gary Lockwood attend science fiction conventions where they meet with fans and autograph books, photos and other memorabilia. Director Brad Bird originally wanted to have a Stanley Kubrick lookalike seen in the 1964 World's Fair flashback sequence in his *Tomorrowland* film, since he knew that the iconic director had visited there. And on it goes.

In the spring of 2015, Kubrick's *2001* was again in the news when the original three-foot-diameter miniature of the globe-shaped Aries 1B moon shuttle, long believed to have been destroyed, along with all the other models created for the film, came to light and was auctioned online by the owner for over $344,000 to the Academy of Motion Picture Arts and Sciences in Los Angeles. Though showing some signs of wear and tear, the 50-year-old prop was in remarkably good condition, a testament to its sturdy construction under Kubrick's exacting standards. As an historical artifact, this surviving example of the model work from the production is a window into the meticulous labor and detail that went into creating the miniature spaceships for the film. Once fully restored, this incredible piece of cinema history will be put on display at the Hollywood History Museum in California.

The Internet has practically exploded with websites and Facebook groups devoted to Kubrick's films, especially *2001*. Some of the more popular Facebook sites include alt. movies kubrick, the Stanley Kubrick Appreciation Society, *2001: A Space Odyssey*, Stanley Kubrick Archives,

2001 Italia, the Keir Dullea Appreciation Society, MGM Borehamwood, Elstree Studio, and Pinewood.

Because of the events of September 11, the horrific images showing the destruction of the World Trade Center towers have replaced the monolith as the iconic emblem of the year 2001. That singular act revealed a level of hatred and divisiveness that could never have been imagined in the cinematic world of Kubrick's *2001*. Now, more than ever, it seems, we need a Star-Child to show us the way. But, on a more positive level, it can be said that we *are* living in the world of *2001*. We've gone to the moon and we have a space station, and though our manned space program has lagged behind what the movie predicted, we have realized some of its visions in other ways. We've explored Jupiter (and Saturn, Uranus, Neptune and Pluto, too!), thanks to the incredible work of the unmanned Pioneer, Voyager, Galileo, Cassini and other probes. And now that we've seen the actual moons of Jupiter, it's astonishing how closely they resemble the orbs created by Kubrick and his effects team, since, at the time, the real ones were only featureless pinpoints of light. Mars is practically a second home, with numerous robotic probes tooling around on its rust-colored plains; we've even gotten up close and personal with asteroids and comets, that were barely specks in the sky when the film was released. The Hubble space telescope has unlocked images that are as breathtaking and alien as anything seen in the Star-Gate. New planets are being discovered around distant suns, and are apparently as common as the stars themselves. We *are* on a "Space Odyssey," and that phrase continues to find purpose and meaning in our cultural milieu.

As time marches on and that iconic date recedes further and further into the past, who knows what the ultimate legacy for Kubrick's film will be once the figures in the ledgers of cinematic art are finally tallied. Right now, *2001* still stands tall as a movie masterpiece. Artists of every stripe can still gaze upon it in wonder and admiration, finding new inspiration in its aging soul. Some may develop a desire to create their own unique images, in whatever form; some may simply acquire an appreciation for classical music; still others may come away from the movie with an expanded vision, whether their gaze is directed outward into the heavens or inward at themselves. That is the movie's great strength as an influential work of art: It is what the viewer brings to it which makes it resonate. As long as there are people around to experience *2001*, whether en masse in a movie theater or on video in the privacy of their own homes, it will have the power to inspire. In an era when many film-makers are satisfied with serving up mindless distractions, *2001* still provokes viewers to continue the quest for answers to life's fundamental question: "Who are we and where are we going?" That is its final triumph; that is its legacy. The Odyssey continues. The Odyssey goes on.

STANLEY KUBRICK'S ODYSSEY
A Cinematic Legend

> To just throw the stuff away would have been like burying Stanley again. It would have been terrifying to just say, "Okay, I don't need this any more."
>
> —Christiane Kubrick, Stanley Kubrick's widow, on preserving his archives

Fifty years after its premiere, *2001: A Space Odyssey* remains one of the greatest movies ever made, spoken of in the hushed and reverent tones reserved for such classics as *Citizen Kane, Casablanca, Rashomon, The Seventh Seal, Lawrence of Arabia* and a handful of other cinematic masterpieces that have stood the half-century (or more) test of time. *All* the movies in Kubrick's oeuvre continue to remain vital, alive and fully original works. Like the films of Powell and Pressburger, Hitchcock and Welles, Kubrick's movies are immediately recognizable and distinct.

Kubrick has become almost as well-recognized a figure in the 21st century as Hitchcock was in the 20th. Thanks to the power of the Internet and the legions of fans banded together to make sure he and his films are remembered, Kubrick, the bearded, reclusive wild man with the intensive, piercing eyes, has taken his place in the pantheon of memorable characters. Ironically, it was his passing which helped inaugurate his return to the public eye, in a manner that had been anathema to the director when he was alive. Family, friends and colleagues have come forward in the subsequent years with books, videos and documentaries that have guaranteed that his legacy will not be forgotten or marginalized, and to soften and humanize the caricature he had become. As astronaut David Bowman was transformed into the Star-Child at the conclusion of *2001*, Kubrick has been reborn to a whole new generation of film enthusiasts.

Kubrick's wife Christiane's book *Stanley Kubrick: A Life in Pictures* (2002) is a scrapbook account of her husband's career: hundreds of photos, many never seen before, along with her observations and reminiscences on their life together. Given her creative background as an actress and artist, and a 40-plus-year intimate relationship with the director, Ms. Kubrick's reflections about their union are both incisive and touching. This amalgam of private family photos and behind-the-scenes pictures of Kubrick on the sets of his films makes for a very engaging mixture of what the director's day-to-day life was like. In her introduction, Christiane states, "It goes without saying that this is a book that Stanley would never have produced himself. He would have seen it as a distraction."[1] She also says that despite all the worthy books written about her husband and his work, she felt they were "a little like *Hamlet* without the Prince of Denmark."[2] She writes that in her book, "I've attempted to put the Prince back into the play."[3] For someone who remained in the wings, so to speak, during her husband's career, it is nice to have her finally take center stage to be the Greek Chorus and illuminate more about the man behind the myth.

The 2005 film *Color Me Kubrick* may be one of the most unusual iterations of Kubrick's life in a public context. Starring John Malkovich, written by Kubrick's longtime assistant Anthony Frewin, and directed by Brian Cook (Kubrick's a.d. on *Barry Lyndon, The Shining* and *Eyes Wide Shut*), it tells the unsavory true story of Alan Conway. Because Kubrick's appearance was mostly unknown in the 1980s and '90s, Conway, a gay British travel agent, passed himself off as the famed director in order to procure money and sexual favors. Frewin and Cook thought this would make for a wonderful comedic romp, but had the good sense to wait a few years after Kubrick's death to bring it to fruition. Co-starring a slate of well-known actors, including Honor Blackman, Richard E. Grant, Marisa Berenson and Robert Powell, the film is a slight, though mildly amusing, bit of fluff on a strange chapter in Kubrick's life. Malkovich's over-the-top wardrobe was designed by Victoria Russell, whose father, director Ken Russell, has a cameo in the film. While there is no depiction of the real Stanley Kubrick, the filmmakers managed to include him in a very clever yet oblique manner. With "The Blue Danube" playing on the soundtrack, punctuated by a ringing telephone, Conway answers the phone, only to faint dead away when he (and the audience) realize that Kubrick is on the other end. The real Alan Conway died of a heart attack in December 1998, three months before Kubrick's passing.

One of the more recent documentaries to shed light on Kubrick and his working methods was the hour-long *Stanley Kubrick Boxes* (2008), available on the special edition Blu-ray of *Full Metal Jacket*. It's the end product of director Jon Ronson's five-year examination of Kubrick's collected archive, which was housed everywhere at the Kubrick estate in over a thousand boxes of various sizes, many of which hadn't been opened in decades. The collection yielded both humorous and peculiar tidbits of arcana that epitomized the director's unique creative process. The film had the full cooperation of the Kubrick family, several of whom were interviewed for the project.

Then there's *Room 237* (2012), directed by Rodney Ascher. This documentary about supposedly hidden clues secreted in the 1980 film *The Shining* (everything from America's Indian genocide to the Nazi Holocaust) was clearly not sanctioned by the Kubrick estate, who considered its premise to be ridiculous. While they definitely had a point, especially concerning some of the more outlandish claims put forth, the film is still quite intriguing on its own terms, and does not take sides regarding what Kubrick did or did not intend. Instead, the film merely presents the theories of various individuals (heard in voiceover, never seen) about the movie. One of the wilder allegations connected to *2001* is that Kubrick was approached by NASA to shoot fake moon landing footage, using the front projection process he helped develop. Most people who watch this documentary will rightly take these speculations with a heavy dose of salt. Still, the movie is never boring, and it does raise some interesting thoughts about the coincidences in *The Shining* that are not easily dismissed. You don't have to believe any of it to enjoy the film. A surprise hit, it helped reinvigorate *The Shining*'s reputation as a cinematic landmark, along with Kubrick's pop culture standing, with a new and younger generation of fans.

The most direct connection to *2001* in a recent documentary is *2001: The Lost Science*, a DVD that accompanied a 2012 book of the same name. The book, written and compiled by Adam K. Johnson, contains a superb assortment of photos, diagrams and documents from the Frederick I. Ordway III collection. Ordway, who passed away in 2014, was one of the scientific advisors to Kubrick during the making of *2001*. The accompanying documentary includes interviews with Ordway as he explains what his work on *2001* entailed and how he carried it out. In addition, there are speeches and anecdotes from Ordway, Keir Dullea, ape choreographer and performer Dan Richter and artist Robert McCall (who did the poster art for *2001's* initial release) recorded at a space science convention in Albuquerque, New Mexico, in 2001. A pre-taped speech by Arthur C. Clarke was also shown at the convention. As you might imagine, all of the talk was about how important *2001* was in the lives of these men, and how proud they were to have been a part of it. A second volume was published in 2016.

Piers Bizony, who wrote the definitive book 2001: *Filming the Future* in 1994, teamed with the publishing company Taschen to update that earlier work. The result was 2014's *The Making of Stanley Kubrick's* 2001: A Space Odyssey, a $1000 behemoth that weighed in at 20 pounds. Consisting of four volumes (two hardcover books in a metal monolith slipcase) and two softcover books of production notes and an early draft of the script, it contained hundreds of color and black-and-white photos and dozens of fold-out pages, along with much new information. It also included a reprint of the classic *Mad* magazine satire of the film. The book was a limited numbered edition and was signed by Christiane Kubrick. The following year, a cheaper, scaled-down version of the main volume was released for those who couldn't afford the expensive limited imprint.

While lacking the flash and opulence of Bizony's Taschen books, *The* 2001 *File*, published in late 2015, contained the collected work of *2001* designer and science advisor Harry Lange. Like Ordway's book, this was a treasure trove of mostly unseen sketches, documents and photos about the film's production. After World War II, Lange worked in advertising and then used his aeronautic drafting skills for Wernher von Braun at NASA, designing spacecraft hardware. Written and compiled by Christopher Frayling, who had previously put out a book on the work of Ken Adam (Adam created sets and designs for *Dr. Strangelove, Barry Lyndon* and most of the James Bond movies), *The* 2001 *File* was a fine addition to the movie's legacy, and was well-received by fans and scholars. It illustrated the working relationship between Lange and Ordway and how they interfaced with Kubrick. Some of the rarest material in this book: preliminary designs of familiar hardware seen in the movie, as well as concepts which never made it beyond the drawing board. Lange, who passed away in 2008, didn't live to see this tribute to his work on *2001*. The book is dedicated to him and his associate Ordway, who passed away in 2014.

The mildly amusing satiric comedy *Moonwalkers* (2015) tells a highly improbable tale of an American CIA operative tasked with hiring Stanley Kubrick to shoot some fake moon landing footage, which the U.S. plans to use if the actual moon landing goes bad. Through some mix-ups, the operative instead hires a guy pretending to be Kubrick, which becomes the catalyst for the rest of the story. Starring Ron Perlman, Rupert Grint and Robert Sheehan and directed by Antoine Bardou-Jacquet, the uneven film never really finds the proper tone as it veers between comedy and violence (unlike Kubrick's *A Clockwork Orange*, which handled the balancing act brilliantly). A great film could have been rendered from such an intriguing premise but, as with *Color Me Kubrick*, the material just wasn't thought through enough and the result is just a mediocre trifle.

One of the most unusual and personal books about Kubrick was Emilio D'Alessandro's touching memoir *Stanley Kubrick and Me* chronicles his 30-year relationship with the director. D'Alessandro left Italy at 18 to become a racecar driver but turned to driving a minicab after the economic crisis in the late 1960s ended his career. He then became Kubrick's personal assistant, chauffeur and confidant, working for him from *A Clockwork Orange* until the director's death. While the book is never gossipy, D'Alessandro was a true insider, and his recollections and anecdotes about his friendship with Kubrick reveal a softer side of the director than was generally supposed. First published in Italian in 2012, the book was released in an English-language edition in 2016. An accompanying documentary, *S Is for Stanley*, has also been released.

Perhaps the greatest tribute to Kubrick and his work has been the ongoing traveling Stanley Kubrick Exhibit. First mounted in Frankfurt, Germany, in 2004, it has since appeared in cities from London to Los Angeles, but has yet to grace the director's own home town of New York. The exhibit contains a vast collection of photographs, props, costumes and other Kubrick memorabilia, displayed in a museum-quality retrospective worthy of a Renaissance master.

The 21st century is the century of digital cinema. Kubrick plied his cinematic trade during the second half of the 20th century, when photochemical processing was still the only game in town. One can only wonder what the maverick director would have thought of the digital filmmaking revolution that took hold following his death. He always considered himself an innovator and looked to modern technology for the latest breakthroughs, be it adapting the Zeiss still camera lens to shoot the candlelit scenes in *Barry Lyndon*, or making full use of the Steadicam handheld camera mount for elaborate camera moves in *The Shining*. Having shot his entire oeuvre on film stock, would he have embraced digital cameras? Would the trade-off that would have allowed him his penchant for shooting many takes without burning through expensive film stock have appealed to him? Then there is the still-developing technology of motion capture, first pioneered for the character of Gollum in Peter Jackson's epic *The Lord of the Rings* trilogy (2001–2003) and then raised to new heights by Robert Zemeckis in *The Polar Express* (2004), *Beowulf* (2007) and *A Christmas Carol* (2009). It allows a filmmaker to record a performance to their satisfaction and later decide how to stage a scene through its realization in CGI. Given Kubrick's drive for perfection and his desire to have as many options as possible, it seems as if this technology might be something he would at least be curious about. To be able to put the camera anywhere, and to move it in any way you wanted; to have complete control over the lighting, the weather, set design, etc., would seem to be an enticing proposition for *any* innovative filmmaker. The only thing we can be sure of is that, like every other film genre or style he's tackled, Kubrick would have taken it to a new level.

For most of his career, Kubrick made films that were about failure, or at least about plans that go wrong. This theme appears most prominently in *The Killing, Paths of Glory, Spartacus, Lolita, Dr. Strangelove, Barry Lyndon* and *The Shining*. There are isolated failures in *2001, A Clockwork Orange, Full Metal Jacket* and *Eyes Wide Shut*. There may be a smidgeon of hope woven into the plots of several of his films, but he was more interested in raising questions about the fallibility of his protagonists, rather than placating his audience with tidy happy endings. *2001* may be the only Kubrick movie with a truly happy—if cryptic—ending, though it does initially show man in decline. This philosophy of human failings is perhaps best exemplified in a comment Kubrick made about Steven Spielberg's Holocaust drama *Schindler's List*. Frederic Raphael, who co-authored the *Eyes Wide Shut* screenplay, recalls Kubrick questioning whether a film could truly represent the Holocaust in its entirety. After Raphael mentioned *Schindler's List*, Kubrick replied: "Think that's about the Holocaust? That was about success, wasn't it? The Holocaust is about six million people who get killed. *Schindler's List* is about 600 who don't. Anything else?"[4] While Spielberg's film has its own validity, one can only wonder what Kubrick might have done with this subject in his aborted film project *Aryan Papers*, based on the book *Wartime Lies*.

In the final analysis, Kubrick's work and talent have transcended the century in which they were created, and live on as timeless examples of true artistic genius. Every film he crafted is a model of a singular scientific experiment on what is possible to achieve in order to extend the genre in question as well as the medium of filmmaking itself. While he never had a blockbuster hit in the larger sense of that term, he nevertheless managed to walk a tightrope between art and commerce, in which he continually was able to make unique and uncompromising movies that were artistically original, while returning enough of a profit to satisfy the studio heads who bankrolled them.

However, financial success is the least measure of any art form's significance. A list of the top 100 grossing movies (or bestselling books for that matter) will yield few, if any, works of lasting value. Walt Disney's boldest gamble *Fantasia* (1940) took 30 years to recoup its costs and turn a profit. Many revered films that have stood the test of time remained financial flops for years. When it comes to artistic success, the only currency of any value is the coin of time and longevity. Kubrick's cinematic canon has continued to be an important barometer of greatness and originality, a testament to an artistic vision that will live on for however long the motion picture remains a vital medium of the human race.

For many, *2001: A Space Odyssey* has occupied the summit of Kubrick's artistic achievement over his 50-year career, though there are those who would champion any number of the director's other films for that position. There can be no real consensus on this matter, especially given the caliber of Kubrick's collected work, and allowing for the peculiarities of individual tastes among his fans. In my view, nothing else has come close in its bold mix of form and content than his work in *2001*. The purpose of this book has been to celebrate a cinematic artist's singular vision, distilled mainly through one specific film, and to make an argument for its place of honor, not just among his own work, but of cinema itself.

APPENDIX

VIEW FROM THE YEAR 2000
A Look Back

> When we have grown used to beautiful strange machines, and the wonder of Kubrick's special effects wears off by duplication in other Hollywood films, then we can probe confidently beyond *2001*'s initial fascination and decide what kind of a film it really is.
> —*Harvard Crimson*, April 1968

Is *2001: A Space Odyssey* a dated film? Well, when the actual year approached, we still had no moon bases, no manned missions to Jupiter (or any *other* planet), not even a halfway decent space station (Russia's Mir Space Station was on its last legs and the new International Space Station was just beginning to take shape in Earth orbit). No, as far as could be seen, we weren't there yet; not even close. If only Stanley Kubrick had called his film simply *A Space Odyssey*, instead of prefacing it with that now famous year date. If so, we'd still be looking forward to *Odyssey*'s "future," rather than seeing it in terms of failed predictions. That date, 2001, anchored the film in a way it was never intended to be.

As modern mythology, though, *2001* transcends the limitations imposed by its numerical moniker. What seemed necessary in 1968, the year the movie was released, now seems superfluous and almost quaint. Metaphorically, it represented a new beginning for mankind (year 001 after the second Millennium), but having a date that could be pointed to on the horizon of history has since caught up with the film and become an unnecessary appendage. Fortunately, the myths endure—the Nietzschean leap from ape to man to superman, orchestrated by forces beyond our understanding; the hero's journey, wherein he must reclaim his lost humanity; and the revelation of the "Divinity" that transforms the hero. All these *2001* elements remain powerful today. Some would say that the mythology of "Kubrick's *Odyssey*" can stand alongside any other, including Homer's original.

Now that we are firmly entrenched in an ongoing space age replete with unmanned planetary exploration and manned Earth orbit science studies, we are very much on a space odyssey of our own. It is a journey along a highway with very different exit ramps from those of the movie. We have not yet acquired much of the technology seen in *2001*, not to mention the huge engineering feats of thousand-foot-diameter "Ferris wheel" space stations, routine shuttle flights to expansive moon bases, or gigantic nuclear-powered interplanetary spaceships. The world of the cinematic 2001 remains in a tentative future, some 30 or so years hence.

So how does *2001*, the movie, remain timely today? Ironically, it may be for what it doesn't show. One of Kubrick's true strokes of genius (and something not generally acknowledged) was his decision not to show any normal Earth-based societal constructs. In *2001* we see no Earth cities, no Earthly dwellings, nothing of the day-to-day of Earth that might become dated. Instead we are treated to images of space plane cabins, space station "airport" lounges, moon base conference rooms and large spacecraft interiors, all of which are still quite believable. Had Kubrick shown us a "typical" 21st-century living room or city street, they would no doubt now look as laughable and unconvincing as those 1950s "futurist" documentaries that promised us a utopian life with robots doing all our chores. History has a way of deflating such speculation. Kubrick wisely chose to avoid that, thus insuring the longevity of his vision.

As a cinematic touchstone, *2001* has made a lasting impression on nearly every facet of filmmaking, as well as permeating our culture beyond the movies. To watch *2001* today is to recognize its artistic brilliance, its innovative single-mindedness in both form and content, and to see just how far ahead of its time it really was. Even in our era of computer-generated imagery, *2001*'s special effects hold up. Current model construction and set design owe their technical sophistication to *2001* and the seriousness it established as the norm. And while *Star Wars* and *Alien* may be the template from which many modern-day science fiction films are now drawn, most professionals in the business, in all branches, can point to *2001* as the catalyst that fueled their creative drive to become a part of the movie industry. And just as Kubrick looked to surrealism and minimalism to appropriate the *mise-en-scène* for *2001*'s visual elegance, the following generation of filmmakers have drunk deep from this cinematic reflecting pool for their own sustenance.

2001 has had a massive influence on our pop culture society in general and sci-fi movies in particular. Every hulking spaceship that lumbers past the camera in extreme close-up is paying homage to Kubrick's vision. Every jump to hyper-space or trip through a wormhole seen in a film has *2001*'s Star-Gate to thank for creating that psychedelic set-piece. Richard Strauss' "Zarathustra" theme is still used in films, commercials, etc., to denote grandeur. The calm voice of Hal the computer has been imitated to the point of parody and, according to Anthony Hopkins, even provided inspiration for his portrayal of Hannibal Lecter in *The Silence of the Lambs*.[5] Musical interludes that showcase special effects sequences must point to the "Blue Danube" segments in *2001* as the source of their creation. The iconic images of Kubrick's film have become so ingrained in our collective consciousness that even people who have never seen the movie still recognize its influence in our contemporary culture.

And that brings us to the actual year itself. In keeping with the mythological theme of beginnings and endings, as well as the idea of returning home, the making of *2001* had Odyssean parallels of its own. The shooting of the film in England was "bookended" by its inception and completion at various spots in New York City. As part of my research for this book, I embarked on an Odyssey of sorts and visited several of these key sites in September 2000. With the fabled year then only a few months away, it seemed too good an opportunity to pass up, as well as being an appropriate pilgrimage for a true fan to make.

Though more than a decade has transpired since I made my visit to New York, with an eye toward seeing these important spaces that still retained the legacy of Kubrick's endeavor, it may be instructive for the reader to experience them within the historic context in which they were made. They are icons of wonder, not just real estate.

My 2001 *New York City Odyssey*

During a span of more than 30 years, much changed in the world and in New York City. But the ghosts and echoes of *2001* can still be found. The city is bred into the bones of Stanley Kubrick, who was born and raised there. Arthur C. Clarke was no stranger there either, making frequent extended business trips over the years. New York has its own energy and personality, a sophisticated blend of high-toned professional bravado and working class immigrant earthiness. It is a world of publishing houses, Wall Street, the garment district and dockworkers. And, for my purposes, it was home to where one of the greatest motion pictures ever made was first conceived and then released to the world. In September 2000 (on the "eve of 2001," as it were), I made a special trip to several important New York sites that figured prominently in the creation of *2001: A Space Odyssey.*

The Chelsea Hotel on 23rd Street between Seventh and Eighth Avenues. This landmark hotel, with its ornate ironwork balconies and

The Chelsea Hotel on 23rd Street between Seventh and Eighth avenues.
AUTHOR PHOTOGRAPH.

imposing facade, has been the haven of artists, writers and numerous eccentric personalities over its storied history. Dylan Thomas, Henry Miller, Allen Ginsberg and William Burroughs all called it home. Inside this establishment, from July to December 1964, in room 1008, writer Arthur C. Clarke toiled away on the first draft of the *2001* novel. Rewrites continued there through June 1965 and over the next couple of years in London, when the film's production moved to England. But here is where it all began.[6]

Inside the Chelsea. At the main desk they seemed to neither know nor care that the *2001* novel was written on the premises. While there was some small acknowledgment of the other writers who had graced

The author inside the Chelsea, standing at its ornate fireplace. Photograph by James R. Hicks, Jr.

the Chelsea, there was nothing at that time to be seen to commemorate Clarke's stay there. On May 1, 1965, Clarke waited anxiously in this lobby while firemen dealt with a fire that had broken out on the third floor. He had visions of the only complete copy of his manuscript going up in smoke. Fortunately, this did not happen. Despite my disappointment at the lack of tribute paid to *2001* or Clarke (especially odd given the approaching year), one cannot deny that the Chelsea is imbued with a great deal of charm. The lobby has many unique works of art, as well as a very eclectic décor, evidenced by the view of the ornate fireplace.[7]

239 Central Park West. In this nondescript building, Kubrick had a penthouse apartment in the early 1960s. It was here that much of the initial *2001* brainstorming went on. Kubrick and Clarke began their "Odyssey" here, developing the themes and ideas that would lead them to create their cinematic masterpiece.

239 Central Park West. Author photograph.

The Grand Foyer at 239 Central Park West. Inside this luxury apartment building was a world that reflected Kubrick's success. However, affluence wasn't just a goal for the famous director; it was a means for him to achieve the freedom to do the kind of movies he wanted

The Grand Foyer at 239 Central Park West. Author photograph.

to do. After Dr. Strangelove's success, Kubrick could more or less write his own ticket for his next project. It was in this atmosphere that he chose to do a film about man's contact with aliens and his place in the cosmic order of the universe, a project that became *2001*.

The Plaza Hotel on Fifth Avenue at Central Park South. Within this well-known establishment, on April 22, 1964 (the same day the New York World's Fair opened), Kubrick and Clarke had their first face-to-face meeting. Nobody realized it at the time, but movie history was about to be made.[8]

The Plaza Hotel on Fifth Avenue at Central Park South. Author photograph.

199

Off limits. With U.N. flags flying, access to the Plaza during my visit on September 10, 2000, was denied. Members of the U.N. Summit were preparing to depart, so only hotel guests were allowed in or out. It didn't matter that I was unable to gain entry that day, since Trader Vic's, the bar in the Plaza where Kubrick and Clarke first met, was long gone.

Exterior of the Plaza. AUTHOR PHOTOGRAPH.

The Uris Building at Paramount Plaza on 51st and Broadway. Things change and things disappear. On this spot once stood the majestic Loew's Capitol Theatre, first opened to live shows in 1919 and then converted for movies. In 1962, it was revamped into a Cinerama movie house and there, in April 1968, *2001* had its world premiere, attended by Kubrick, Clarke and the principal actors. It was the last film to play there. After its premiere, Kubrick trimmed 19 minutes from *2001* in the basement of the MGM Building at 1540 Broadway. Later that same year, the Loew's Capitol fell to the wrecking ball and was replaced by this imposing edifice, which stands like a huge black monolith in the heart of the city. How ironic!

The Uris Building at Paramount Plaza on 51st and Broadway. AUTHOR
PHOTOGRAPH.

Corona Park in Flushing Meadows, Queens. The entrance to the
World's Fair site at Corona Park still has the power to impress. Both the
1939 and 1964 World's Fairs were held here, and both were a tribute to
the future of mankind. Kubrick and Clarke visited the 1964 Fair together
to gain inspiration about "the future" for their fledgling movie project.
Celebrating the dawn of the space age, the 1964 Unisphere still stands

Corona Park in Flushing Meadows, Queens.

201

proud 36 years later. And, as 2001 the year approached, society was still looking toward space as the next frontier.

The Future. A romanticized notion of "futuristic" design as envisioned by famed architect Philip Johnson. These "space age" viewing platforms, which look like something from *The Jetsons*, were created for the 1964 World's Fair. *2001*'s own predictions about the future may have been just as inaccurate, but at the time they certainly seemed to be a valid extrapolation of our progress.

"Space age" viewing platforms created for the 1964 World's Fair by architect Philip Johnson. Photograph by James R. Hicks, Jr.

CHAPTER NOTES

Chapter 1

1. Arthur C. Clarke, *The Lost Worlds of 2001* (New York: Signet, 1972), 29–31.
2. Vincent LoBrutto, *Stanley Kubrick: A Biography* (Boston: Da Capo, 1999), 7.
3. Ibid., 10.
4. Ibid., 19–20.
5. Kirk Douglas, *The Ragman's Son: An Autobiography* (New York: Simon & Schuster, 1988), 275.
6. Audio interview with Jeremy Bernstein, 1966.
7. Kirk Douglas, *I Am Spartacus! Making a Film, Breaking the Blacklist* (New York: Open Roads Media, 2012), 146–147.
8. Neil M. McAleer, *Arthur C. Clarke: The Authorized Biography* (Chicago: Contemporary Books, 1992), 176.
9. Ibid., 2.
10. Ibid., 11.
11. Ibid., 8.
12. Ibid., 53–55.
13. Ibid., 61.
14. Ibid., 66–67.
15. Ibid., 105.
16. Arthur C. Clarke, interview, *Playboy*, 1986.
17. McAleer, *Arthur C. Clarke*, 176.
18. *Ibid.*
19. Clarke, *The Lost Worlds of 2001*, 29.
20. McAleer, *Arthur C. Clarke*, 185.
21. Clarke, *The Lost Worlds of 2001*, 18.
22. *Ibid.*, 31.
23. *Ibid.*
24. Ibid., 34.
25. McAleer, *Arthur C. Clarke*, 185.
26. Eric Norden, "Stanley Kubrick, the Playboy Interview," *Playboy*, September 1968, 94.
27. LoBrutto, *Stanley Kubrick*, 262.
28. *Ibid.*, 270.
29. *Ibid.*, 264.
30. Ron Miller and Frederick C. Durant III, *The Art of Chesley Bonestell* (London: Paper Tiger, 2001), 63–65.
31. Clarke, *2001*, 220.
32. Joseph Campbell, *The Hero with a Thousand Faces* (New York: MFJ Books, 1949), 382.
33. Ibid., 30.
34. Edith Hamilton, *Mythology* (New York: Grand Central Publishing, 1942), 312.
35. Stanley Lombardo, trans., *Homer's Odyssey* (Indianapolis: Hackett, 2000), 334–335.
36. Clarke, *The Lost Worlds of 2001*, 38.
37. *Ibid.*
38. Jerome Agel, *The Making of Kubrick's 2001* (New York: Signet, 1970), photo insert.
39. *Ibid.*
40. Clarke, *The Lost Worlds of 2001*, 32.
41. *Ibid.*, 34.
42. Carl Sagan, *The Cosmic Connection* (Garden City: Anchor Press, 1973), 182.
43. *Ibid.*
44. Clarke, *The Lost Worlds of 2001*, 188.

Chapter 2

1. Agel, *The Making of Kubrick's 2001*, 289.
2. Clarke, *The Lost Worlds of 2001*, 44.
3. *Ibid.*
4. *Ibid.*
5. Agel, *The Making of Kubrick's 2001*, 355.
6. Al Hall, ed., *Petersen's Book of Man in Space* (Los Angeles: Petersen, 1974), Vol. 4, 50.
7. Agel, *The Making of Kubrick's 2001*, 98.
8. *Ibid.*
9. Hamilton, *Mythology*, 24.
10. Agel, *The Making of Kubrick's 2001*, 76.
11. *Ibid.*, 88.

12. Rene Magritte, Belgian Surrealist artist (1898–1967).
13. Agel, *The Making of Kubrick's 2001*, 115.
14. Penelope Gilliatt, "After Man," *The New Yorker*, April 13, 1968.
15. Jeremy Bernstein, "Profile: Stanley Kubrick," *The New Yorker*, November 12, 1966.
16. Gene D. Phillips, ed., *Stanley Kubrick Interviews* (Jackson: University Press of Mississippi, 2001), 103.
17. *Ibid.*
18. Sergei Eisenstein, *Film Form*, rev. ed. (San Diego: Harcourt Brace Jovanovich, 1949), 78–80.
19. "Stanley Kubrick, the Playboy Interview," 94.

Chapter 3

1. Agel, *The Making of Kubrick's 2001*, 313.
2. LoBrutto, *Stanley Kubrick*, 291.
3. Agel, *The Making of Kubrick's 2001*, photo insert.
4. I communicated with Allen Hawthorne in 1977 about his work for Eliot Noyes on *2001*, and he kindly gave me print outs of his design concepts for the film.
5. Agel, *The Making of Kubrick's 2001*, 193–195.
6. Adam K. Johnson, *2001: The Lost Science* (Burlington, ON: Apogee Prime, 2012), Vol. 2, 2016, DVD interview.
7. Johnson, *2001: The Lost Science*, 26–30.
8. (A. K. Johnson, 2001: The Lost Science 2012) DVD interview.
9. Clarke, *The Lost Worlds of 2001*, 80.
10. *Ibid.*, 33.
11. Johnson, *2001: The Lost Science*, 75.
12. Clarke, *The Lost Worlds of 2001*, 34.
13. *Ibid.*, 78.
14. Agel, *The Making of Kubrick's 2001*, photo insert.
15. Don Shay and Jody Duncan, "2001: A Time Capsule," *Cinefex*, April 2001, 86.
16. Hall, *Petersen's Book of Man in Space*, Vol. 3, 95.
17. Johnson, *2001: The Lost Science*, Vol. 2, 29.
18. Johnson, *2001: The Lost Science*, 47.
19. Piers Bizony, *2001: Filming the Future* (London: Aurum Press Limited, 1994), 94.
20. Mark Wolverton, *The Depths of Space* (Washington, D.C.: Joseph Henry Press, 2004), 57.
21. *Ibid.*, 111.
22. *Johnson, 2001: The Lost Science*, 56.
23. *Ibid.*, 77.
24. Allen Hawthorne from Eliot Noyes gave me a Xerox photo in 1977 of the original push button design with a TV monitor screen incorporated into the unit.
25. Author's personal collection.
26. Norden, "Stanley Kubrick, the Playboy Interview," 184.

Chapter 4

1. Agel, *The Making of Kubrick's 2001*, 313.
2. *Ibid.*, 314.
3. Dan Richter, *Moonwatcher's Memoir* (New York: Carroll & Graf, 2002), 3.
4. Martin Scorsese, ed., *The Making of 2001: A Space Odyssey* (New York: The Modern Library, 2000), 249.
5. Richter, *Moonwatcher's Memoir*, 136.
6. Agel, *The Making of Kubrick's 2001*, photo insert.
7. *Ibid.*
8. 2001 shooting script continuity sheets from the Kubrick Archives,
9. LoBrutto, *Stanley Kubrick*, 273–274.
10. Herb A. Lightman, *"Filming 2001: A Space Odyssey," American Cinematographer*, June 1968, 7–8.
11. Douglas Trumbull, *"Creating Special Effects For 2001," American Cinematographer*, June 1968, 15–16.
12. Shay and Duncan, "2001: A Time Capsule," 105–106.
13. Bizony, *The Making of Stanley Kubrick's 2001: A Space Odyssey* (Cologne: Taschen, 2014), 324–325.
14. Herb A. Lightman, "Front Projection for 2001," *American Cinematographer*, June 1968, 11.
15. *Ibid.*, 12.
16. *Ibid.*, 13.
17. *Ibid.*, 14.
18. *Ibid.*, 11.
19. Richter, *Moonwatcher's Memoir*, 108.
20. Lightman, "Front Projection for 2001: A Space Odyssey," 14.
21. *Ibid.*
22. Shay and Duncan, "2001: A Time Capsule," 94
23. Dan Richter email correspondence with the author.
24. Lightman, "Front Projection For 2001: A Space Odyssey," 14.

25. Richter, *Moomwatcher's Memoir.*
26. Lightman, "Front Projection for 2001: A Space Odyssey," 14.
27. *Ibid.*
28. Shay and Duncan, "2001: A Time Capsule," 96.
29. Dan Richter email correspondence with the author.
30. Clarke, *The Lost Worlds of 2001*, 50.
31. Shay and Duncan, "2001: A Time Capsule," 81.
32. *Ibid.*
33. *Ibid.*, 82.
34. Dan Persons, "Retrospect: 2001: A Space Odyssey," *Cinefantastique*, June 1994, 33.
35. Lightman, "Filming 2001: A Space Odyssey," 6.
36. *Ibid.*
37. *Ibid.*
38. *Ibid.*
39. Persons, "Retrospect: 2001," 38.
40. Shay and Duncan, "2001: A Time Capsule," 109.
41. *Ibid.*, 85.
42. Persons, "Retrospect: 2001," 35.
43. Shay and Duncan, "2001: A Time Capsule," 110.
44. *Ibid.*, 110–111.
45. Agel, *The Making of Kubrick's 2001*, photo insert.
46. *Ibid.*
47. Shay and Duncan, "2001: A Time Capsule," 113.
48. Agel, *The Making of Kubrick's 2001*, photo insert.
49. Persons, "Retrospect: 2001," 38–39.
50. Shay and Duncan, "2001: A Time Capsule," 113.
51. LoBrutto, *Stanley Kubrick*, 290.
52. *Ibid.*, 288.
53. Shay and Duncan, "2001: A Time Capsule," 113.
54. Persons, "Retrospect: 2001," 46.

Chapter 5

1. Agel, *The Making of Kubrick's 2001*, 306.
2. Shay and Duncan, "2001: A Time Capsule," 112.
3. Robert and James Adam, 18th-century neoclassic designers.
4. Martin Scorsese, ed., *The Making of 2001: A Space Odyssey* (New York: The Modern Library, 2000), 249.
5. Agel, *The Making of Kubrick's 2001*, photo insert.
6. Alex Eisenstein, *2001: The Odyssey Explained*, Science Fantasy Film Classics, 1977, 12–16, 69.
7. When I first read Alex Eisenstein's article in 1977, I had already seen *2001* 24 times in a theatre. I found his comments about the meaning of the Star-Gate reinforced my own previously-determined interpretation. When I wrote the Star-Gate chapter for this book (in the early 2000s) I relied solely on my own memories of viewing the movie as well as studied the sequence repeatedly on DVD but did not revisit Mr. Eisenstein's article of 25 years before. Whatever similarities remain are based strictly on our separate interpretations of that sequence in the movie.

Chapter 6

1. LoBrutto, *Stanley Kubrick*, 66.
2. Clarke, *The Lost Worlds of 2001*, 45.
3. Matthew Boyden, *Richard Strauss* (Boston: Northeastern University Press, 1999), 123.
4. *Ibid.*, 121.
5. Liner notes from *Spartacus* CD, 1995.
6. Bizony, *The Making of Stanley Kubrick's 2001: A Space Odyssey*, 428.
7. Agel, *The Making of Kubrick's 2001*, 12.
8. *Ibid.*, 65.
9. *Ibid.*, 198.
10. *Ibid.*, 198–199.
11. David Hughes, *The Complete Kubrick* (London: Virgin, 2000), 143.
12. *Ibid.*
13. Liner notes Alex North *2001* CD.
14. *Ibid.*
15. Pleasantville DVD commentary.
16. Christopher Frayling, *Once Upon a Time in Italy* (New York: Harry N. Abrams, 2005), 82.

Chapter 7

1. Steven Spielberg interview in *Stanley Kubrick: A Life in Pictures* DVD documentary.

Chapter 8

1. Agel, *The Making of Kubrick's 2001*, 170.
2. Audio commentary with Trumbull on *Silent Running* DVD.
3. *Variety*, April 9, 1975.

Chapter 9

1. Audio commentary *Moon* DVD.
2. LoBrutto, *Stanley Kubrick*, 131–132.
3. *Ibid.*, 317.
4. Andrew Chaikin, "2001: The Odyssey and the Ecstasy. A Conversation with Tom Hanks," *Space Illustrated*, December 2000, 28.

Afterword

1. Christiane Kubrick, *Stanley Kubrick: A Life in Pictures* (New York: Little, Brown, 2002), 10.

2. *Ibid.*
3. *Ibid.*
4. Richard Brody, "Stanley Kubrick on Schindler's List and the Holocaust," *The New Yorker*, March 24, 2011.

Appendix

1. Anthony Hopkins, commentary in *Silence of the Lambs* DVD Criterion.
2. Clark, *The Lost Worlds of 2001*, 33.
3. Clark, *The Lost Worlds of 2001*, 37.
4. Clark, *The Lost Worlds of 2001*, 29.

BIBLIOGRAPHY

Books

Agel, Jerome, ed. *The Making of Kubrick's 2001*. New York: Signet, 1970.

Anderson, Craig W. *Science Fiction Films of the Seventies*. Jefferson, NC: McFarland, 1985.

Aronofsky, Darren. *The Fountain*. New York: Rizzoli, 2006.

Baxter, John. *Stanley Kubrick: A Biography*. New York: Carroll & Graf, 1997.

Bizony, Piers. *The Making of Stanley Kubrick's 2001: A Space Odyssey*. Cologne: Taschen, 2014.

_____. *2001: Filming the Future*. London: Aurum Press Limited, 1994.

Boyden, Matthew. *Richard Strauss*. Boston: Northeastern University Press, 1999.

Brosnan, John. *Movie Magic*, rev. and ex. ed. New York: Plume, 1976.

Campbell, Joseph. *The Hero with a Thousand Faces*. New York: MFJ Books, 1949.

Castle, Alison, ed. *The Stanley Kubrick Archives*. Cologne: Taschen, 2003.

Ciment, Michel. *Kubrick: The Definitive Edition*, rev. and ex. ed. New York: Faber & Faber, 1999.

Clarke, Arthur C. *Astounding Days: The Science Fictional Autobiography*. London: Victor Gollancz, 1989.

_____. *The Lost Worlds of 2001*. New York: Signet, 1972.

_____. *The Odyssey File*. New York: Ballantine Books, 1984.

_____. *2001: A Space Odyssey*. New York: New American Library, 1968.

Davidson, Keay. *Carl Sagan: A Life*. New York: John Wiley & Sons, 1999.

Douglas, Kirk. *I Am Spartacus! Making a Film, Breaking the Blacklist*. New York: Open Roads Media, 2012.

_____. *The Ragman's Son: An Autobiography*. New York: Simon & Schuster, 1988.

Eisenstein, Sergei. *Film Form*, rev. ed. San Diego: Harcourt Brace Jovanovich, 1949.

_____. *The Film Sense*, rev. ed. San Diego: Harcourt Brace Jovanovich, 1969.

Finch, Christopher. *Special Effects: Creating Movie Magic*. New York: Abbeville Press 1984.

Frayling, Christopher. *Once Upon a Time in Italy*. New York: Harry N. Abrams, 2005.

_____. *The 2001 File*. London: Reel Art Press, 2015.

Gelmis, Joseph. *The Film Director As Superstar: Stanley Kubrick*. New York: Doubleday, 1970.

Greenberg, Harvey R., M.D. *The Movies on Your Mind*. New York: E.P. Dutton, 1975.

Hall, Al, ed. *Petersen's Book of Man in Space*, Los Angeles: Petersen, 1974.

Hamilton, Edith. *Mythology*. New York: Grand Central Publishing, 1942.

Hardy, Phil, ed. *Science Fiction: The Complete Film Sourcebook*. New York: William Morrow, 1984.

Hieronimus, Robert R., Dr. *Inside The Yellow Submarine*. Iola, WI: Krause Publishing, 2002.

Hughes, David. *The Complete Kubrick*. London: Virgin, 2000.

Johnson, Adam K. *2001: The Lost Science*. Burlington, ON: Apogee Prime, 2012.

_____. *2001: The Lost Science Vol. 2*. Burlington, ON: Apogee Prime, 2016.

Johnson, William, ed. *Focus on the Science Fiction Film*. Englewood Cliffs, NJ: Prentice-Hall, 1972.

Kagan, Norman. *The Cinema of Stanley Kubrick*, rev. and ex. ed. New York: Continuum, 2000

Kubrick, Christiane. *Stanley Kubrick: A Life in Pictures*. New York: Little, Brown, 2002.

LoBrutto, Vincent. *Stanley Kubrick: A Biography*. Boston: Da Capo, 1999.

Lombardo, Stanley, trans. *Homer's Odyssey*. Indianapolis: Hackett, 2000.

Marsh, Madeleine. *Miller's Collecting the 1960s*. London: Octopus Publishing Group, 1999.

McAleer, Neil M. *Arthur C. Clarke: The Authorized Biography*. Chicago: Contemporary Books, 1992.

Menville, Douglas, and R. Reginald. *Future Visions*. North Hollywood: Newcastle Publishing Company, 1985.

Miller, Ron, and Frederick C. Durant III. *The Art of Chesley Bonestell*. London: Paper Tiger, 2001.

Nelson, Thomas Allen. *Kubrick: Inside a Film Artist's Maze*, rev. and ex. ed. Bloomington: Indiana University Press, 2000.

Olander, Joseph D., and Martin Harry Greenberg. *Arthur C. Clarke*. New York: Taplinger Publishing Company, 1977.

Phillips, Gene D. *Stanley Kubrick: A Film Odyssey*. New York: Popular Library, 1975.

_____, ed. *Stanley Kubrick Interviews*. Jackson: University Press of Mississippi, 2001.

Phillips, Gene D., and Rodney Hill. *The Encyclopedia of Stanley Kubrick*. New York: Checkmark Books, 2002

Pohl, Frederick. *Science Fiction Studies in Film*. New York: Ace Books, 1981.

Pudovkin, V. I. *Film Technique and Film Acting*. London: Vision Press Limited, 1954.

Richter, Dan. *Moonwatcher's Memoir*. New York: Carroll & Graf, 2002.

Sagan, Carl. *The Cosmic Connection*. Garden City: Anchor Press, 1973.

Schechter, Harold, and David Everitt. *Film Tricks: Special Effects in the Movies*. New York: Harlin Quist, 1980.

Scorsese, Martin, ed. *The Making of 2001: A Space Odyssey*. New York: The Modern Library, 2000.

Sobchack, Vivian. *Screening Space*, rev. and ex. ed. New Brunswick: Rutgers University Press, 1987.

Stork, David G. Ed. *Hal's Legacy*. Cambridge: MIT Press, 1997.

Walker, Alexander. *Stanley Kubrick, Director*, rev. and ex. ed. New York: Norton, 1999.

Wolverton, Mark. *The Depths of Space*. Washington, D.C.: Joseph Henry Press, 2004.

Periodical Articles

Bernstein, Jeremy. "Profile: Stanley Kubrick." *The New Yorker*, November 12, 1966.

Boyd, David. "Mode and Meaning in *2001*." *The Journal of Popular Film* 6, no. 3 (1978).

Brody, Richard. "Stanley Kubrick on Schindler's List and the Holocaust." *The New Yorker*, March 24, 2011,

Chaikin, Andrew. "2001: The Odyssey and the Ecstasy. A Conversation with Tom Hanks." *Space Illustrated*, December 2000.

Clarke, Arthur C. "The Playboy Interview." *Playboy*, July 1986.

Eisenstein, Alex. "2001: The Odyssey Explained." *Science Fantasy Film Classics*, 1977.

Gilliatt, Penelope. "After Man." *The New Yorker*, April 13, 1968.

Lightman, Herb A. "Filming 2001: A Space Odyssey." *American Cinematographer*, June 1968.

_____. "Front Projection for 2001." *American Cinematographer*, June 1968.

Norden, Eric. "Stanley Kubrick, The Playboy Interview." *Playboy*, September 1968.

Persons, Dan. "Retrospect: 2001: A Space Odyssey." *Cinefantastique*, June 1994.

Petkovic, John. "The Secret Odyssey of Stanley Kubrick." *Your Flesh*, Spring/Summer 2001.

Shay, Don, and Jody Duncan. "2001: A Time Capsule." *Cinefex*, April 2001.

Trumbull, Douglas. "Creating Special Effects for 2001." *American Cinematographer*, June 1968.

Variety, April 9, 1975.

INDEX